Martin Heidegger
AND
National Socialism

Martin Heidegger

AND

National Socialism

•

Questions and Answers

GÜNTHER NESKE

AND

EMIL KETTERING

•

Introduction by Karsten Harries

Translated by Lisa Harries

French portions translated by
Joachim Neugroschel

PARAGON HOUSE
New York

First American edition, 1990

Published in the United States by

Paragon House
90 Fifth Avenue
New York, NY 10011

Scattered French phrases translated by Yvonne Shafir.

Designed by Jules Perlmutter, Off-Broadway Graphics

Library of Congress Cataloging-in-Publication Data

Antwort—Martin Heidegger im Gespräch. English.
  Martin Heidegger and National Socialism : questions and answers /
[edited by] Günther Neske and Emil Kettering ; introduction by Karsten
Harries ; translated by Lisa Harries ; French portions translated by
Joachim Neugroschel. — 1st American ed.
    p.   cm.
  Translation of: Antwort—Martin Heidegger im Gespräch.
  Includes bibliographical references.
  ISBN 1-55778-310-1 : $21.95
    1. Heidegger, Martin, 1889–1976—Political and social views.
2. National socialism.   3. Heidegger, Martin, 1889–1976—Interviews.
4. Philosophers—Germany (West)—Interviews.   5. Philosophy.
I. Neske, Günther.   II. Kettering, Emil, 1957–   . III. Title.
B3279.H49A7513   1990
193—dc20   90-33349
                                                                 CIP

Manufactured in the United States of America

This book is printed on acid-free paper

10 9 8 7 6 5 4 3 2 1

Contents

THE TELEVISION INTERVIEW

POSITIONS

RECOLLECTIONS

APPRECIATIONS

APPENDICES

NOTES

Translator's Preface

The task of translating Martin Heidegger—or even essays on Heidegger—is, as many translators before me have remarked, no easy one. His special use of the German language to express his thinking, a language that others necessarily use when writing about him, is difficult to capture in language other than his own. Heidegger himself said in the *Spiegel* interview contained in this volume: "Thinking can be translated as little as poetry can. At best it can be paraphrased." Despite the danger that this language barrier could also prove a barrier to an understanding of Heidegger the thinker and Heidegger the man, it is to be hoped that the essays, interviews, and comments collected here will add necessary information to the discussion that has arisen since Heidegger and his involvement in National Socialism have once again become a focus of attention. Perhaps here and there they will provide an access that will help overcome the barrier.

Small accesses may be found in the explanatory footnotes I have given in places where I thought the reader might want additional information. In some cases, I have used footnotes to explain passages that are especially difficult to translate. In general, I have used accepted translations of Heideggerian terminology, but where they did not satisfy me I have explained my own translation decision in a footnote. Where words that are peculiarly Heideggerian or peculiarly German are used, words whose meaning or feel is close to impossible to translate into English, I have included the German word in brackets in the text. Some of the pieces have previously been translated into English but in the interest of consistency have been retranslated here.

Throughout my work on the translation of this book, I have

pestered people with questions—too many for me to thank them all
here. But thanks are due especially to Roman Schumann for answering more questions than anyone else; to Don Fehr, my editor at
Paragon House, for his comments and his humor in putting up with
the distance between New York and Hamburg; and to my father,
Karsten Harries, for his careful reading of and suggestions on many
of the pieces included here.

Hamburg, West Germany   LISA HARRIES
January 1990

Introduction

1

On 23 September, 1889 Martin Heidegger was born in the small town of Messkirch, which now honors him as her greatest son. And with good reason. For although Heidegger has been widely attacked or simply dismissed as a mystifying wordsmith, the fact remains that with the possible exception of Wittgenstein no philosopher of the twentieth century has had a wider and more profound impact on the spiritual life of our time. Regardless whether we welcome or deplore it, the worldwide influence of his thought cannot be denied; it extends far beyond philosophy to literary theory, theology, and psychoanalysis and beyond the academy to poets, artists, and architects.

Heidegger's impact has been especially profound in France: Sartre, Merleau-Ponty, Ricoeur, Levinas, Foucault, Lacan, and Derrida have all acknowledged their indebtedness to Heidegger's thought. Poststructuralist, postmodern theory is unthinkable without his questioning.

In Germany Gadamer's hermeneutics testifies to the fecundity of Heidegger's teaching; so, in a very different way, does the critical theory of the Frankfurt School, especially that of Heidegger's student Herbert Marcuse, although Heidegger has also had a profound if unacknowledged impact on the work of Theodor Adorno and on such younger scholars as Karl-Otto Apel and Jürgen Habermas. Both Hannah Arendt and Hans Jonas owed much to Heidegger, as did theologians like the Protestant Rudolf Bultmann and the Catholic Karl Rahner, or psychoanalysts like Ludwig Binswanger and Medard Boss. It would be easy to go on.

Although not nearly as pervasive as in Germany, let alone in France, Heidegger's influence in the United States too has been growing ever since some of his essays first appeared in English in 1949.[1] How many philosophers are there on whom as many articles and dissertations have been written in the past ten years? Heidegger's American success is all the more remarkable given his insistence that translation threatens to sever the translated discourse from the thinking to which it originally gave expression. Most translations of his works and much that has been written about him illustrate this danger: Genuine communication threatens to give way to a mode of idle talk as Heidegger's laboring and labored, often opaque, but at times astonishingly illuminating German is replaced with Heideggerian English, a strange language that tends to follow its own rules. And yet, despite such obstacles, the challenge presented by his thought and style, which have long called not just academic philosophy but the university as we know it, and indeed modernity, into question, makes it increasingly difficult to get around what he has thought. With good reason Richard Rorty has called Heidegger "as original a philosopher as we have had in this century."[2]

The past year should then have been a year for honoring the memory of a thinker who has transformed the intellectual landscape of our time by thoughtfully questioning the legacy he has left us. Such questioning, however, has been made difficult by the way this legacy has become entangled with Heidegger's support of National Socialism, which some of his critics have taken as a welcome excuse simply to dismiss his thought: How can someone who chose to associate himself with this "main example of absolute evil in our time"[3] still deserve our serious attention as a thinker? Such a dismissal spares one the labor that reading Heidegger's texts demand and of trying to understand that choice and its significance.

Some of his supporters, on the other hand, have been all too ready to make light of that association. But even they have had to admit that, in one sense at least, Heidegger was of course a Nazi: He did join the National Socialist Party on 1 May 1933 and remained a dues-paying member until the very end of the war.[4] But did this mean that the philosopher ever was (let alone remained) committed to Nazi ideology? Did the apologetic account Heidegger first presented to the rectorate of the University of Freiburg in a letter of 4 November 1945, requesting that he be allowed to resume teaching, not say as much as needed to be said? It is substantially the same account Heidegger gave in the *Spiegel* interview and in "Facts and Thoughts," both included in this volume. Heidegger's apology was first made public by Alfred de Towarnicki, who reported in Sartre's journal *Les Temps Modernes* on a visit with Heidegger.[5] His account has been repeated over and over again by those loyal to the philosopher: Heidegger, a fundamentally apolitical academic, did indeed allow himself in 1933 to be swept up by the storm of enthusiasm that carried the Nazis to power, but very soon recognized how misplaced his enthusiasm had been. Much in the volumes of the *Gesamtausgabe* that have so far been published, especially in the Nietzsche lectures (1936–1940), can be cited in support of this.

Heidegger's critical confrontation with the nihilism implied by modern technological culture did indeed include an increasingly outspoken critique of aspects of official National Socialist ideology, including its racism, its attempt to politicize science and the university, and its invasion of the private sphere. But that critique in no way implied an endorsement of liberal democracy. There is indeed a sense in which Heidegger may be said to have looked forward to a quasi-religious spiritual revolution far more radical than anything the Nazis envisioned.

The distinctly academic radicality of Heidegger's thinking rendered it ineffective: There was no need for the Nazis to take this potentially subversive collaborator very seriously. To be sure, it took very little time for Heidegger to fall out of favor with certain influential party members—as early as 1934 the office of Alfred Rosenberg, whom Hitler had appointed the Party's chief ideologue, had begun to compile a dossier on the increasingly suspect Heidegger that soon included a long denunciation by Heidegger's former colleague, the Marburg philosopher Erich Jaensch, who called him a "dangerous schizophrenic," a "German talmudist," who "owed his fame to Jewish propaganda."[6] And Jaensch was by no means the only Nazi professor who, with good reason, had difficulty recognizing in Heidegger one of their own. He was upset when he heard of serious plans to make Heidegger head of a planned academy that was to be in charge of the ideological training of university teachers.[7] Especially the influential Party ideologue Ernst Krieck,[8] with whom Heidegger had once hoped to collaborate in his effort to transform the German university, soon missed no opportunity to question the German character of Heidegger's thinking.[9]

Still, even after Heidegger had resigned the rectorate his opposition to the Party, and its opposition to him, was not as clear-cut as he later claimed. This is made clear by the facts that (1) he could still be seriously considered for an important Party office and (2) by his participation in the Academy of German Law[10] and in the *Deutsche Hochschule für Politik*—its list of lecturers for 1933 included, besides Heidegger, Goebbels and Göring, Rosenberg and Krieck.[11] There was indeed a significant overlap between the philosopher's hope for a spiritual renewal of the German people and aspects of the Nazi program—a hope he never, in fact, renounced entirely even after the disappointments of 1933 and 1934. We can now see that this hope intertwined with dreams of what we can call a postmodern culture born of the destruction of what Heidegger took to be the fundamentally nihilistic rationalism presupposed by both democratic liberalism and technological thinking.

What led Heidegger to look expectantly first to Hitler and, later, to the poet Hölderlin, is difficult to understand unless we keep in mind that the reasons were both very personal and rooted in the widely shared distress in Germany of that time. There was deep disillusionment and widespread discontent with the social order that had been established in Germany following the First World War. There was also Heidegger's strong Catholic upbringing. Although he outgrew this while a student at Freiburg, he could never quite leave it behind; just as he could never quite leave behind his native Messkirch, where his father had been a sexton at the church of St. Martin.[12] Because of these personal ties Heidegger never stopped struggling against Nietzsche's proclamation of the death of God, just as he never stopped struggling against the rootlessness and spiritual mobility technology has brought into our lives, even as he recognized that attempts to rid ourselves of technology would be both irresponsible and doomed to failure. Only against the background of this twofold nostalgia for a saving God and a return to the earth can we understand the hopes that first made him vulnerable to Nazi rhetoric and later led him to search out traces of the absent God and shadows of the earth in the dark poetry of Hölderlin.

Are we today free of such nostalgia, which would appear to be a presupposition of the continuing appeal of Heidegger's thinking? Because Heidegger continues to speak to so many who share his deep unease with the shape of the modern world, who dream of a postmodern, post-technological culture that once again would give the earth its due, there still remains the task of thoughtful confrontation with what he thought. As Heidegger himself insisted, his work is profoundly *fragwürdig*, questionable in the sense of both demanding and deserving to be questioned.

2

Whenever a new publication brings the matter of Heidegger's association with National Socialism to the surface once more, controversy tends to spill beyond academe into the larger world, beyond learned journals into the public press.[13] This first happened shortly after the end of the Second World War. Only a few months after Towarnicki reported in *Les Temps Modernes* on his visit with Heidegger, Karl Löwith published in the same journal an article he had written in 1939 when, neither welcome nor safe in his native Germany, he had found refuge in Japan. In that piece Löwith sought to demonstrate both the nihilism and the profoundly disturbing political significance of Heidegger's special brand of existentialism, drawing attention to the affinities between his understanding of resolute authenticity and Carl Schmitt's political decisionism.[14] By then French thinkers had already rehabilitated and appropriated Heidegger: Alfonse de Waelhens and Eric Weil were quick to come to Heidegger's defense, the former claiming that Heidegger's analysis of authenticity demanded a respect for the freedom of the other incompatible with fascism, the latter insisting that we separate Heidegger's thinking from his politics.[15]

The controversy flared up again in 1953, when the *Introduction to Metaphysics*, a lecture course Heidegger had given in 1935, was finally published and Heidegger chose to let what he had said earlier about the "inner truth and greatness" of the National Socialist movement stand without comment (although in other places he did edit and comment on the earlier lectures). Jürgen Habermas, then still a student, was sufficiently outraged to criticize Heidegger in the *Frankfurter Allgemeine Zeitung* (25 July 1953) for allowing this passage to stand while passing over the planned murder of millions without a word.[16] Much discussed, the passage deserves to be quoted yet one more time:

> What, today, finally, is being passed around as philosophy of National Socialism, but has not the least to do with the inner truth and greatness of the movement (namely the encounter of planetarily determined technology and modern man) goes fishing in these murky waters of "values and wholes."[17]

While the passage suggests that by 1935 Heidegger had grown quite critical of such Party philosophers as Krieck and Bäumler, it also shows that his high opinion of what he took to be the real significance of the movement remained unshaken. The reader is forced to conclude that Heidegger himself thought his turn to National Socialism to have been much more than just an unfortunate, perhaps opportunistic but all too human mistake: as genuine and not to be erased from his thought.

Should it really surprise us that in 1953 Heidegger left what he had said in 1935 about the "inner truth and greatness" of the Nazi movement standing without comment that he felt, would only be misunderstood? Should he have suppressed it? Or added a lengthy interpretation? What could he have said? Even if he had admitted publicly that he had been stupidly and tragically mistaken about the Nazis, he could not have disowned what had made him vulnerable to their rhetoric of blood and soil: his romantic dream of Germany's redemption from decadence. Heidegger continued to believe in what he once took to be the promise of the National Socialist revolution even if he very soon came to recognize how difficult it was to reconcile his understanding of that promise with the Party's actual words and actions. But just for that reason he thought it important to join with those who shared his concerns to try to save the revolution from those small-minded Nazis who, he thought, could not even begin to understand the greatness of the historical moment.

But what reason was there in 1933 or 1935 to attribute greatness to what was actually happening? How could Heidegger have allowed his hope and grand ontological-historical perspective so to blind him to Nazi excesses that even then demanded active opposition rather than Heidegger's often much more than half-hearted collusion, shadowed by essentially private misgivings? We cannot leave unchallenged the quite characteristic way in which Heidegger in "Facts and Thoughts" dismisses both the charges leveled against him in connection with his rectorate and his own apologetic remarks in that essay with the comment that "within the context of the entire movement of the planetary will to power," they "are so insignificant they cannot even be called tiny."[18]

But does Heidegger's remark about the movement's "inner truth and greatness" actually demonstrate that his commitment to an admittedly idealized National Socialism remained unshaken in 1935 and perhaps in 1953? Challenging Habermas, Christian E. Lewalter, editor of the prestigious German weekly *Die Zeit*, claimed that in context the passage should not be read as an expression of support for National Socialism; quite the opposite: especially the explanatory parenthetical remark showed that by 1935 Heidegger understood the National Socialist movement as "a symptom of the tragic collision of technology and man"; only "as such a symptom" did it have "greatness," because the danger that here became terrifying reality extended to the entire Western world.[19] The discussion continued in the *Frankfurter Allgemeine Zeitung* and in *Die Zeit.* Heidegger himself contributed a letter to the editor, one of the rare occasions after 1934 when he decided to enter the public arena. In that letter he endorsed Lewalter's interpretation, insisting that the parenthetical remark did indeed belong to the lectures as originally written and would not be misunderstood by a reader who had learned "the craft of thinking"—a dig at Habermas, who had read the passage as not at all implying a critique of National Socialism.[20] The context of the lectures makes it difficult not to agree with Habermas. Even if endorsed by Heidegger himself, the reading offered by Lewalter projects Heidegger's much later understanding of the essence of both technology and National Socialism back into the lecture of 1935.[21] There can be no doubt that in 1935 Heidegger still saw in National Socialism the possibility of a national renewal, even if the Nazis themselves had difficulty relating the philosopher's concerns to their own.

Publications like Georg Lucács' *Die Zerstörung der Vernunft* (1954),[22] Paul Hühnerfeld's journalistic and quite superficial *In Sachen Heidegger. Versuch über ein deutsches Genie* (1959), [23] Theodor W. Adorno's *Jargon der Eigentlichkeit* (1964),[24] which subjected Heidegger's style to withering critique, and especially Guido Schneeberger's *Nachlese zu Martin Heidegger* (1962), an important if one-sided collection of material relating to Heidegger's political engagement, including fifteen compromising short pieces by Heidegger himself, once again challenged those who would dismiss his engagement of the thirties as a regrettable but pardonable excursion into the world of politics.[25] And once more his defenders did not wait long to reply. Among them François Fédier, a student of Jean Beaufret[26] and, like his mentor, a faithful Heideggerian, deserves to be singled out.

The smoldering controversy was given new life when the *Spiegel* published its now-famous interview in 1976. Given ten years before, it was not published until just after Heidegger's death, in accord with his wishes.[27] And public discussion was stirred up again by the republication in 1983 of Heidegger's notorious Rectorial Address of 1933 along with the already-mentioned disturbingly self-serving retrospective essay, "The Rectorate 1933/34: Facts and Thoughts"—as illuminating for what it failed to say as for what it said.[28]

Today the discussion not only continues, but was raised in 1987 to a new level of intensity by the appearance of Victor Farías' *Heidegger et le nazisme*[29], to which I shall return. Once more Heidegger has become newsworthy, although many of the concerns that have kept the current discussion alive seem to be anything but philosophical: Whatever has to do with the Nazis still can count on wide interest, unfortunately not only (indeed, not even primarily) because it is important for our moral health not to forget. The hold that the events of these years continue to have on so many, where horror mingles all too readily with fascination, helps explain why the case of Heidegger's involvement with National Socialism will not be closed.

But why should the often-disturbing details of Heidegger's life concern us today—the rector's actions and public statements, which present him as a naïve and uncritical follower of Hitler; or his denunciation of his colleague, the chemist and later Nobel Prize laureate Hermann Staudinger, for his earlier pacifism, and of the philosopher Eduard Baumgarten when the latter was being considered for a professorship at Göttingen? (Baumgarten, a German-American, had come to Freiburg to write his *Habilitationsschrift* on Dewey under Heidegger, only to have—as was perhaps to be expected—a philosophical and soon personal falling out with his hoped-for mentor.[30])

Still, was Eric Weil not right to insist on a separation of Heidegger's thought from his politics? Can new biographical details, no matter how compromising, render the considerations advanced in *Being and Time* or in essays like "The Origin of the Work of Art" or "The Question of Technology" any less compelling?

Yet, can we separate Heidegger's thought from his politics? The more that is written about Heidegger and the more volumes of his collected works appear, the more difficult it becomes to escape the conclusion that there is indeed an essential connection between Heidegger's embrace of National Socialism and his philosophical thinking. But if careful reading of the relevant texts should indeed force us to acknowledge such a connection and if Heidegger nevertheless remains a thinker who presents us with a continuing challenge, then this must also mean that we cannot relegate the considerations that led Heidegger to be so receptive to National Socialism to a past so thoroughly contaminated by Auschwitz as to deserve only condemnation, not thoughtful reflection. If so, this must also mean that there is a sense in which the historical appeal of National Socialism presents us (especially us philosophers) a continuing, deeply disturbing challenge. Because Heidegger is at once a genuinely important and highly questionable thinker, it remains important to question his thought in the light of both his misguided attempt to enter the world of politics and his later attempt to retreat altogether from the political arena into a sublime realm of thought.[31]

3

Antwort: Martin Heidegger im Gespräch (Answer: Martin Heidegger in Conversation) is the title of the German edition of the present collection of materials that relate to the controversy that continues to swirl around Heidegger's thinking and political engagement. Translations of the Rectorial Address and of "Facts and Thoughts" have been added to help fill in at least part of the necessary background.

Antwort means "answer" or "response." Who is responding here? To what question? And to whom?

Anyone who expects clear answers to these questions from the present volume will be disappointed. The editors—Günther Neske, for many years Heidegger's loyal publisher and friend, and Emil Kettering, who wrote his dissertation under Richard Wisser (the Mainz philosopher who succeeded in persuading the publicity-shy Heidegger to grant his only television interview)—point out in their preface to the German edition that their title is deliberately ambiguous: "Answer" here should not be thought in opposition to "question." The editors invoke the authority of Heidegger, who understands answers as only the last step of a questioning in which they must remain rooted and to which they must remain open. "Genuine philosophical answers do not have a character that defines and concludes but that opens and closes. They do not take leave of questioning but keep it open and going. In that spirit, this book, too, is an attempt to achieve pioneering work on the problem of the connection between Heidegger's thinking and actions."[32] This collection is indeed less likely to give answers (much less one definitive answer) than to raise further questions.

"The title of this book—"response"—does not mean to imply that the last word has been spoken. Rather it should be understood in two different ways: as Martin Heidegger's direct responses to the questions posed him by Richard Wisser and Rudolf Augstein, and as a response or as responses [given by renowned philosophers and authorities on Heidegger] to the question asked by the public on the topic "Heidegger and National Socialism."[33] The second meaning is the more important: First of all, the present volume is meant as "a supplement to the public discussion that has once more focused on Martin Heidegger."[34]

As the book's title is ambiguous, so is its subtitle: *Martin Heidegger im Gespräch* (*Martin Heidegger in Conversation*). The two interviews do indeed show us Heidegger in conversation, although the supplementary essays by Richard Wisser and Heinrich W. Petzet, which tell us how these "conversations" came about, also make us aware of how carefully prepared they both were. There is little spontaneity in these interviews. That is especially true of the first, the television interview Heidegger granted. Richard Wisser was a very deferential questioner. Questions that would have allowed or even forced Heidegger to address what the editors themselves call *the* question their volume hopes to address—the question of his involvement with National Socialism—were eliminated by Heidegger in his preparatory discussion with Wisser.

That question is, however, addressed in the course of the much longer and widely discussed *Spiegel* interview. The magazine's editor, Rudolf Augstein, did ask often pointed, albeit still deferential, questions. A comparison of the answers given by Heidegger in this interview with his retrospective apology "The Rectorate 1933/34: Facts and Thoughts" is instructive. It suggests that Heidegger had rehearsed many of his answers for many years. The "answer" given to Augstein is thus essentially the same "answer" that he had already given in the letter to the rectorate of the University of Freiburg of 4 November 1945 in which he requested the restoration of his right to teach.

But, as already pointed out, in this book it isn't really Heidegger who gives us his answer. The interviews take up only a small part of the volume, a miscellany that also includes (besides the explanatory commentaries by Wisser and Petzet) a useful survey of the controversy by Emil Kettering; four brief contributions to the heated debate that followed the appearance of Farías' *Heidegger et le nazisme* by Hugo Ott, Hans-Georg Gadamer, Jacques Derrida, and Emmanuel Lévinas; reminiscences by Karl Löwith, Georg Picht, Hans L. Gottschalk, Max Müller, and Hans Jonas; tributes by Hannah Arendt, Jean Beaufret, and Walter Jens; and a number of shorter documents in an appendix. Of special interest is Löwith's report on his last meeting with Heidegger in 1936, in Rome: Even on that occasion Heidegger is said to have worn the Nazi Party pin. Confronted with Löwith's assertion that he thought Heidegger's endorsement of National Socialism grounded in the very essence of his philosophy, Heidegger is reported to have agreed "without reservations" and to have pointed to the discussion of historicity in *Being and Time* as "the basis of his political 'engagement,' "[35] one more bit of evidence that Heidegger himself recognized an essential connection between his philosophical thought and his National Socialist engagement.

Also important are the two interviews with the philosophers Max Müller and Hans Jonas. In his nuanced, thoughtful replies to questions by the Freiburg historians Bernd Martin and Gottfried Schramm, Müller helps to correct Heidegger's self-presentation in the *Spiegel* interview and in "Facts and Thoughts." From 1928 to 1933 Müller had belonged to the small circle of Heidegger's preferred students. He broke with him in 1939 when Heidegger, asked about Müller's attitude to the Nazi state (Müller's activities on behalf of Catholic students had rendered him suspect) testified to his former student's superb academic qualifications but also to his political unreliability and thus helped block his academic career. Despite this falling-out, they renewed their friendship in 1945.

In this interview Müller gives us some understanding of Heidegger's charismatic teaching style, remarks on his lack of "civil courage," points out ambiguities in his character, and confirms what critical readers of the *Spiegel* interview and of "Facts and Thoughts" had to suspect: that while Heidegger had indeed lost confidence in the Party by 1934, his trust in Hitler and the Movement lasted much longer. Like Löwith, Müller insists on an essential connection between Heidegger's philosophical thinking and his politics.

The nature of that connection is made clearer by Hans Jonas, another former Heidegger student, in an interview originally broadcast in Switzerland.[36] Jonas too gives us a sense of Heidegger's appeal as a teacher. More important, given the focus of this volume, is the way Jonas links Heidegger's embrace of Hitler and the Nazi Movement to the analysis of authenticity and resolve developed in *Being and Time*.

Among the remaining material Karl Jaspers' brief letter of 23 September 1933 to Martin Heidegger deserves to be singled out. Although Jaspers does remark on certain features of the Rectorial

Address he finds all too timely and a bit forced and hollow, he is full of admiration: Heidegger's use of the Greeks strikes him as a "new and, at the same time, self-evident truth." He praises the address' style and density. "Everything considered, I am only glad that someone can speak in a way that touches on the genuine limits and origins."[37] This letter by someone whose attitude to National Socialism has often been compared favorably with that of Heidegger helps to recall us to the historical context in which the address was delivered and should be placed.

Hannah Arendt's sympathetic birthday tribute "Heidegger at Eighty," which first appeared in English in the *New York Review of Books*, concludes by likening Heidegger's work to Plato's, his political engagement to Plato's Syracusan venture.[38] Arendt, another former student with whom Heidegger was once romantically involved,[39] speaks of a *déformation professionelle* that lets great thinkers lean toward tyranny. But if, at least for a time, Heidegger allowed himself to be swept up by the evil storm that in the thirties swept through Germany, in this tribute at least Arendt does not dwell on the fact that Heidegger failed to stand up to that storm. "For the storm that blows through Heidegger's thinking—like the one that still sweeps toward us from Plato's work after thousands of years—does not originate from the century he happened to live in. It comes from the primeval, and what it leaves behind is something perfect that, like all that is perfect, returns home to the primeval."[40]

4

Given the editors' loyalty and intention, it is hardly surprising that voices sympathetic to Heidegger should dominate their collection, that it should read a bit like a brief submitted by an amicus curiae. We have already encountered some of Heidegger's accusers, including their current leader; as the introduction explains, "The present volume is a collection of texts Günther Neske put together as his contribution to the heated discussion that followed the appearance of Victor Farías' *Heidegger et le nazisme* in 1987."[41] Farías' testimony is to be countered with Heidegger's own testimony in the interviews and with that of the witnesses gathered in this volume. This, then, is very much a friendly collection, assembled in a hurry to help undo the damage done by Farías' widely publicized image of Heidegger as a committed Nazi, an image very much at odds with Heidegger's own self-representation.

After 1945 Heidegger presents himself as a profoundly apolitical thinker who, by his own testimony, in 1933 not only saw no alternative to Hitler but was convinced that the storm that was sweeping through Germany, sweeping away so much of the established and accepted, was the harbinger of a new dawn. Swept up by the enthusiasm that carried the National Socialist movement to power, he readily seized the opportunity thrust upon him, especially by some of his younger colleagues, who first besieged him to lead the university in troubled times and then elected him rector. Despite his lack of experience as an administrator, it was his hope to be able to channel the enormous energy that had been released so that it would not destroy the German university and, more importantly, science, but rather give both a new, more vigorous life.[42] He seized that opportunity all the more eagerly since the reality of German university life had forced him to question Wilhelm von Humboldt's grand image of the university as a place of free inquiry whose removal from the political arena was a presupposition of the academic freedom on which the pursuit of truth had to insist.[43] Had the university not long ago strayed from this lofty ideal and degenerated into a collection of schools serving the different professions?

The National Socialist state threatened the university in a very different way: by insisting on the primacy of political interests that university and science had to serve. Heidegger describes himself as having hoped to rescue the university from both its professionalization and its politicization. Does the very title of the Rectorial Address—"The Self-Assertion of the German University"—not speak for itself? Does self-assertion here not imply opposition to all attempts to subordinate the university to foreign interests?[44]

After only ten turbulent months in office Heidegger was forced to recognize how misplaced had been his hopes for reform; he had come to see that the gulf that separated the National Socialist conception of university and science from his own could not be bridged.[45] But Heidegger at least had the courage to risk the consequences and to resign the rectorate, to leave the public arena for the thinker's proper sphere: the relative privacy of study and classroom. The lectures of the following years did not hide his increasingly outspoken opposition to National Socialism. Security Service and Gestapo had good reason to suspect the philosopher of subversive activities. In only a few years the would-be collaborator of 1933 had joined the ranks of at least a spiritual resistance. This, in brief, is Heidegger's apology.

Farías has assembled more than enough material, much of it already quite familiar, to unmask Heidegger's self-serving narrative as in good part a fabrication. The impact of this unmasking was heightened by the centenary of Heidegger's birth in 1989, which saw the appearance of countless critical and not-so-critical publications. According to Farías, Heidegger's public decision to join the National Socialist party on 1 May 1933 was not at all a merely strategic maneuver, as Heidegger's own apology would have it. Farías attempts to show that it had its roots in the milieu that helped shape Heidegger's thinking, a milieu dominated as much by "the Austrian movement of Christian Socialism, with its conservatism and antisemitism, and in the attitudes he had found in his native region [Messkirch and Konstanz], where he had begun his studies."[46] In this connection Farías places great weight on an essay by the twenty-one-year-old Heidegger (then a student at the university of Freiburg, expecting to pursue a career in theology) on the occasion of the dedication of a monument honoring a compatriot, the famous baroque preacher Abraham a Santa Clara, in 1910. In this rather slight early effort, which celebrates the preacher as a doctor and healer of the people's soul (*Volksseele*), Farías finds the key to "the progressive connections in a thought process nourished in traditions of authoritarianism, antisemitism, and ultranationalism that sanctified the homeland in its most local sense."[47] This understanding of Heidegger's cast of mind makes it easy for Farías to link *Being and Time* to his decision to join the Nazi Party, which now appears to have been anything but a merely strategic maneuver or an opportunistic aberration. If Heidegger became disaffected with the Party, this, according to Farías, was not at all because he had come to reject National Socialism but because he felt that after June 1934, when Hitler eliminated Ernst Röhm and the Party's right wing, "the Nazis had become traitors to the truth that was at the root of their movement."[48] If Farías is right, Heidegger was to remain faithful to that "truth" long after the end of World War II, indeed to the very end.

Not surprising therefore that the old Heidegger should have returned to his intellectual beginnings with another public lecture honoring Abraham a Santa Clara, whom Heidegger now calls "a teacher for our life and a master of language."[49] As Farías once more reminds us, this "teacher for our life" was not only an unusually gifted rhetorician but also a rabid nationalist and antisemite who for good reasons was a favorite with Nazi literary historians.[50]

Farías makes a great deal of the fact that in his address Heidegger cites a remark by Abraham a Santa Clara that peace is as distant from war as Sachsenhausen is from Frankfurt—i.e., not distant at all: Sachsenhausen is now part of Frankfurt. Another Sachsenhausen, not too far from Berlin,[51] was of course the site of a concentration camp and Frankfurt the scene of the Auschwitz trial. How then are we to understand Heidegger's use of a passage using place names with such connotations—as an insignificant accident, or as a slip of the tongue betraying the depth of Heidegger's continued if now perhaps unconscious commitment to Nazi ideology, or as a deliberate provocation? Without further documentation, Farías suggests, the question must remain open, although the book leaves no doubt that its author at least finds it highly significant. As so often in this book, Farías relies on suggestion and association more than on facts to support his portrayal of Heidegger as an unrepentant National Socialist.

To those familiar with the earlier literature, especially with the essays the Freiburg historian Hugo Ott had published in a number of rather obscure journals,[52] the new facts adduced by Farías could hardly have come as a surprise. Still, Heidegger's own self-representation had been successful enough, especially in France, to allow *Le Monde* to compare the book's impact to that of a bomb.[53] The academic world seemed to have been left a shambles.

To understand that impact it is important to keep in mind the profound influence of Heidegger's work on many of the most influential French thinkers. With good reason Christian Jambet could claim in his introduction to the French edition of Farías' book that since the war Heidegger had become a French philosopher, that it was in France that his thinking found the most echoes, that it was here that he was celebrated as the philosopher who had most thoughtfully confronted modernity, a genius worthy of being placed beside Plato and Aristotle, Kant and Hegel.[54] Could this last giant of the history of philosophy, the spiritual father of French existentialism and of different brands of postmodernism, have been an unregenerate Nazi?

We also should not lose sight of the fact that not only Germany but also France had proved vulnerable to National Socialism. This makes it important to understand the sources of this vulnerability. Those who insist that there is indeed an intimate connection between Heidegger's philosophical thought and his embrace of National Socialism should find it easy to agree with Philippe

Lacoue-Labarthe and Jacques Derrida when they claim that an engaged reading of Heidegger can help us thoughtfully approach what we condemn so that we may better understand just what it is that we condemn.[55]

A considerably revised German version that takes into account some of the criticisms made of the French edition appeared in 1988, accompanied by an important introduction by Jürgen Habermas.[56] Habermas challenges Jaspers' maxim that "the true content of a philosophical doctrine would have to mirror itself in the personality and life style of the philosopher." The autonomy of a philosopher's work and of the history of its reception must be respected[57]—and Habermas, too, understands *Being and Time* as the most significant event in German philosophy since Hegel,[58] dismissing the suggestion that a work such as this could be discredited by the compromising biographical details documented by Farías.[59] But if Habermas is quite willing to grant that much in Heidegger, especially aspects of his critique of reason, will prove of lasting significance, he also insists that the ideological contamination of his thinking forces the thoughtful reader to consider "the *inner* connections that exist between Heidegger's political engagement and his changing attitude to Fascism, on the one hand, and his critique of reason, which is also not without its political motivation, on the other,"[60] where Habermas suggests that what should interest us today first of all is Heidegger's attitude *after 1945*, the attitude that informs the two interviews.

Almost as soon as it appeared, Farías' critique met with vigorous opposition from very different quarters. Expected was the countercritique by such loyal Heideggerians as François Fédier, who wrote *Heidegger: anatomie d'un scandale* to prove that Farías' representation of the philosopher as a Nazi constituted a calumny.[61] Fédier accused Farías of having grossly misused the facts, an accusation made easier than it should have been by the latter's often careless scholarship and penchant for hyperbole. But Fédier's own brief in support of Heidegger is so blatantly a case of special pleading that the reader is immediately put on guard.

Then there were those who, like Gadamer and Derrida in the essays included in this volume, insisted with good reason that apart from a few new details the main story was already quite familiar, that only a prior refusal to acknowledge what was so evidently there to be seen could explain why Farías' rather careless book should have had such an impact especially in France. Gadamer and Derrida, however, differ sharply in their understanding of the significance of Heidegger's political engagement. Long a disciple and friend, Gadamer does not question that Heidegger once "believed" in Hitler, but also insists that Heidegger soon came to see that the revolution of which he dreamed had nothing to do with the reality of what was happening in Germany. Heidegger felt that he had nothing to do with the horrors that issued from Hitler's rise to power; accordingly, he felt no responsibility. Like Hannah Arendt, Gadamer likens Heidegger's political engagement of 1933–1934 to Plato's Syracusan venture, a comparison that implies that (far from now being done with Heidegger) what awaits us is rather the task of a more critical, more careful reading.[62]

Jacques Derrida, too, has only contempt for suggestions that Farías, having unmasked Heidegger, had made it unnecessary to read him. But unlike Gadamer, Derrida insists on the importance of thoughtful consideration of what links Heidegger's work and his political engagement, thoughtful consideration especially of the significance of Heidegger's silence on Auschwitz and on so much else that continues to weigh on us. Such consideration has to begin with a careful reading of what Heidegger has written, above all of *Being and Time*, and with an equally careful, open attention to what is communicated by Heidegger's silence.[63]

Very different in tone was historian Hugo Ott's critical discussion of the Farías book, also reprinted here. The fact that Farías had relied heavily on Ott's research gave it added weight. (Ott's very recent and also very critical *Martin Heidegger: Unterwegs zu seiner Biographie* offers the best discussion of the facts relating to Heidegger's involvement with National Socialism.) Unlike Farías, Ott makes no claim to address the philosophical problems raised by Heidegger's activities. But, as a historian, he finds Farías' method unacceptable, especially his reliance on often all-too-free association, as when he finds in Abraham a Santa Clara the key to Heidegger's political engagement or when he attempts to link Heidegger to the Röhm faction of the Party.[64] But Ott agrees with Farías about what would seem to be most important: that Heidegger's self-representation misrepresents his past involvement with National Socialism. The facts assembled by Ott and Farías do indeed leave no doubt about the genuineness of Heidegger's commitment to National Socialism and about the extent of his soon-to-be-disappointed ambitions.[65]

5

Why should such biographical details matter? Was Habermas not right to insist on the autonomy of philosophical argument? To be sure, most of us are curious about the lives of those thinkers and artists, scientists and statesmen who are part of our inheritance. And we take a special delight in revelations that show them to have been human—all too human in their faults and moral lapses. Is it our easily injured self-esteem that demands that we cut our heroes down to size, thus diminishing the distance between them and us?

But more than self-serving curiosity is involved when, as with Heidegger, going astray means identification with something we have come to recognize as so unquestionably evil that it seems our only response can be condemnation. Especially Heidegger's admirers should find it difficult not to agree with his former student Herbert Marcuse, who in a letter dated 28 August 1947 deplores his once revered teacher's silence and implores him to publicly confess his mistake and thus cleanse himself and his thinking of the stain of Nazism:

> Publicly, you have not denounced a single one of the actions
> and ideologies of the regime. Under these circumstances you
> are identified with the Nazi regime even today. Many of us
> have waited for a long time for a word from you that clearly
> and definitively would free you from this identification, a word
> that expresses what you, today, really think of what happened.
> You never spoke such a word—at any rate it never went
> beyond the private realm. I—and a great many others—have
> venerated you as a philosopher and have learned infinitely
> much from you. But we cannot make the distinction between
> the philosopher and the human being Martin Heidegger—it
> contradicts your own philosophy. A philosopher can be
> mistaken about politics—then he will openly admit his error.
> But he cannot be mistaken about a regime that murdered
> millions of Jews merely because they were Jews, that made
> terror part of everyday life and turned everything that ever was
> really tied to the concept of spirit and freedom and truth into
> its bloody opposite. A regime that in every respect was the
> deadly caricature of that Western tradition you yourself have
> presented and defended in such penetrating fashion. And if
> that regime was not the caricature, but the real fulfillment of

that tradition—even then there was no deception, then you had to accuse and abjure this entire tradition. . . . Are you really to enter intellectual history in this manner? Every attempt to combat this cosmic misunderstanding suffers shipwreck over the general resistance to occupy oneself seriously with a Nazi ideologue. Common sense (even of those who live a life of the spirit) refuses to see in you a philosopher because it considers philosophy and Nazism incompatible. In this conviction it remains correct. Once more: You can only combat (and we can only combat) the identification of your person and work with Nazism (and thus the obliteration of your philosophy) if you make a public confession of your change and transformation.[66]

Heidegger did not remain completely silent. Twice he was to address the horror of the Holocaust in the course of four lectures that were first given in the Club of Bremen on 1 December 1949. But although both go some way toward showing that Heidegger had indeed come close to adopting one of the alternatives sketched by Marcuse (that he had come to understand National Socialism as something like "the real fulfillment" of the metaphysical culture of the West and had come to distance himself from that tradition), he did so in a way that could hardly have lessened Marcuse's concerns. Consider this remark from the third Bremen lecture, *"Die Gefahr"* ("The Danger"), the only one of the four Heidegger chose to leave unpublished:

Hundreds of thousands die *en masse.* Do they die? They perish. They are cut down. Do they die? They become items of the material available for the manufacture of corpses [*Sie werden Bestandstücke eines Bestandes der Fabrikation von Leichen*]. Do they die? Hardly noticed, they are liquidated in extermination camps. And even apart from that, in China millions now perish of hunger.

Dying, however, means bearing death in its essence. To be capable of dying means to be capable of bearing this death. But we are able to do so only when the essence of death has an affinity to our essence.[67]

Heidegger, too, understands the extermination camps as factories of death. Presupposed is a reduction of human beings to human material that denies what is a condition of true humanity, according to Heidegger: the possibility of really dying. To be sure, the victims of the Holocaust perished. But to perish thus is to suffer a fate that all but precludes the authentic appropriation of death. "To die, however, means to carry out death in its essence. To be able to die means to be capable of this carrying-out. We are capable of this only if the essence of death has an affinity to our essence."[68] *Being and Time* had tied authenticity to resolute being unto death. But circumstances can be such that they make such resolve all but impossible. Thus the death the Nazis dealt to uncounted innocent victims denied them the possibility of a genuine dying and thus full humanity. "Only those able to die become mortals in the full sense of the word. A mass of misery, of countless, dreadfully undied deaths everywhere—and all the same, the essence of death remains blocked. Not yet are human beings mortals."[69]

As it obscures the distinction between the victims of the Holocaust and the many who have lived and continue to live contentedly, caught up in and lost to the modern world, Heidegger's lament also obscures his own quite personal failure. An inhuman detachment, very much like the detachment Heidegger himself connected with that technological age which, so he came to think, revealed its inhuman essence in National Socialism, allowed him to include the following remark in the second Bremen lecture:

> Agriculture is now a motorized food industry: in its essence
> it is the same thing as the manufacture of corpses in gas
> chambers, the same thing as blockades and the reduction of a
> region to hunger, the same as the manufacture of hydrogen
> bombs.[70]

In the wake of the French edition of the book by Farías, such different thinkers as Blanchot, Lacoue-Labarthe, Lévinas, and Sheehan cited this passage as an example of an inhuman detachment that refuses to recognize the evil of the Holocaust in its terrifying specificity.[71]

Not that we cannot make sense of Heidegger's equations. They are indeed demanded by his understanding of the essence of technology as the fulfillment of what is demanded by the essence of metaphysics.

Metaphysics is determined by the question What is the essence of being? It seeks to determine that essence, to seize and secure it in such a way that being will no longer elude us. But we can secure only what is sufficiently stable and enduring to be comprehended. The attempt to secure being thus invites a refusal to count as being simply what presents itself to us. Being comes to be linked to what abides, to what transcends destructive time. Greek metaphysics thus already opposed what truly is to the shadowy world that presents itself to our senses. Being and becoming are divorced, as whatever becomes is declared to possess only an inferior kind of being: to be mere appearance, dependent in its being on true being. In the Middle Ages this understanding allied itself with the conception of an omnipotent, all-seeing creator-God: Everything is created by Him and therefore open to His gaze. Metaphysics enters a third stage, decisive for modernity, with Descartes. The knowing subject now becomes the measure of reality, which comes to be understood as what can in principle become the object of clear and distinct knowledge. And just as things were thought to lie open to God's gaze just because He had created them, so Descartes suggests that we understand nature precisely to the extent that we can recreate her works. In this sense the metaphysician's attempt to lay hold of being may be said to triumph in natural science and technology. In the age of technology all that is comes to be understood as always available manipulable material. Inseparable from the history of modernity thus understood is an increasing leveling or homogenization of what is. Human beings, too, come to be understood increasingly as human material.

The collision of technology with the requirements of genuine humanity remained for Heidegger *the* problem facing modern culture. And can we dismiss his often-repeated claim that the technological spirit ruling the modern world threatens to reduce human beings, too, to material for planning as just another resource? But even those who share Heidegger's concern about technology should question his all-too-easy identification of extermination camps with modern agriculture. With good reason has Habermas charged Heidegger with *Abstraktion durch Verwesentlichung* ("abstraction by essentializing"). "Under the leveling glance of the philosopher of Being, the extermination of the Jews, too, appears as a happening, where everything can be replaced as one likes with anything else."[72]

Heidegger never made the kind of confession Marcuse demanded; no more did he engage the poet Paul Celan in the conversation the latter so desperately sought, a conversation that would find words that would not be totally inappropriate to the horror of the Holocaust.[73] The thinker of Being failed the poet. Heidegger remained silent.

What could he have said? What should he have said? That he abhorred the horror of Auschwitz and felt profoundly ashamed for once having aligned himself with those responsible? Derrida may well be right to suggest that, had he done so, we probably would no longer be occupying ourselves with the question of the significance of Heidegger's involvement with the Nazis. Would this constitute a more adequate response to the challenge of his thought? To the challenge of the Holocaust? Heidegger's silence leaves us the task of thinking what he himself could not or would not think.[74]

As the piece by Gadamer and the *Spiegel* interview make clear, Heidegger himself saw no reason to utter a public peccavi; he could not hold himself responsible for the horrors of the Holocaust, nor did he think himself mistaken in that critique of modernity that once let him link "the inner truth and greatness" of the Nazi movement to "the encounter between global technology and contemporary man." He did come to admit that he had misjudged the depth of the rule of technology and therefore had been wrong to hope where no reason was left to hope: National Socialism, Heidegger came to insist, was unable to confront the problematic essence of technology because it was itself just an extreme manifestation of that essence.[75] Heidegger did come to recognize that he had been wrong to project onto the Nazis his dream of a new politics and a new religion that would result in the spiritual renewal of the German people. But he could not condemn himself for having thus dreamed of revolution, and if the holding of this dream is sufficient to make someone a Nazi, then Heidegger remained a Nazi to the very end. That dream he never did surrender, even as he came to recognize that the shape of the modern world condemned it to remain no more than a dream.

But what did this dream have to do with the monster that National Socialism turned out to be? Otto Wacker, at the time of the Rectorial Address Nazi secretary of education in Baden, was quite on target when (if we are to believe Heidegger's report) he accused him of subscribing to a " 'private National Socialism' that circumvented the perspectives of the Party program."[76] This private National Socialism Heidegger saw no reason to renounce.

6

Heidegger's silence did not mean the obliteration of his philosophy, as Marcuse had predicted. Quite the opposite.

Should it have? How should the personal failings of great artists and thinkers affect our appreciation of the achievements for which we remember them? Does an understanding of the not always edifying details of Mozart's biography help us hear his music better? Is the case different for the philosopher? Does he owe us, as Jaspers thought, a life that supports his teachings? Max Scheler is said to have answered an admirer who wondered why his life-style was so much at odds with his lofty philosophical teaching by comparing the philosopher to a signpost: No one asks the signpost to stand where it points. Could Heidegger have answered those of his admirers who found it difficult to square his life and thought in similar fashion? But do the often-disturbing facts to which Ott and Farías have called our attention diminish the value of Heidegger's ontological reflections? Of his determination of our historical place? Of his thinking of the essence of technology and art?

Heidegger introduced a lecture course on Aristotle with the all-but-empty laconic observation: "Aristotle was born, worked, and died."[77] No doubt Heidegger would have liked his readers to approach the many volumes he was to leave them in the same spirit, bracketing the too-personal, and he took great pains to keep his life private. Writers like Farías and Ott have invaded that privacy, and the same can be said of many of the pieces included in this volume. What justifies such invasion? In their foreword to the English edition of Farías' *Heidegger and Nazism* Joseph Margolis and Tom Rockmore claim that "the strong case" there assembled "now quite properly affects the reading of Heidegger's *philosophy*."[78] But just how should it affect our reading? Should philosophers not respect the autonomy of philosophical reflection and allow what Heidegger has written to speak for itself? What does it mean to "allow a text to speak for itself"?

No text can be understood without an understanding of its context. Who could disagree with René Wellek when he points out that to understand even the first lines of Ariosto's *Orlando Furioso*

Of *Loves* and *Ladies, Knights* and *Arms* I sing,
Of *Courtesies,* and many a *Daring Feat;*

we must already have some understanding of what is meant by *lady* and *knight*—that is to say, we must have entered into the spirit of a particular language game.[79] The requirement is easily extended. Must the interpreter not also have some familiarity with the tradition of the epic to allow this text to "speak for itself"? In countless cases interpretation must draw on historical scholarship. How far should we pursue this? Certain words may carry a particular aura for a writer, rooted in his own very personal experiences. Should we not turn to biography to discover that aura?

Wellek was of course speaking of a work of literature. Different types of text require different kinds of reading. A textbook in chemistry demands a very different reading than does Ariosto's poem. How then should philosophical texts be read? And are philosophical texts sufficiently alike for all to require the same kind of reading? Does "allowing a text to speak for itself" mean the same thing when reading Frege and when reading Heidegger? What is the proper context for reading one of Heidegger's works, say, *Being and Time*? Does it require us to examine his association with the Nazis, as Margolis and Rockmore suggest? Is that context not provided by the philosophical, more especially the phenomenological tradition?

Heidegger's own words prevent us from answering with a simple yes. As Marcuse points out, *Being and Time* quite explicitly refuses to sever the philosopher from the concrete person and his inevitably specific ethos. There Heidegger raises the question "Is there not, however, a definite ontic way of taking authentic existence, a factical ideal of Dasein, underlying our ontological interpretation of Dasein's existence?" In other words, does Heidegger's analysis of the essential structures of human being in the world and with others, of care and guilt, of authenticity and resolve, not presuppose the choice of a particular way of being in the world, the adoption of what we can call a specific ethical stance? Heidegger's unambiguous answer: "That is so indeed. But not only is this Fact one that must not be denied and that we are forced to grant; it must also be conceived in its positive necessity, in terms of the objects we have taken as the theme of our investigation."[80] This means that, unlike natural science, fundamental ontology can never be a disinterested, "objective" pursuit of the truth; it is inevitably rooted in the thinker's specific ethos, in his stance toward persons and things.

In *Being and Time* mood is said to rule the way we stand in the world.[81] This implies that adequate interpretation of a text presupposes that we have understood its ruling mood. Despite the enormous importance granted to mood in *Being and Time*, Heidegger does not develop there the implications of the ontological significance of mood for interpretation. We are given no more than a hint when Heidegger suggests that mood communicates itself in what we can call the music of a discourse, in "intonation, modulation, and tempo"[82]—a text's distinctive style.

The importance of style for interpretation is addressed in more detail in Heidegger's correspondence with Emil Staiger. Staiger had raised the question What form does the hermeneutic circle actually take when we interpret a work of literature? On first hearing or reading a literary text we are unlikely to come away with an adequate grasp of its structure or meaning—if we did, what would be the point of interpretation? Instead we seize on details and, more importantly, on the work's particular rhythm. Before we have understood, say, a poem, this rhythm communicates the mood that animates the whole. It is this mood that should guide subsequent interpretation. On this point Heidegger found himself in agreement with Staiger: even on a first reading, a text communicates a basic mood or *Grundstimmung*. That mood should guide subsequent interpretation.

Heidegger and Staiger were discussing a poem by Mörike, but Heidegger's understanding of the fundamental importance of mood demands that we apply his insight into the significance of mood to all interpretation. That goes even for the interpretation of scientific texts; they, too, are written in a particular style that communicates a definite mood—call it the mood of objectivity. Sharing that mood is a presupposition of joining in the language game of science. Scientific texts accordingly do not demand that the reader attend to and struggle with the presupposed mood.

The case is quite different when the mood presupposed by a text is different from and challenges our own. Interpretation then demands that we not neglect the author's stance in the world. Such neglect would condemn us to a correspondingly superficial understanding: we would find ourselves in the position of someone struggling with a text in a language he had not quite mastered. This is the position in which many of Heidegger's texts place us.

Consider once more the Rectorial Address. In "Facts and Thoughts" Heidegger complains that the address had been misunderstood. There he also tells us what is required of a responsible reading: "In this case, as with every spoken [and, we can add, every written] word, everything depends on the interpretation and on the readiness to enter into what is essential and to get it into view at all."[83] Because the *Grundstimmung* or fundamental mood governing what he had written had been misunderstood, the address also failed to communicate its meaning.

If the address was indeed misunderstood, its author must have known that he invited such misunderstanding. Consider, for example Heidegger's willful translation of Socrates' "*ta . . . megála pánta episphale*" as "all that is great stands in the storm," a collage of Platonic thought and Nazi jargon that lends a misleading timeliness to the former even as it lends respectability to the Nazi revolution by placing it in the light of Greek philosophy.[84] This holds for the address' style in general, which in the way it forces together classical Greek thought and an all-too-timebound ideology invites comparison with the style of Nazi architecture. Heidegger's choice of words could leave no doubt in the audience that the Rectorial Address' fundamental mood was in some sense "oriented toward 'battle' "[85]—and in those years there was a great deal of talk of "battle." But how many of those who then responded to Heidegger's impassioned use of that word could have been expected to understand "battle" with Heidegger as meaning first of all the Heraclitean *pólemos*, an *Auseinandersetzung* (confrontation) or setting apart that lets those who are thus set apart truly come into their own? How convincing is Heidegger's subsequent insistence in "Facts and Thoughts" that "This is the sense of 'battle' thought philosophically and what is said in the address is only thought philosophically,"[86] his protestation that nothing was further from his mind than a celebration of the warlike? The style of the address is deliberately ambiguous where such ambiguity gives expression to Heidegger's attempt to reappropriate the Greek paradigm invoked in the address, to "repeat" (a term that should be understood in the sense Heidegger had given "repetition" in *Being and Time*[87]) a heroic past in the present.

Heidegger complains in "Facts and Thoughts" that the address was understood neither by the academic community that was its intended audience nor by the Nazis, who, as Heidegger knew, would take a keen interest in what the much-heralded philosopher-rector would have to say, nor by those later critics who would hear in it only what aligned him with the Nazis, not his opposition. Such manifold misunderstanding was hardly an accident. If Heidegger's readers failed to grasp what its author considered essential, this was because of the address' ambiguous style, which fused an all-too-familiar National Socialist jargon with the dark, suggestive rhetoric of fundamental thinking.

In the letter to Heidegger included in this volume, Karl Jaspers praises the style and density of the address, which make it "of all the documents of a present academic will, the only one up to now that will endure," even as he tempers such praise somewhat by speaking of "characteristics of this address that are in keeping with the times," of "something in it, that seems a little forced to me," of "sentences that appear to me to have a hollow sound."[88] Jaspers here touches on a central feature of Heidegger's style, and not only in the Rectorial Address: its ambiguous position between jargon and authenticity. The sharply divergent responses to Heidegger's reading of "The Origin of the Work of Art" included in this volume illustrate this ambiguity. Hans Barth, in a report published in the *Neue Zürcher Zeitung*, says of Heidegger's language: "often it is violent, often playful, feigning depths where a sober description of the findings would be more desirable."[89] Only to have Emil Staiger counter by calling that same language "primordial" rather than violent, "masterful" and "regal" rather than playful, "sober" as everything genuine is sober, where only such sobriety allows things to present themselves as the things they are.[90] Neither characterization can simply be dismissed; jointly they show something about the ambiguity of Heidegger's style, which, inviting both uncritical rejection and equally uncritical fascination, makes the genuine appropriation of his thought enormously difficult.

7

In the *Spiegel* interview Heidegger makes the startling claim:

> My thinking has an essential connection (*in einem unumgänglichen Bezug*) to Hölderlin's poetry. But I do not think Hölderlin is just any poet, whose work is a subject, among many others, for literary historians. I think Hölderlin is the poet who points toward the future, who expects the god, and who therefore cannot remain simply a subject for Hölderlin research in the literary historical imagination.[91]

This late pronouncement forces the reader to wonder how Heidegger had come to understand his writings up to and including the Rectorial Address, of which it would seem impossible to claim that they stand in an unavoidable relationship to the poetry of Hölderlin. Neither his dissertation "The Doctrine of Judgment in Psychologism" nor his *Habilitationsschrift* on Duns Scotus, nor *Being and Time*, nor the immediately following essays even mention Hölderlin. Until 1933 Heidegger would appear to have remained convinced of the autonomy of philosophical thinking. The later claim that all his thinking stands in an essential relationship to Hölderlin's poetry implies a renunciation of such autonomy.

It is significant that it was only in the winter semester 1934/1935, following the disappointment of his hope to help bring about a spiritual revolution of the German people, that Heidegger, having resigned his political ambitions and with it political responsibility, offered for the first time a lecture course on Hölderlin; and again no accident that he chose for his texts the hymns *Germanien* and *Der Rhein.* Something of the mood in which Heidegger then found himself is communicated by the preface to this lecture course:

> He still has to be passed over in silence for a long time, especially now that "interest" in him is rising and literary history looks for new themes. One now writes about "Hölderlin and his gods." This may well be the most extreme misinterpretation by means of which one pushes this thinker, whom the Germans still need to confront, into irrelevance under the guise of finally doing him justice. As if his work needed that, especially from the bad judges who do their work today. One takes Hölderlin historically and misunderstands what alone is essential: that standing beyond time and place, his work has already surpassed our historical busy-work and has founded the beginning of another history, the beginning of the history that begins with the advent or flight of the God.[92]

Apocalyptic pathos fuses with Nietzschean longing for a discourse beyond mere poetry and mere philosophy, as these have come to be understood.

Heidegger calls the poet here a thinker the Germans still need to confront. The introductory first paragraph of the lecture expands on this.

> Hölderlin is one of our greatest thinkers—that is to say, the thinker who belongs most to the future—because he is our greatest poet. The poetic turn to his poetry is possible only as the thinking confrontation with the revelation of being that has been achieved in his poetry.[93]

Heidegger is addressing his fellow Germans. But he also insists that Hölderlin has unique significance for the entire West and claims that this presents the German people with a special task and responsibility.

"Revelation of being" recalls the divine revelation made known to John to show God's servants "what must soon take place." Heidegger understands Hölderlin as the prophet of modernity, who has found words for "what must soon take place," not in the sense of predicting coming events but of naming the still-hidden destiny that presides over the history of the German people. If, as the *Spiegel* interview reminds us, in 1933 Heidegger had been able to say "The *Führer* himself, and only he, is the current and future reality of Germany, and his word is your law,"[94] it now is the poet Hölderlin who is supposed to teach the Germans who they are and thus gather them into a genuine community. Both the brief embrace of Hitler's leadership and the far more decisive idealization of Hölderlin into a poetic prophet-leader presuppose an inability to make sense of a pure practical reason able to tell us where to stand.

Heidegger calls Hölderlin "our greatest poet." Rather like a lover's assertion of the unsurpassed beauty of the beloved, this is a claim that cannot be supported by argument. It presupposes a decision grounded in affect. Heidegger calls on the German people to follow his example and to gather itself into a genuine community by choosing Hölderlin their common hero.

Heidegger hints at how he understands the greatness of Hölderlin when he calls the "seeming prose" of the hymn *Germanien* "more poetic than the smoothest versifying and jingling of rhymes of one of Goethe's songs or some other singsong.[95] This suggests that the greatness of Hölderlin's poetry shows itself not so much in what it says as in how it says it, in its unique style. This sublime style is contrasted with the beautiful style of Goethe, whom the Germans have traditionally honored as their greatest poet. Heidegger describes what he calls the *Grundstimmung*, the fundamental mood, of Hölderlin's poetry as *Trauer*, as mourning over the flight of the gods. By placing his thinking in an unavoidable relationship to Hölderlin, Heidegger suggests that it must be understood as ruled by the same mood. And this mood already governs the Rectorial Address, which quite appropriately invokes Nietzsche's pronouncement: God is dead. But even though God and the gods have fled and the words of their prophets have a hollow ring, the need for words that will tell us where to stand, for prophet-leaders, remains. Hölderlinian *Trauer* invites seduction by false prophets. For a brief time Heidegger succumbed to such a prophet.

But of greater significance than Heidegger's soon-to-be-reconsidered and revoked decision for Hitler is the mood that made it possible. Understanding that mood remains a task. And while the distinctive style of Heidegger's discourse provides the indispensable first access and for this reason demands much more attention than it has received, Heidegger's own understanding of authentic thinking and speaking demands that we interpret that style by placing it against the background of his style of life.

Martin Heidegger
AND
National Socialism

THE
RECTORIAL
ADDRESS

Preface to the Rectorial Address*

HERMANN HEIDEGGER

FIFTY YEARS AFTER Martin Heidegger gave his rectorial address "The Self-Assertion of the German University," it seems necessary to make the text of this address once again available to the public, a text that many discuss, some even write about, without having read it. Six old misprints were corrected; two minor linguistic corrections made by Martin Heidegger in his own copy were inserted. Otherwise the text is an unchanged reprint of the first edition from the year 1933.

At the instigation of the NSDAP, the address was withdrawn from sale soon after Martin Heidegger resigned in protest at the end of February 1934—he had refused to dismiss deans he had appointed who were not National Socialists—and shortly after the second edition was published.

Much has been said about the content of this address that is false and untrue. From 1945 to the present, even university professors have cited statements that are supposed to be in Martin Heideg-

* Translator's note. Hermann Heidegger's "Preface" and the following two pieces, Martin Heidegger's "The Self-Assertion of the German University" and "The Rectorate 1933/34: Facts and Thoughts," were published together in 1983, fifty years after the National Socialists came to power, in Martin Heidegger, *Die Selbstbehauptung der deutschen Universität / Das Rektorat 1933/34. Tatsachen und Gedanken* (Frankfurt: Vittorio Klostermann, 1983). They have been previously translated by Karsten Harries and were published in the *Review of Metaphysics, 38* 3 (March 1985): 467–502. These three translations were done in collaboration with him.

ger's rectorial address but that cannot be found in it. The words *National Socialism* and *National Socialist* do not appear in this address; neither the *Führer*, the *Chancellor of the Reich*, nor *Hitler* is mentioned.

At the time, the title of the address alone caught people's interest. Without a doubt, Martin Heidegger was at first, like many of those who later became resistance fighters, seized by the mood of national change. He never denied his temporary entanglement in the movement at the time. He certainly also made mistakes during his rectorate. He did not deny his own inadequacies. But he was neither an uncritical fellow traveler nor an active Party member. From the very beginning, he kept a clear distance from the Party leadership. This showed itself in a number of ways, for example in his prohibition of book burnings and of the posting of the "Jewish Notice"[1] at the university, in his appointment of only non-National Socialists as deans, and in that he was able to keep the Jewish professors von Hevesy[2] and Thannhauser[3] at the university during his rectorate.

Shortly after the collapse [of the National Socialist regime] in 1945, Martin Heidegger wrote a retrospective essay: "The Rectorate 1933/34: Facts and Thoughts." He later gave the handwritten manuscript to the undersigned with the instruction to publish it at the proper time. The necessary new edition of the rectorial address, which was published as a bilingual edition in France in 1982,[4] seems to be the right moment for the first publication of this essay, which covers some of the same points as the *Spiegel* interview, given in September 1966.[5]

Attental, January 1983   HERMANN HEIDEGGER

The Self-Assertion of the German University

MARTIN HEIDEGGER

THE ASSUMPTION OF the rectorate is the commitment to the *spiritual* leadership of this institution of higher learning.[1] The following of teachers and students only awakens and strengthens through a true and common rootedness in the essence of the German university. This essence, however, only gains clarity, rank, and power if the leaders, first and foremost and at any time, are themselves led—led by the relentlessness of that spiritual mission that forces the destiny of the German people into the shape of its history.

Do we know about this spiritual mission? Whether we do or not, the question must inevitably be faced: *are* we, teachers and students of this "high" school, truly and commonly rooted in the essence of the German university? Does this essence have genuine strength to shape our existence [*Dasein*]?[2] Only if we fundamentally *will* this essence. But who would want to doubt this? The dominant characteristic of the university's essence is generally thought to be its "self-administration"; it is to be preserved. However—have we really fully considered what this claim to self-administration demands of us?

Self-administration means that we set ourselves our own task and determine the way and manner of its realization ourselves, so that in doing so we ourselves will be what we ought to be. But do we know *who we ourselves* are, this body of teachers and students of the highest school of the German people? Can

5

we know this at all without the most constant and unsparing *self-examination*?

Neither awareness of the present state of the university nor acquaintance with its previous history are enough to guarantee sufficient knowledge of its essence—unless we first, with clarity and severity, delimit this essence for the future, and in such self-limitation, *will* it, and in such willing, *assert* ourselves.

Self-administration can only exist when it is grounded in self-examination. Self-examination, however, can only take place in the strength of the German university's *self-assertion*. Will we carry it out? And how?

The self-assertion of the German university is the primordial, common will to its essence. We regard the German university as the "high" school that, grounded in science and by means of science, educates and disciplines the leaders and guardians of the destiny of the German people. The will to the essence of the German university is the will to science as will to the historical spiritual mission of the German people as a people that knows itself in its state [*Staat*]. *Together*, science and German destiny must come to power in the will to essence. And they will do so and *only* will do so, if we—teachers and students—*on the one hand*, expose science to its innermost necessity and, *on the other hand*, are able to stand our ground while German destiny is in its most extreme distress.

However, we will not experience the essence of science in its innermost necessity as long as we—when speaking of the "new concept of science"—only contest the self-sufficiency and lack of presuppositions of an all-too-contemporary science. Such action is merely negative. Hardly looking back beyond the past decades, it becomes a mere semblance of a true struggle for the essence of science.

If we want to grasp the essence of science, we must first face the decisive question: Should there still *be* science for us in the future, or should we let it drift toward a rapid end? It is never unconditionally necessary that science should be at all. But if there should be science and if it should be *for* us and *through* us, then under what condition can it truly exist?

Only if we again place ourselves under the power of the *beginning* of our spiritual-historical existence. This beginning is the departure, the setting out, of Greek philosophy. Here, for the first time, Western man rises up, from a base in a popular culture [*Volkstum*] and by means of his language, against the *totality of what is* and questions and comprehends it as the being that it is. All science is philosophy, whether it knows and wills it—or not. All science remains bound to that beginning of philosophy. From it science draws the strength of its essence, assuming that it still remains at all equal to this beginning.

Here we want to regain two distinguishing properties of the original Greek essence of science for *our* existence.

An old story was told among the Greeks that Prometheus had been the first philosopher. Aeschylus has this Prometheus utter a saying that expresses the essence of knowing:

τέχνη δ'ἀνάγκης ἀσθενεστέρα μακρῷ

(Prom. 514, ed. Wil).

"Knowing, however, is far weaker than necessity." That means that all knowing about things has always already been surrendered to the predominance of destiny and fails before it.

Precisely because of this, knowing must unfold its highest defiance. Only then will the entire power of the concealedness [*Verborgenheit*] of what is rise up and knowing will really fail. In this way, what is opens itself in its unfathomable inalterability and lends knowing its truth. In this Greek saying on the creative impotence of knowledge, one all too readily hopes to find a prototype for a knowing that is based purely on itself, when actually such knowing has forgotten its own essence. This knowing is interpreted for us as the "theoretical" attitude. But what does θεωρία mean to the Greeks? It is said: pure contemplation, which only remains bound to the matter in question and all that it is and demands. This contemplative behavior is said, with reference to the Greeks, to be pursued for its own sake. But this reference is mistaken. For on the one hand, "theory" is not pursued for its own sake, but only in the passion to remain close to and under the pressure of what is. On the other, the Greeks fought precisely to comprehend and carry out this contemplative questioning as one, indeed as *the* highest, mode of human ἐνέργεια, of human "being-at-work." They were not concerned with aligning practice with theory. Rather, the reverse was true: theory was to be understood as the highest realization of genuine practice. For the Greeks, science is not a "cultural asset" but the innermost determining center of all of popular [*volklich*] and national [*staatlich*] existence. The Greeks thought science not merely a means of bringing the unconscious to consciousness, but the power that hones and encompasses all of existence.

Science is the questioning standing of one's ground in the midst of the constantly self-concealing totality of what is. This active perseverance knows about its impotence in the face of destiny.

This is the initial essence of science. But does this beginning not already lie two and half millennia behind us? Has not the progress of human actions changed science as well? Certainly! The Christian-theological interpretation of the world that followed and the later mathematical-technological thinking of the modern age have distanced science, both in time and in its concerns, from its beginning. But this does not mean that the beginning has been overcome, let alone that it has been negated. Assuming that the primordial Greek science is indeed something great, then the *beginning* of this greatness remains what is *greatest*. The essence of science could not even be emptied out or used up, as is happening today despite all the results and "international organizations," if the greatness of the beginning did not *still* endure. The beginning still *is*. It does not lie *behind us*, as something that was long ago, but stands *before* us. As what is greatest, the beginning has passed in advance over all that is to come and thus already over us as well. The beginning has invaded our future. There it stands as the distant command to us to catch up with its greatness.

Only if we resolutely submit to this distant command to regain the greatness of this beginning, only then will science become the innermost necessity of our existence. Otherwise it will remain an accident into which we fall or the dispassionate contentment of a safe occupation, serving to further a mere progress of information.

But if we submit to the distant command of the beginning, science must become the fundamental happening of our spiritual and popular [*volklich*] existence.

And if our most authentic existence itself stands before a great transformation, and if it is true what that passionate seeker of God and last German philosopher, Friedrich Nietzsche, said: "God is dead"—and if we must be serious about this forsakenness of modern human beings in the midst of what is, then what is the situation of science?

Then, the initial, awed perseverance of the Greeks in the face of what is transforms itself into a completely uncovered exposure to the hidden and uncertain; that is, the questionable. Questioning is then no longer merely a preliminary step that is surmounted on the way to the answer and thus to knowing; rather, questioning itself becomes the highest form of knowing. Questioning then unfolds its most authentic strength to unlock the essential in all things. Questioning then forces our vision to focus, with the utmost simplicity, on the inevitable.

Such questioning shatters the encapsulation of the sciences in separate specialities, brings them back from their boundless and aimless dispersal in individual fields and corners, and directly exposes science once again to the productivity and blessing of all world-shaping powers of human-historical existence, such as nature, history, language; people, custom, state; poetry, thought, faith; disease, madness, death; law, economy, technology.

If we will the essence of science understood as the *questioning, uncovered standing one's ground in the midst of the uncertainty of the totality of what is*, then *this* will to essence will create for our people its world of innermost and most extreme danger, i.e. its truly *spiritual* world. For "spirit" is not empty cleverness, nor the noncommittal play of wit, nor the boundless drift of rational dissection, let alone world reason; spirit is the primordially attuned, knowing resoluteness toward the essence of Being. And the *spiritual world* of a people is not the superstructure of a culture any more than it is an armory filled with useful information and values; it is the power that most deeply preserves the people's earth- and blood-bound strengths as the power that most deeply arouses and most profoundly shakes the people's existence. Only a spiritual world guarantees the people greatness. For it forces the constant decision between the will to greatness and the acceptance of decline to become the law for each step of the march that our people has begun into its future history.

If we will this essence of science, then the teachers of this university must really advance to the outermost post, endangered by constant uncertainty about the world. If they stand their ground there; that is to say, if a common questioning and a communally tuned saying arises from there—in essential nearness to the pressing insistence of all things—then they will gain the strength for leadership. For what is decisive in leading is not just walking ahead of others but the strength to be able to walk alone, not from obstinacy or a craving for power, but empowered by the deepest purpose and the broadest obligation. Such strength binds to what is essential, selects the best, and awakens the genuine following of those who have new courage. But we do not need to first awaken this following. German students are on the march. And *whom* they are seeking are those leaders through whom they want to elevate their own purpose so that it becomes a grounded, knowing truth, and to place it into the clarity of interpretive and effective word and work.

Out of the resoluteness of the German students to stand their ground while German destiny is in its most extreme distress comes a will to the essence of the university. This will is a true will, provided that German students, through the new Student Law,[3] place themselves under the law of their essence and thereby first define this essence. To give oneself the law is the highest freedom. The much-lauded "academic freedom" will be expelled from the German university; for this freedom was not genuine because it was only negative. It primarily meant lack of concern, arbitrariness of intentions and inclinations, lack of restraint in what was done and left undone. The concept of the freedom of the German student is now brought back to its truth. In future, the bond and service of German students will unfold from this truth.

The first bond binds to the national community [*Volksgemeinschaft*]. It obligates to help carry the burden of and to participate actively in the struggles, strivings, and skills of all the estates and members of the people. From now on, this bond will be fixed and rooted in the existence of the student by means of *Labor Service* [*Arbeitsdienst*].

The *second* bond binds to the honor and the destiny of the nation in the midst of all the other peoples. It demands the readiness, secured by knowledge and skill and tightened by discipline, to give the utmost in action. In future, this bond will encompass and penetrate the entire existence of the student as *Military Service* [*Wehrdienst*].

The *third* bond of the students binds them to the spiritual mission of the German people. This people works at its fate by opening its history to all the overwhelming world-shaping powers of human existence and by continually fighting for its spiritual world anew. Thus exposed to the most extreme questionableness of its own existence, this people wills to be a spiritual people. It demands of itself and for itself that its leaders and guardians possess the strictest clarity of the highest, broadest, and richest knowledge. Young students, who at an early age have dared to act as men and have extended their willing to the future destiny of the nation, force themselves, from the very ground of their being, to serve this knowledge. These students will no longer permit *Knowledge Service* [*Wissensdienst*] to be a dull and rushed training for a "distinguished" profession. Because the statesman and the teacher, the doctor and the judge, the minister and the architect lead the existence of people and state, because they guard and hone it in its fundamental relations to the world-shaping powers of human being, these professions and the education for them are entrusted to Knowledge Service. Knowledge does not serve the professions but the reverse: the professions effect and administer that highest and essential knowledge of the people concerning its entire existence. But for us this knowledge is not the dispassionate taking note of essences and values as such, but the most severe endangerment of existence in the midst of the overwhelming power of what is. The very questionableness of Being forces the people to work and fight and forces it into its state [*Staat*], to which the professions belong.

The three bonds—*by* the people, *to* the destiny of the state, *in* spiritual mission—are *equally primordial* to the German essence. The three services that arise from it—Labor Service, Military Service, and Knowledge Service—are equally necessary and of equal rank.

The primordial and full essence of science, whose realization is our task, provided we submit to the distant command of the beginning of our spiritual-historical existence, is only created by knowledge about the people that actively participates and by knowledge about the state's destiny that always keeps itself prepared, both at one with knowledge about the spiritual mission.

It is *this* science that is meant when the essence of the German university is delimited as the "high" school that, grounded in science and through science, educates and disciplines the leaders and guardians of the German people.

This primordial concept of science obligates us not only to "objectivity," but, above all, to make our questioning in the midst of the historical-spiritual world of the people essential and simple. Indeed, it is only then that objectivity can truly ground itself—i.e., discover its nature and its limit.

Science, in this sense, must become the power that shapes the body of the German university. This contains a twofold task: Teachers and students, each in their own way, must become *seized* and *remain* seized by the concept of science. At the same time, however, this concept of science must intervene in and rearrange the basic forms in which the teachers and students each act in a scientific community: in the *faculties* and as *student bodies of specific departments* [*Fachschaften*].

The faculty is a faculty only if it becomes capable of spiritual legislation, and, rooted in the essence of its science, able to shape the powers of existence that pressure *it* into the *one* spiritual world of the people.

The student body of a certain department is a student body only if it places itself in the realm of this spiritual legislation from the start and thus tears down departmental barriers and overcomes the staleness and falseness of superficial professional training.

At the moment when faculties and departmental student bodies set the essential and simple questions of their science into motion, teachers and students are already encompassed by the *same* final necessities and pressing concerns of the existence of people and state.

The unfolding of the primordial essence of science, however, demands such a degree of rigor, responsibility, and superior patience that, in comparison, the conscientious adherence to or the eager alteration of established procedures hardly matter.

But if the Greeks needed three centuries just to put the *question* of what knowledge is onto the right ground and on a secure track, *we* have no right to assume that the elucidation and unfolding of the essence of the German university will occur in the current or coming semester.

But there is *one* thing we do know from the indicated essence of science: The German university will only gain shape and power if the three services primordially coalesce to become *one* formative force. That is to say:

The teachers' will to essence must awaken to the simplicity and breadth of knowledge about the essence of science and thus grow strong. The students' will to essence must force itself to rise to the highest clarity and discipline of knowing and integrate, demanding and determining, engaged knowledge [*Mitwissenschaft*] about the people and its state into the essence of science. The two wills must confront one another, ready for *battle*. All abilities of will and thought, all strengths of the heart, and all capabilities of the body must be unfolded *through* battle, heightened *in* battle, and preserved *as* battle.

We choose the knowing battle of those who question, and we profess with *Carl von Clausewitz*:[4] "I renounce the frivolous hope of salvation by the hand of accident."

This battle community of teachers and students, however, will only recreate the German university into a place of spiritual legislation and establish in it the center of the most disciplined preparation for the highest service to the people in its state if teachers and students arrange their existence more simply, more unsparingly, and more frugally than all the other members of their people [*Volksgenossen*]. All leading must concede its following its own strength. All following, however, bears resistance in itself. This essential opposition of leading and following must not be blurred let alone eliminated.

Battle alone keeps this opposition open and implants in the entire body of teachers and students that basic attitude that allows self-limiting self-assertion empower resolute self-examination to come to genuine self-administration.

Do we, or do we not, will the essence of the German university? It is up to us whether, and to what extent, we concern ourselves with self-examination and self-assertion, not just in passing, but starting from its foundations, or whether we—with the best of intentions—merely change old institutions and add new ones. No one will keep us from doing this.

But no one will even ask us whether we do or do not will, when the spiritual strength of the West fails and its joints crack, when this moribund semblance of a culture caves in and drags all forces into confusion and lets them suffocate in madness.

Whether this will or will not happen depends solely on whether we, as a historical-spiritual people, still and once again will ourselves—or whether we no longer will ourselves. Each individual *participates* in this decision even when, and especially when, he evades it.

But we do will that our people fulfill its historical mission.

We do will ourselves. For the young and the youngest strength of the people, which is already reaching beyond us, *has* already *decided* the matter.

But we will only fully understand the magnificence and greatness of this new departure when we carry within us that profound and far-reaching thoughtfulness that gave ancient Greek wisdom the saying:

τὰ ... μεγάλα πάντα ἐπισφαλῆ ...
[All that is great stands in the storm ...]

(Plato, *Republic*, 497 d. 9).

The Rectorate 1933/34: Facts and Thoughts

MARTIN HEIDEGGER

IN APRIL 1933, I was unanimously elected rector by the plenum of the university. My predecessor, von Möllendorff,[1] had been forced to resign, on the instructions of the Minister [of Culture and Education in Baden, Otto Wacker], after a brief term in office. Von Möllendorff himself, with whom I spoke about the succession in detail numerous times, wanted me to assume the rectorate. Similarly, the man who had been rector before him, Sauer,[2] tried to persuade me to assume the office in the interest of the university. As late as the morning of the election day, I hesitated and wanted to withdraw my candidacy. I had no contact to the influential governmental and [National Socialist German Workers'] Party agencies, was neither a member of the Party, nor had I been politically active in any way. Thus it was uncertain whether my conception of necessity and task would be heard in places where political power was concentrated. But it was just as uncertain to what extent the university would go along with it, of its own accord, and find and shape its own essence in a more primordial manner. I had already publicly presented this task in my inaugural lecture delivered in the summer of 1929.

In the introductory sentences of the inaugural lecture, "What Is Metaphysics?" the following is stated: *"We* question, *here* and *now,* for *ourselves.* Our *existence [Dasein]*—as members of a community of scientists, teachers, and students—is determined by *science.* What essential thing is happening to us at the foundation of our existence, assuming science has become our *passion*? The areas of the sciences lie far apart. The ways they treat their subject matter are fundamentally different. This disintegrated multiplicity of the disciplines is only held together today by the technical organization of the universities and faculties and only retains some meaning because of the practical purposes set for the departments. However, the roots of the sciences in their essential ground have died."[3] By the year 1933 this speech had already been translated into French, Italian, Spanish, and Japanese.

Everyone was in a position to know what I thought about the German university and what I considered its most urgent concern. It was to renew itself starting from its essential ground, which is precisely the essential ground of the sciences, that is to say from the essence of truth itself; and, instead of persisting in a technical organizational-institutional pseudo-unity, it was to regain the primordial vital unity of those who question and those who know.

In 1930 I spoke on the essence of truth. I even repeated the lecture in a number of German towns until 1932, and it was known through duplicated transcripts. The lecture was not published until 1943.[4] At the time I gave that lecture, I also gave a two-hour lecture course on the Greek concept of truth, approaching the topic with an interpretation of the Platonic allegory of the cave. This lecture course was repeated during my rectorate in the winter semester 1933/34 and was supplemented by a very well-attended seminar on "People [*Volk*] and Science." The interpretation of the allegory of the cave was published in 1942 in the *Jahrbuch für geistige Überlieferung II* under the title *"Plato's Doctrine of Truth"* [*"Platons Lehre von der Wahrheit"*].[5] The Party officially prohibited mention and review of this essay; the production of offprints and their distribution by the book trade were similarly prohibited.

What made me hesitate to assume the rectorate up to the very last day was the knowledge that with what I intended I would necessarily run into a twofold conflict with both the new and the old. The new had meanwhile appeared in the form of political science,[6] the idea of which is based on a falsification of the essence of truth. The old was the endeavor to remain in one's own department, to support its progress and utilize this progress in classes, to reject all reflection on the essential foundations as abstract and philosophical, or at most to admit it as superficial decoration, but not to engage in it as reflection and to think and belong to this university *from the base of this engagement.*

Thus there was a danger that my attempt would be fought

against, and made impossible, in the same way by both the new and the old, opposed as they were to one another. What I admittedly did *not yet* see and could not expect when I assumed the rectorate, is what happened in the course of the first semester: that the old and the new finally joined, at one in their desire to paralyze my efforts and to finally eliminate me.

Despite this double threat to my intention to found the essence of the university in a primordial manner, I finally decided to assume the office, moved by the urging of many colleagues at the university, especially of the dismissed rector von Möllendorff and of his predecessor and vice-rector at the time, Sauer. I was especially moved by the possibility, pointed out by Canon Sauer, that, should I refuse, the university might be faced with a rector chosen by outsiders.

On the whole, a threefold consideration determined me to assume the rectorate:

1. At the time, I saw in the movement that had come to power the possibility of an inner self-collection and of a renewal of the people, and a path toward the discovery of its historical-Western purpose. I believed that the university, renewing itself, might also be called to significantly participate in the inner self-collection of the people.

2. For that reason, I saw the rectorate as a possibility to lead all capable forces—regardless of party membership and party doctrine—toward this process of reflection and renewal, and to strengthen and secure the influence of these forces.

3. In this manner I hoped to oppose the advance of unsuited persons and the threatening hegemony of Party apparatus and Party doctrine.

It is a fact that at that time much that was inferior and incapable, much that was selfish and envious, already carried on its terrible business. But in view of the total situation of our people, I thought that this was precisely one more reason to bring the capable forces and the essential aims into play. It was certainly more comfortable to stay on the side, to turn up one's nose at the "impossible people," and to praise what had been without a glance at the historical situation of the Western world. A reference might suggest how I saw the historical situation even at that time. Ernst Jünger's essay on "Total Mobilization" ["*Die totale Mobilmachung*"] was published in 1930; in this essay the basic features of his book *The Worker* [*Der Arbeiter*], which was published in 1932, announced themselves.[7] With my assistant Brock,[8] I discussed these writings in a small circle and attempted to show how they express an essential understanding of Nietzsche's metaphysics, insofar as the history and present of the Western world are seen and foreseen within the horizon of this metaphysics. Using these writings and, still more essentially, their foundations, as a base for our thoughts we were able to think what was coming, that is to say, we attempted to face it in our confrontation with it. Many others also read these writings at the time; but they laid them aside along with many other interesting things they read and did not comprehend their far-reaching implications. In the winter of 1939/40, I once again discussed parts of Jünger's book *The Worker* with a circle of colleagues; I learned that these ideas still seemed strange and disconcerting even then, until they were verified by "the facts." What Ernst Jünger means by his idea of the rule and figure of the worker and what he sees in the light of this idea is the universal rule of the will to power within planetary history. Today everything is a part of this reality, whether it is called communism, or fascism, or world democracy.

From the vantage point of this reality of the will to power, I saw even then what *is*. This reality of the will to power can be expressed, with Nietzsche, in the proposition "God is dead." Essential reasons led me to cite this proposition in my rectorial address. This proposition has nothing to do with the assertion of ordinary atheism. It means: the supersensible world, especially the world of the Christian God, has lost its effective force in history. (See my lecture, 1943, on Nietzsche's word "God is dead."[9]) If things had been different, would the First World War have been possible? And especially, if things had been different, would the Second World War have become possible?

Was there not, then, enough reason and essential distress to think in primordial reflection toward an overcoming of the metaphysics of the will to power, and that means to begin a confrontation with Western thinking by returning to its beginning? Was there not, then, enough reason and essential distress to attempt, for the sake of this reflection on the spirit of the Western world, to awaken and lead into battle, here in Germany, that place that was considered the seat of the cultivation of knowledge and insight—the German university?

Certainly, in the face of the course of history, an argument that begins with "What would have happened, if . . . and if not . . ." is always risky. Yet the question may still be posed: What would have happened and what would have been prevented, if, around 1933, all capable forces had set out, in secret cohesion, to slowly purify and moderate the "movement" that had come to power?

Certainly—it is always a presumption when human beings calculate the guilt of other human beings or charge them with it. But if one is indeed looking for those who are guilty and is judging them by their guilt, is there not also a guilt incurred by failing to do what is essential? Those who were so prophetically gifted then that they foresaw what was to come (I was not so wise), why did they wait almost ten years to oppose the threatening disaster? Why did not those who thought they knew it, why did precisely they not set out to direct everything, starting from its foundations, toward the good in 1933?

Certainly it would have been difficult to gather all capable forces; difficult, too, to slowly influence the movement in its entirety and its position of power, but not more difficult than to bear the burden that we were consequently forced to bear.

With the assumption of the rectorate, I had risked the attempt to save and to purify and to strengthen what was positive.

It was never my intention to merely put Party doctrines into effect and to act in accordance with the "idea" of a "political science." But I was equally unwilling to defend only what had been previously established and, by merely mediating and balancing, to level everything and to keep it in mediocrity. My clear conviction was that the things that were at stake were too essential, towering far above all that concerned the university.

However, it was also clear to me that first of all the positive possibilities that I then saw in the movement had to be emphasized and affirmed in order to prepare for a gathering of all capable forces that would be based not only on facts but also on what mattered. Immediate and mere opposition would neither have corresponded to my conviction at the time (which was never blind faith in the Party) nor would it have been prudent.

To characterize my basic attitude while I was rector, let the following be noted:

1. I was never asked by any Party agency for any kind of political advice; I also never sought such participation.
2. I never maintained any other personal or political relations to Party functionaries in any other way, either.

The intention and attitude of my rectorate are expressed in the rectorial address of May 1933. However, in this case as with every spoken word, everything depends on the interpretation and on the readiness to enter into what is essential and to get it into view at all. The heart of the rectorial address, which is already apparent by the space given it, is the exposition of the essence of knowing and science; the university is to be grounded on that essence, and on that ground it is to assert itself in its essence as German university. Knowledge Service is named in third place after Labor Service and Military Service, not because it is subordinated to them, but because knowing is what is authentic and highest, that unto which the essence of the university and therefore reflection gathers itself. As far as Labor Service, which is mentioned in second place, goes: I may be permitted to remind the reader that this "service" grew out of, and was shaped by, the plight of the times and the will of the young long before 1933. I did not name Military Service in either a militaristic or an aggressive sense but understood it as defense in self-defense.

The heart of the address serves the explanation of the essence of knowing, science, and profession that is based on a training in science. Four major points should be singled out with respect to content:

1. The grounding of the sciences in the experience of the essential area of their subject matter.
2. The essence of truth as the letting be of what is, as it is.
3. Preservation of the tradition of the beginning of Western knowledge in the Greek world. (See my two-hour lecture course given in the summer semester 1932: "The Beginning of Western Philosophy.")
4. In keeping with this, the responsibility of the Western world.

In all this lies the decisive rejection of the idea of "political science," which was announced by the National Socialists as a cruder doctrine of Nietzsche's understanding of the essence of truth and knowledge. But beyond this, the rectorial address clearly rejects the idea of "political science."

The attitude of reflection and questioning is oriented toward "battle." But what does *battle* mean in the address? If what is essential in this reflection returns to the Greek ἐπιστήμη and that means to ἀλήθεια, then one may conjecture that the essence of battle is also not conceived arbitrarily. Battle is thought in the sense of Heraclitus, fragment 53. But to understand this often-cited and equally often misunderstood saying, two things should first be taken into consideration, as I have said often enough in my lectures and seminars:

1. The word πόλεμος, with which the fragment begins, does not mean "war" but what is meant by the word ἔρις, which Heraclitus uses in the same sense. But that means "strife"—not strife as discord and squabbling and mere disagreement and certainly not as the use of violence and beating down the opponent but as confrontation[10] in which the essence of those who confront one another exposes itself to the other and thus shows itself and comes to appearance, and that means in a Greek way: into what is unconcealed and true. Because battle is reciprocal recognition that exposes itself to what is essential, the address, which orients this questioning and reflecting toward "battle," continually speaks of "being exposed." That what is said here lies in the direction of the Heraclitan saying is very clearly shown by the saying itself. One must only take a second point into consideration.

2. Not only must we not think πόλεμοσ as war and, furthermore, not use the supposedly Heraclitan proposition "War is the father of all things" to proclaim war and combat as the highest principle of all being and to philosophically justify the warlike. Above all and at the same time, we must take into consideration that Heraclitus' saying—cited in the usual manner—falsifies everything, because the saying in its entirety is thus suppressed and with it what is essential. The complete saying goes: "Although confrontation sows all things, it is also (and above all) of all things that which is highest that which preserves, and this is because it lets some show themselves as gods, the others, however, as humans, because it lets some step into the open as bondsmen, but the others as free beings."

The essence of πόλεμος lies in δεικνύναι, to show, and in ποιεῖν, to produce [*her-stellen*], as the Greeks say, make-it-stand-out [*hervorstellen*] in open view. That is the essence of *battle* as it is philosophically thought, and what is said in the address is only thought philosophically.

This confrontational reflection on the essential realm of science must take place in each science or it will remain science [*Wissenschaft*] without knowing [*Wissen*]. From such reflection on the totality of the sciences, the university will bring itself, through itself, to its essential ground, which is only accessible to the knowing that it cultivates. That is why its essence cannot be determined from some other place, by "politics" or by some other purpose established for it.

In accordance with this fundamental conception and fundamental attitude, the address bears the title "The Self-Assertion of the German University." Only very few clearly understood what this title alone meant in the year 1933, because only a few of those whom it concerned took the trouble to clearly think through what was said, without bias and without the matter having been obscured by idle talk about it.

Admittedly, one could deal with it in another way. One could excuse oneself from reflection and hold onto the seemingly obvious thought that, shortly after National Socialism seized power, a newly elected rector gives an address on the university, an address which "represents" National Socialism—that is to say, proclaims the idea of "political science," which, crudely understood, says "True is what is good for the people." From this one concludes, and rightly so, that this betrays the essence of the German university in its very core and actively contributes to its destruction; for this reason, the title should be "The Self-Decapitation of the German University."[11] One *could* proceed in this way, if one is sufficiently ignorant and incapable of reflection, if one is lazy enough and ready to escape into idle talk, if one only summons up a sufficient degree of malevolence.

One *could* proceed in such an irresponsible manner when interpreting the address; but then one should not pose as someone who knows himself responsible for the spirit and the welfare of the German university. For to think so superficially and to spend one's days with such superficial chatter corresponds perhaps to political methods, but contradicts the innermost spirit of the objectivity of thinking, the spirit one is pretending to have to save.

The address was not understood by those whom it concerned; neither was its content understood, nor was it understood that it states what it was that guided me during my term in office in distinguishing between what was essential and what was less essential and merely external.

Although the address, and with it my attitude, was grasped even less by the Party and the relevant agencies, it was "understood" inasmuch as one immediately sensed the opposition in it. Following the inaugural banquet in the [Hotel] Kopf, Minister Wacker told me his opinion of the address on the very same day he had heard it:

1. That this was a kind of "private National Socialism," which circumvented the perspectives of the Party program.
2. Most importantly, that the whole address had not been based on the concept of race.
3. That he could not accept the rejection of the idea of "political science," even if he were willing to admit that this idea had not yet been given sufficient foundation.

This opinion of the Minister mattered inasmuch as it was immediately announced to Party friends, to Scheel,[12] then the Gau student leader, and to Dr. Stein, lecturer in medicine, and to Krieck[13] in Frankfurt. Incidentally, these three dominated the Ministry of Culture in Karlsruhe from the start. Fehrle,[14] the Ministerial Counselor responsible for the universities, who was actually harmless and good-natured, was completely under their control.

When I visited the ministry shortly after the inaugural celebration, I was given to understand the following: (1) That in future the presence of the archbishop at such celebrations was not welcome; (2) that the speech I gave at the banquet following the inaugural celebration was inappropriate in that I had superfluously singled out my colleague Sauer from the theological faculty and had emphasized how much I owed him for my own academic education.

The fact that such issues were raised in the ministry was not only characteristic of its standpoint as a whole, but it also showed that one was not at all willing to even consider what I, against a background of squabbling and disagreement, was striving to accomplish for the sake of the inner renewal of the university.

By then I had already been in office for a few weeks. My first official action was, on the second day of my rectorate, to prohibit the posting of the "Jewish notice"[15] in any of the rooms belonging to the university. The notice had already been posted in all German universities. I told the student leader that as long as I was rector, this notice would have no place in the university. Thereupon he, with his two companions, left with the comment that he would report this prohibition to the Reich student leadership. About eight days later, I received a telephone call from a Dr. Baumann, SA Group Leader, from the SA Office of Higher Education of the Supreme SA Leadership. He demanded that the "Jewish notice" be posted. If I refused, I should expect to be removed from office or even that the university might be closed. I continued to refuse. Minister Wacker declared that he could do nothing in opposition to the SA, which then played a role that was later taken over by the SS.

These events were only the first signs of a state of affairs that became more and more apparent during the course of my year as rector: The most diverse groups with political power or common interests intervened in the university with their claims and demands; the ministry often played a minor role and was also busy trying to secure an autonomy against Berlin. Struggles for power were going on everywhere; the actors in these struggles took an interest in the university only to the extent that it, as an institution, as the body of students and teachers, was a factor that entered into the power equation. In addition, the professional associations of doctors, judges, and teachers announced their political claims and demanded the removal of professors who seemed troublesome and suspicious to them.

This atmosphere of confusion, which dominated everything, offered me no possibility to cultivate or even call attention to those efforts that were my sole concern and that had moved me to assume the rectorate: the reflection on the ethos that should govern knowing and the essence of teaching. The summer semester went by and was wasted with the discussion of personnel and institutional questions.

The only productive thing, although productive only in a negative sense, was that I was able to prevent injustices and damages to the university and to colleagues during the "Cleaning-up operation" [*Säuberungsaktion*; a purge], which often threatened to exceed its goals and limits.

The achievements of this merely preventive work did not call themselves to public attention, and it was also unnecessary that colleagues should find out about them. Respected and meritorious colleagues in the faculties of law, medicine, and natural science would be amazed if they knew what had been intended for them then.

During my first weeks in office, it was called to my attention that the minister thought it important that the rectors belong to the Party. One day Dr. Kerber, the county leader at the time, the deputy county leader, and a third member of the county leadership visited me at my office to invite me to join the Party. Only in the interest of the university, which played no role in the play for political power, did I, who had never belonged to any political party, accept the invitation. But I only accepted it on the expressly acknowledged condition that I would never, not as an individual, let alone in my capacity as rector, take over a Party office or engage in any Party activity. I stuck to this condition, which was not difficult, because after my resignation as rector in the spring of 1934 (see below), I was considered politically unreliable and was surveilled more and more with each passing year.

My joining of the Party remained simply a matter of form insofar as the Party leadership had no intention of consulting me in discussions of questions pertaining to the university, culture, and education. During the entire time of my rectorate, I never participated in any deliberation or discussion, let alone in the decision-making, of the Party leadership and of the various Party organs. The university remained suspect, but at the same time it was used for purposes of cultural propaganda.

With every passing day I became steadily more occupied with things that, given my real intention, I had to consider unimportant. I was not only uninterested in the formal execution of such empty official business, but at the same time I was inexperienced, since up to that point I had refused every academic office and thus was a novice. The unfortunate circumstance that the head of the university's administrative office had also only been in office for a short time and was similarly inexperienced in university affairs made things worse. Therefore quite a few things happened that were inadequate, incorrect, and careless. This, it seems, exclusively occupied my colleagues. The rectorial address was a waste of breath and was forgotten the day after the inaugural celebration. During my rectorate, not one of my colleagues discussed any aspects of the address with me. They moved in the tracks of faculty politics that had been worn out for decades.

All this confusion and the predominance of the inessential that arose with it would have been bearable if two dangers for the university had not announced themselves more and more plainly in the course of the summer semester 1933.

On the occasion of a lecture I gave at the University of Heidelberg on the essence of science, I heard from Dr. Stein and Scheel about plans to replace the present holders of several chairs at the University of Freiburg. The university was to be infiltrated with reliable Party members, and this was to make it possible to appoint Party members, especially to the deanships. It was claimed that in making such appointments what mattered, at least for the time being, was not so much an individual's significance as a scholar or his

teaching ability, but his political reliability and activistic effectiveness. These remarks and plans showed once again that Krieck's
influence was spreading from Frankfurt and growing stronger in
Heidelberg and Karlsruhe. In Karlsruhe I was given to understand
that it was unacceptable to leave the present deans in their offices.
The faculties needed a National Socialist leadership. I thus faced
the task of acting in a way that would forestall this threat to the
genuine essence of the university.

The second danger that threatened was an external one, as became apparent at the conference of rectors held during the summer semester in Erfurt. It consisted of efforts to let the entire
teaching activity of the faculties be determined by the medical,
legal, and teaching professions and by their claims and needs and
thus to split up the university once and for all into professional
schools. Not only the inner unity of the university was threatened
by this, but also the basic mode of academic training, which is what
I was trying to save by means of a renewal and for whose sake
alone I had assumed the rectorate.

I tried to confront the dangers threatening from Heidelberg and
from the tendency toward professional schools by proposing a
change in the university's constitution. This change was to have
made it possible to make decanal appointments in such a way that
the essence of the faculties and the unity of the university could be
saved. The motive for this change in constitution was not at all
revolutionary fervor and eagerness for innovation but the insight
into the dangers named above, which were, in view of the distribution and nature of political power, by no means merely imagined.

Within the university, where one stared more and more one-
sidedly at what had been, this change in constitution was only
considered from an institutional and legal point of view. Similarly,
the new decanal appointments were only judged from the point of
view of personal favors or slights.

For the winter semester 1933/34, I appointed colleagues as deans
who had, not only in my personal opinion but also in the general
judgment of the scholarly world, names in their fields and who, at
the same time, guaranteed that each in his own way would place the
spirit of science at the center of his work within the faculty. None of
the deans was a member of the Party. The influence of Party functionaries was eliminated. There was hope that a tradition of scientific spirit would be preserved and revived in the faculties.

But this is not what happened. All hopes were disappointed.
Every effort on behalf of what really mattered was in vain.

The Todtnauberg camp became a strange omen for the winter semester 1933/34. The camp was to have prepared teachers and students for work during the actual semester and to have clarified my understanding of the essence of science and of scientific work and, at the same time, to have presented it for consideration and discussion.

The selection of the participants in this camp was *not* made according to Party membership and National Socialist engagement. After the plan for the camp had become known in Karlsruhe, an insistent request also to be allowed to send participants soon arrived from Heidelberg. Heidelberg communicated with Kiel in a similar vein.

In a talk about university and science, I attempted to clarify the core section of the rectorial address and, in consideration of the dangers mentioned above, to present the task of the university more forcefully. Productive discussions in individual groups were the immediate result, discussions on knowledge and science, knowledge and faith, faith and Weltanschauung. On the morning of the second day, Gau student leader Scheel and Dr. Stein suddenly appeared unannounced by car and had an animated discussion with the camp participants from Heidelberg. Their function gradually became apparent. Dr. Stein asked to be permitted to give a talk. He spoke on race and the principle of race. The camp participants listened to the talk but did not discuss it further. The Heidelberg group had the mission to sabotage the camp. But it was not really the camp that was at issue, it was the University of Freiburg, whose faculties were not to be led by Party members. Unpleasant occurrences, some of them painful, followed. I had to swallow them, however, if I did not want to let the entire coming winter semester fail before it had even begun. Perhaps it would have been more correct to have resigned from office at that time. But at that point I still had not reckoned with what would soon become apparent: the increasing opposition from both the minister and the group in Heidelberg that controlled him and from colleagues.

Although the minister agreed formally with the new decanal appointments, he still thought it strange that not only were no Party members appointed but also that I had dared to appoint as dean of the medical school exactly the man the minister had dismissed as rector half a year earlier because he was unacceptable. Furthermore, the ministry expressed, with increasing clarity, the desire that the idea of "political science" be taken far more seriously at the University of Freiburg than had previously been the case.

It was striking that in the course of the winter semester it was suggested to me numerous times by members of the medical and law schools that I appoint new deans and replace our colleagues von Möllendorff and Wolf.[16] I attributed these wishes to squabbling and rivalries within the two faculties and took no further notice of them. Until, late in the winter toward the end of the semester 1933/34, I was asked to come to Karlsruhe, where Ministerial Counselor Fehrle informed me, in the presence of Gau student leader Scheel, that the minister wanted me to relieve these deans, von Möllendorff and Wolf, of their posts.

I immediately declared that I would do so under no circumstances and that I could not justify such a change of appointments either personally or objectively. If the minister were to insist on his request, I would have no choice but to resign from office under protest against this imposition. Herr Fehrle then said to me that the law school also wanted a new decanal appointment as far as colleague Wolf was concerned. I thereupon declared that I was resigning from office and asked for a meeting with the minister. During my declaration, Gau student leader Scheel had a grin on his face. In this way one had achieved what one wanted. It had become unambiguously clear that circles at the university that were incensed by anything that looked like National Socialism did not hesitate to conspire with the ministry and the group that controlled it in order to push me out of office.

In my meeting with the minister, who immediately accepted my resignation, it became clear that there was a rift between the National Socialist conception of the university and of science and my own, a rift that could not be bridged. The minister explained that he did not want this opposition, which presumably was based on the incompatability of my philosophy with the National Socialist Weltanschauung, to become known to the public as a conflict between the University of Freiburg and the ministry. I responded that I could have no interest in that, if only because the university was agreeing with the ministry and I did not want to became a topic for public discussion because of a conflict. The minister replied that, after I had resigned from the rectorate without attracting any attention, I would be free to act as I thought necessary.

And I did act in that I refused to take part in the ceremonial handing over of the rectorate as the departing rector and to give my report, as was the tradition. This refusal was understood at the

university, and I was not, of course, further consulted as the departing rector, as was the custom, before and since. I did not expect
anything of the sort.

After April 1934, I lived outside the university inasmuch as I no
longer concerned myself with "what went on," and instead tried, to
the best of my ability, to carry out only what was absolutely necessary in my teaching obligations. But in the following years even
teaching was more of a conversation of essential thinking with
itself. Perhaps it touched and awakened people here and there, but
it did not shape itself into a developing structure of a definite
conduct, which might in turn have given rise to something primordial.

The case of the rectorate 1933/34, unimportant as it is in itself, is
probably a sign of the metaphysical state of the essence of science,
a science that can no longer be determined by attempts at renewal
and whose essential transformation into pure technology[17] can no
longer be checked. This I only recognized in the following years
(see "The Foundation of the Modern World View Through Metaphysics").[18] The rectorate was an attempt to see something in the
movement that had come to power, beyond all its failings and
crudeness, that was much more far-reaching and that could perhaps one day bring a concentration on the Germans' Western
historical essence. It will in no way be denied that at the time I
believed in such possibilities and for that reason renounced the
actual vocation of thinking in favor of being effective in an official
capacity. In no way will what was caused by my own inadequacy in
office be played down. But these points of view do not capture what
is essential and what moved me to accept the rectorate. The various assessments of this rectorate, made within the boundaries of
the usual academic business, may be correct and justified, but they
never capture what is essential. And today there is even less of a
possibility than there was then to open blinded eyes to the horizon
of what is essential.

What is essential is that we are in the midst of the consummation
of nihilism, that God is "dead," and every time-space for the god-
head is covered. The surmounting of nihilism nevertheless announces itself in German poetic thinking and singing.[19] The
Germans, admittedly, still have the least understanding of this
poetry, because they are striving to adapt themselves to the stan-
dards of the nihilism that surrounds them and thus to misjudge the
essence of a historical self-assertion.

The Time after the Rectorate

Let the following be listed for those, and only for those, who take pleasure in fixedly staring at what were, in their judgment, the mistakes of my rectorate. Taken by itself, the following is as unimportant as the unproductive rummaging through past attempts and measures, which are, within the context of the entire movement of the planetary will to power, so insignificant they cannot even be called tiny.

The possible consequences of my resignation from office in the spring of 1934 were clear to me; after 30 June of the same year,[20] they were completely clear to me. Anyone who assumed an office in the leadership of the university after that was in a position to know very clearly with whom he was getting himself involved.

How my rectorate was then judged by the Party and the ministry, by the teachers and students is set down in a statement that was circulated by the press when my successor assumed office. It said that this successor was the first National Socialist rector of the University of Freiburg, a man who, as a veteran, guaranteed a fighting-soldierly spirit and its propagation at the university.

Suspicions, which at times degenerated into rudeness, began to be voiced against me. A reference to volumes of E. Krieck's journal *Volk im Werden*, which was first published at that time, is enough proof. Hardly an issue of this journal appeared in which open or seemingly unaware polemics did not disparage my philosophy. Because I never, until today, took note of these carryings on and absolutely never got involved in a refutation, the rage of those who were so pathetic that I had never attacked them steadily increased. A. Bäumler[21] went into the same business of voicing suspicions, although in a somewhat different form, in his journal of education, which he published on behalf of Rosenberg's office. The Hitler Youth's journal, *Wille und Macht*, served as a preview. My rectorial address, which had been published, became a popular target for polemics in the teachers' camps. (Verified by H. G. Gadamer, Gerh. Krüger, W. Bröcker.[22])

Even my lectures, which I gave rarely enough and in purely academic spheres, were attacked very rudely every time by the local Party newspaper in a disgusting manner and, every time, the university leadership only roused itself with difficulty to intervene in these doings. The following lectures were given: 1935, "The Origin of the Work of Art";[23] 1938, "The Foundation of the Modern

World View through Metaphysics"; 1941, "Hölderlin's Feast-Day Hymn";[24] and 1943, "Hölderlin's Memorial Celebration".[25]

This hounding, which also extended to my lecture courses, gradually had its intended effect. In the summer semester 1937, a Dr. Hancke from Berlin, very gifted and interested, appeared in a seminar and worked with me. He soon confessed to me that he could no longer conceal from me that he was working for Dr. Scheel, who was then the head of the South-West Section of the SD [*Sicherheitsdienst*; Security Service]. Dr. Scheel had called to his attention that my rectorate had been the real reason for the *non*-National Socialist appearance and the lukewarm attitude of the University of Freiburg. I do not want to count this as a merit. I only mention it to suggest that the opposition that had begun in 1933 had continued and grown stronger.

The same Dr. Hancke also told me that the SD thought I was collaborating with the Jesuits. It is true that members of Catholic orders (especially Jesuits and Franciscans from the Freiburg House) attended my lectures and seminars up until the very end. These gentlemen had the opportunity to participate in and benefit from my seminars just like other students. For a number of semesters, the Jesuit Fathers Prof. Lotz, Rahner, and Huidobro were members of my advanced seminar; they were often in our house. One only has to read their writings to recognize the influence of my thinking; this influence is, furthermore, not denied.[26]

Later, too, the Gestapo's inquiries of me concerned only Catholic members of my seminar: Father Schumacher, Dr. Guggenberger, Dr. Bollinger (in connection with the Scholl student action[27] in Munich; they were looking for a source of that action in Freiburg and searched for it in my lectures).

Even before that time, after my resignation from office, there were complaints that I allowed former students (non-Aryans) to attend my lectures.

Furthermore, it is well known that my three most capable students (Gadamer, G. Krüger, and Bröcker), all three well above the average of the new generation in philosophy at the time, were kept back for years because they were Heidegger students. They were only appointed to professorships when it became impossible not to acknowledge their qualifications and the scandal became apparent.

After 1938 it was forbidden to mention my name in newspapers and journals and to review my writings, insofar as they could still appear in new editions. Finally the publication of new editions of

Being and Time and the book on Kant was not allowed, although the publishers had the necessary paper.

Despite the complete silence within the country, attempts were made to use my name abroad for purposes of cultural propaganda and to get me to give lectures. I turned down all such lecture trips to Spain, Portugal, Italy, Hungary, and Romania; I also never participated in the lectures the faculty held in France for the armed forces.

The following facts may speak for the ways in which my philosophical work was judged and attempts were made to eliminate it:

1. At the International Congress of Philosophy in Prague in 1935, I neither belonged to the German delegation nor was I even invited to participate.

2. I was to have been excluded from the Descartes Congress in Paris in 1937 in the same way. This action against me seemed so strange to those in Paris that Prof. Brèhier from the Sorbonne asked me, on behalf of the executive committee, why I did not belong to the German delegation; the Congress wanted to invite me on its own to give a lecture. I replied that they should inquire at the Reich Ministry of Education in Berlin about this case. After a while I received an invitation from Berlin to join the delegation. The whole matter was handled in such a way that it became impossible for me to go to Paris with the German delegation.

During the war a publication of accounts of the humanities in Germany was being prepared. Nic. Hartmann[28] was in charge of the section "Systematic Philosophy." A three-day conference was held in Berlin to plan this undertaking. All professors of philosophy were invited except for Jaspers and myself. We were of no use because an attack on "existential philosophy" was being planned in connection with this publication, which was indeed later carried out.[29]

In this case, too, as earlier during the rectorate, my opponents showed a strange willingness to ally themselves, despite the oppositions that divided them, against everything by which they felt spiritually threatened and put into question.

But these events, too, are only a fleeting appearance on the waves of a movement of our history, whose dimensions the Germans still do not suspect, even after the catastrophe has descended upon them.

Preface to the German Edition of "Antwort: Martin Heidegger im Gespräch"

"QUESTIONING IS THE piety of thinking." This often-cited sentence with which Heidegger concluded his lecture *The Question Concerning Technology*, given in the year 1953, is characteristic of his understanding of philosophizing, or thinking. Throughout his life, Heidegger understood thinking to be a path, as being under way in asking the *one* fundamental question around which all of his writings circle: the "question of Being," or, more precisely, the question on the nearness between Being and human beings, on the *belonging* together of Being and human beings in turn, and their origin in the happening.

For Heidegger answers only constitute the last step of questioning, and as such they must remain rooted in questioning. He thinks genuine philosophical answers do not have a character that defines and concludes but that opens and discloses. They do not take leave of questioning but keep it open and going. In that spirit, this book, too, is an attempt to achieve pioneering work on the question of the connection between Heidegger's thinking and actions that has recently been raised again.

Following numerous requests, it had first been planned to re-edit Richard Wisser's television interview with Martin Heidegger in 1969, which had been out of print for years, and supplement it with Wisser's description of the history and circumstances of this very literally unique venture.

In the case of the relatively short television interview, such a documentation of the precise circumstances of the conversation, the background, and the atmosphere when the interview took place are extremely informative and absolutely necessary. For example, Wisser gives all the questions he had originally planned to ask but that Heidegger did not want to answer in front of the television camera, and he gives us information on the background of Heidegger's refusal. Only the interview text and the recollection text together give a complete and thus rounded picture of this venture. The proportion between the quite short television interview and the description of the background, which is almost three times as long, should be understood in this light.

Beyond presenting information on the omitted questions, Wisser is concerned with giving a detailed description of Heidegger's character (even if consciously personal), especially with regard to the younger generation who can no longer have the privilege of hearing Heidegger themselves, let alone meeting him, but who might nonetheless be highly interested in his personal character.

Heidegger avoided publicity and was critical of mass media. Despite numerous suggestions and strong urging, he only gave two interviews in his life: the television interview in 1969 and an interview with the magazine *Der Spiegel*, given in 1966 on the condition that it would be published only after his death, which was in 1976. Since the *Spiegel* interview has not yet appeared in book form (is therefore not even available in the libraries of philosophy departments, and is only accessible through periodical archives) it seemed necessary to include it in this volume. In addition, the interview is published here for the first time in the version authorized by Heidegger, which differs considerably in places from the version published in *Der Spiegel*.

An eyewitness account by Heinrich W. Petzet, who "assisted" Heidegger in the *Spiegel* interview with Rudolf Augstein and Georg Wolff, is added here as well to describe the circumstances of the interview.

On the basis of their rarity alone, both interviews hold a special place for research on Heidegger, especially since Heidegger did not often retrospectively comment on his own work or publicly answer critical questions.

Whereas the television interview limits itself primarily to Heidegger's thinking, the significance of the considerably more extensive *Spiegel* interview lies in Heidegger's statements on his political engagement during the era of National Socialism. There has been heightened interest in this topic since Dr. Hermann Heidegger, his son and executor, republished Heidegger's rectorial address "The Self-Assertion of the German University" (1933) in 1983, supplemented by Martin Heidegger's notes "The Rectorate 1933/34: Facts and Thoughts," written in 1945, and since the Freiburg historian Hugo Ott has made revelations about Heidegger's rectorate in 1933/34 in several essays written after 1983. This interest reached a high point when Victor Farías' book *Heidegger and Nazism,* published in France in 1987, struck like "a bomb" (*Le Monde*) and kindled an unusually vehement and controversial discussion that has meanwhile spread from France to Germany and is still burning.

The immense interest in the discussion on Heidegger, especially on his political conduct during the National Socialist era as well as the possible link between his thinking and his at least temporary support of National Socialism, that is apparent not only in philosophical circles but also in the mass media, caused the editors to add a third section in which a documentation of pieces on Heidegger's thinking and actions is given.

In view of the still-continuing flood of newspaper articles, essays, and books on the topic "Heidegger and Politics" and the different statements and evaluations of this question, which are so varied it is hard to keep track of them, it must be emphasized that the documentation does not claim to be a complete collection. Rather, we have consciously limited ourselves to a few fragments of this discussion.

Primarily, texts that describe Heidegger's personality or comment on his political conduct were chosen. Precedence was given to philosophers who belong or once belonged to Heidegger's circle, like Hans-Georg Gadamer, Karl Löwith, Hannah Arendt, Hans Jonas, Max Müller, and Jean Beaufret, or whose own philosophy has been substantially influenced by Heidegger's thinking, like Emmanuel Lévinas and Jacques Derrida.

On the one hand, we wanted to call attention to previously unprinted documents, or at least documents that have not been previously published in German, for example the contributions by Hans-Georg Gadamer and Jacques Derrida. On the other hand, we wanted to make publications that are hard to find and thus forgotten accessible, for example Hannah Arendt's article in *Merkur* written for Heidegger's eightieth birthday in 1969. For this reason we could, for example, leave out the statements by Theodor W. Adorno and Jürgen Habermas because these are easily available.

The documents were divided into four sections according to their nature: positions, recollections, appreciations, and contemporary documents.* They are preceded by a summary of the stages of the discussion up to now and a detailed bibliography on the topic "Heidegger and Politics."

Because the Chilean Victor Farías' publication *Heidegger and Nazism* directly brought about the current feverish preoccupation with the question of the connection between Heidegger's political error during the era of National Socialism and his thinking, it seemed appropriate to start with several positions on Farías' book. All the contributions focus on the question whether the case of Heidegger's thinking is closed because of his political failure, as Farías contends. Hugo Ott, who deserves credit for revealing new insights, earlier than Farías, into Heidegger's political engagement during the National Socialist era on the basis of his extensive study of the sources, concisely summarizes the crucial accusations in his review of Farías' book and also points out faults and insufficiencies in Farías' research. The oldest living Heidegger student and the Nestor of German philosophy, Hans-Georg Gadamer, expresses his astonishment at the great sensation Farías' book caused in France, since most of what Farías presents has long been known in Germany. He agrees with Jacques Derrida that Heidegger's political conduct and his silence after 1945, however one perceives it, do not release us from the obligation to take his thinking seriously and to study his writings. Emmanuel Lévinas, who could never forget Heidegger's political misconduct and in whose opinion Heidegger never freed himself from the guilt of his involvement with National Socialism, also thinks Heidegger's thinking remains "a great event of our century."

These positions are supplemented in the second section by recollections of encounters with Heidegger during the twenties and thirties. They give insight into the events after 1933 and describe the atmosphere at the time. Karl Löwith, the first student at the University of Marburg to receive his qualification to teach at the university level [*Habilitation*] under Heidegger describes his meeting with Heidegger in Rome in 1936, which he supposed would be his last, when Heidegger unambiguously declared his support of National Socialism. Georg Picht's recollections of several episodes from his years as a student at the University of Freiburg (from 1933

---

* In this English-language edition many of the texts originally included under the heading "Contemporary documents" have been moved to the appendix.

to 1944), however, testify that Heidegger by no means adhered to the usual Party line and that it was more a case of a "power of thinking." Hans Gottschalk, son of the Freiburg philosopher Jonas Cohn, and Max Müller are two further trustworthy witnesses to the situation in Freiburg during the years 1933/1934. Müller's contribution gives a detailed account of the atmosphere at the time and of constellations in the faculty. Hans Jonas' recollections of his teacher Heidegger's appearance and effect go further back to Heidegger's years in Marburg and early years in Freiburg, and they conclude the second section.

In a third section, four appreciations of Heidegger's life and work are given. They primarily give information on his personality and his direct effect. Hannah Arendt, one of Heidegger's first students from the time he spent at the University of Marburg, from 1923 to 1929, describes in an unsurpassed way the rumors about and the personal aura of the young philosophy professor who, despite his youth, had already become the "secret king" of German philosophy before the publication of *Being and Time.* The great effect Heidegger had in France, against the background of which the tremendous sensation caused by Farías' book should be seen, is the focus of Jean Beaufret's contribution. Beaufret was long a friend of Heidegger and contributed a great deal toward making Heidegger's writings known in his native France. In his "Words in Memory of Martin Heidegger from the Academy of the Arts in Berlin" written in 1977, Walter Jens emphasizes the contradictoriness and greatness of Heidegger's poetical thinking. In a letter to Günther Neske written on 18 August 1988, the Protestant theologian Eberhard Jüngel honors Heidegger as the "thinker of what is possible."

The contemporary comments collected in the fourth section naturally have special importance. They include Karl Jaspers' letter to Heidegger written on 23 September 1933, a letter in which (contrary to his later statements) Jaspers still emphatically praises Heidegger's rectorial address, and Jaspers' letter from 5 June 1949 to the then-rector of the University of Freiburg, Gerd Tellenbach, which initiated repeal of the prohibition of Heidegger teaching and the conferral of the honorable status of emeritus professor upon him. The public debate between Hans Barth and Emil Staiger on the occasion of Heidegger's lecture "The Origin of the Work of Art" given on 17 January 1936 in Zürich is paradigmatic of the contradictory evaluations of the connection between Heidegger's rectorial address and his other works and of his language in the mid-thirties. Especially noteworthy for the discussion of Heidegger's political engagement is the fact that a symposium was held in Beirut in 1974 in honor of his eighty-fifth birthday. Although Heidegger could not attend the symposium because of his age, he did write a greeting.

All of the documents are accompanied by a short commentary, in which, in addition to the sources and biographical notes, references to further publications or important passages on Heidegger are given, and (where this plays a role) the development of the personal relationship to Heidegger is outlined.

The title of this book—"response"—does not mean to imply that the last word has been spoken. Rather it should be understood in two different ways: as Martin Heidegger's direct responses to the questions posed him by Richard Wisser and Rudolf Augstein, and as a response or as responses given by renowned philosophers and authorities on Heidegger to the question asked by the public on the topic "Heidegger and National Socialism." This "response," in contrast to other publications, does not cut conversation short but contributes interesting opinions and convincing arguments.

"Discussion" can also be understood in two ways. This book shows Martin Heidegger in direct discussion with Richard Wisser and Rudolf Augstein, and it supplements the public discussion that has once more focused on Martin Heidegger. It should become clear from all of these contributions that the simple response to the phenomenon "Heidegger" that some hope for does not exist.

Mainz, West Germany   GÜNTHER NESKE
September 1988   EMIL KETTERING

THE
SPIEGEL
INTERVIEW

Der Spiegel Interview
*with Martin Heidegger**

SPIEGEL: Professor Heidegger, we have noticed again and again that your philosophical work is somewhat overshadowed by incidents in your life that, although they didn't last very long, were never clarified, either because you were too proud or because you did not find it expedient to comment on them.

HEIDEGGER: You mean 1933?

SPIEGEL: Yes, before and afterward. We would like to place it in a greater context and then to move on from there to a few questions that seem important to us, such as: What possibilities does philosophy have to influence reality, including political reality? Does this possibility still exist at all? And if so, what is it composed of?

HEIDEGGER: Those are important questions. Will I be able to answer them all? But let me start by saying that I was in no way politically active before I became rector. In the winter of 1932/33, I had a leave of absence and spent most of my time up in my cabin.[1]

---

* Translator's note. A previous translation of the *Spiegel* interview by Maria Alter and John D. Caputo appeared in *Philosophy Today* 20 (Winter 1976): 267–284.

Source: *"Nur noch ein Gott kann uns retten,"* Der Spiegel, *31 May 1976, pp. 193–219. The interview with Rudolf Augstein and Georg Wolff took place on 23 September 1966. Reprinted with the kind permission of Martin Heidegger's executor, Dr. Hermann Heidegger. The text was corrected using Martin Heidegger's own copy.*

SPIEGEL: Then how did it come about that you became rector of the University of Freiburg?

HEIDEGGER: In December of 1932, my neighbor von Möllendorff,[2] professor of anatomy, was elected rector. At the University of Freiburg, the new rector assumes his post on April 15. During the winter semester 1932/33 we often spoke about the situation, not only about the political situation, but especially about the situation of the universities, about the situation of the students—which was, in some ways, hopeless. My opinion was: As far as I can judge things, the only possibility that remains is to try to counterbalance the coming development with those of the constructive powers that are still really vital.

SPIEGEL: So you saw a connection between the situation of the German university and the political situation in Germany in general?

HEIDEGGER: I certainly followed the course of political events between January and March 1933 and occasionally talked about it with younger colleagues as well. But at the time I was working on an extensive interpretation of pre-Socratic thinking, and at the beginning of the summer semester I returned to Freiburg. In the meantime Professor von Möllendorff had assumed his office as rector on April fifteenth. Just under two weeks later, his office was taken away from him again by the Minister of Culture in Baden at the time, Wacker. The fact that the rector had prohibited the posting of the so-called Jewish Notice[3] at the university was, presumably, a welcome cause for the minister's decision.

SPIEGEL: Herr von Möllendorff was a Social Democrat. What did he do after his dismissal?

HEIDEGGER: The day of his dismissal von Möllendorff came to me and said: "Heidegger, now you must take over the rectorate." I said that I had no experience in administration. The vice-rector at the time, Sauer (theology), however, also urged me to run in the new rectorial election because there was a danger that otherwise a functionary would be appointed as rector. Younger colleagues, with whom I had discussed questions of the structure of the university for many years, besieged me with requests to take over the rectorate. I hesitated a long time. Finally I declared myself willing to take over the office, but only in the interest of the university, and only if I could be certain of the plenum's unanimous approval. Doubts about my aptitude for the rectorate remained, however, and on the morning of the day set for the election I went to the rector's office and told my colleagues von Möllendorff (who, although dismissed from his office as rector, was present) and vice-rector Sauer that I could not take over the office. Both these colleagues responded that the election had been prepared in such a way that I could no longer withdraw from my candidacy.

SPIEGEL: After that you declared yourself finally ready. How did your relationship to the National Socialists then develop?

HEIDEGGER: The second day after my assumption of the rectorate, the Student Leader appeared with two others in the office I had as rector and again demanded that the Jewish Notice be posted. I refused. The three students left with the comment that the Reich Student Leadership [*Reichsstudentenführung*] would be notified of the prohibition. A few days later I got a telephone call from the SA Office of Higher Education in the Supreme SA Command, from SA-Group Leader Dr. Baumann. He demanded that the said notice, which had already been put up in other universities, be posted. If I refused, I would have to expect that I would be dismissed or even that the university would be closed. I refused and tried to win the support of Baden's Minister of Culture for my prohibition. He explained that he could do nothing in opposition to the SA. I still did not retract my prohibition.

SPIEGEL: This was not known in that way before.

HEIDEGGER: I had already named the fundamental motive that made me decide to take over the rectorate in my inaugural lecture "What Is Metaphysics?" given in Freiburg in 1929: "The areas of the sciences lie far apart. The ways they treat their subject matter are fundamentally different. This disintegrated multiplicity of the disciplines is only held together today by the technical organization of the universities and its faculties and only retains some meaning because of the practical purposes set for the departments. However, the roots of the sciences in their essential ground have died."[4] What I attempted to do during my term in office with respect to this state of the universities (which has, by today, become extremely deteriorated) is explained in my rectorial address.

SPIEGEL: We are attempting to find out how and if this statement from 1929 corresponds to what you said in your inaugural address as rector in 1933. We are taking one sentence out of its context here: "The much-lauded 'academic freedom' will be expelled from the German university; for this freedom was not genuine because it was only negative."[5] We believe we can assume that this statement expresses at least a part of opinions that are not foreign to you even today.

HEIDEGGER: Yes, I still stand by it. For this "academic freedom" was basically purely negative: the *freedom from* the effort of getting involved in the reflection and contemplation scholarly study demanded. Incidentally, the sentence you picked out should not be isolated, but placed in its context. Then it will become clear what I wanted to have understood as "negative freedom."

SPIEGEL: Fine, that's understandable. We believe, however, that we hear a new tone in your rectorial address when you speak, four months after Hitler was named Chancellor of the Reich, about the "greatness and magnificence of this new departure."[6]

HEIDEGGER: Yes, I was convinced of that as well.

SPIEGEL: Could you explain that a bit more?

HEIDEGGER: Gladly. At the time I saw no other alternative. In the general confusion of opinions and political tendencies of thirty-two parties, it was necessary to find a national, and especially a social, point of view, perhaps along the lines of Friedrich Naumann's attempt.[7] I could refer here, to give only one example, to an essay by Eduard Spranger that goes way beyond my rectorial address.[8]

SPIEGEL: When did you begin to deal with the political conditions? The thirty-two parties had been there for a long time. There were already millions of unemployed in 1930.

HEIDEGGER: During that time, I was still completely taken up by the questions that are developed in *Being and Time* (1927) and in the writings and lectures of the following years. These are fundamental questions of thinking that indirectly also concern national and social questions. As a teacher at the university, I was directly concerned with the question of the meaning of the sciences and, therefore, the determination of the task of the university. This effort is expressed in the title of my rectorial address, "The Self-Assertion of the German University." In no other rectorial address at the time was such a title risked. But have any of those who polemicize against this speech really read it thoroughly, thought it through, and understood it from the standpoint of the situation at the time?

SPIEGEL: Self-assertion of the university, in such a turbulent world, does that not seem a little inappropriate?

HEIDEGGER: Why? "The Self-Assertion of the University" goes against so-called political science, which had already been called for by the Party and National Socialist students. This title had a very different meaning then. It did not mean "politology," as it does today, but rather implied: Science as such, its meaning and its value, is appraised for its practical use for the nation [*Volk*]. The counter position to *this* politicization of science is specifically expressed in the rectorial address.

SPIEGEL: Do we understand you correctly? In including the university in what you felt to be a "new departure," you wanted to assert the university against perhaps overpowering trends that would not have left the university its indentity?

HEIDEGGER: Certainly, but at the same time self-assertion was to have set itself the positive task of winning back a new meaning, in the face of the merely technical organization of the university, through reflection on the tradition of Western and European thinking.

SPIEGEL: Professor, are we to understand that you thought then that a recovery of the university could be achieved with the National Socialists?

HEIDEGGER: That is incorrectly worded. The university was to have renewed itself through its own reflection, not with the National Socialists, and thereby gain a firm position against the danger of the politicization of science—in the sense already given.

SPIEGEL: And that is why you proclaimed these three pillars in your rectorial address: Labor Service [*Arbeitsdienst*], Military Service [*Wehrdienst*], Knowledge Service [*Wissensdienst*]. Through this, you seem to have thought, Knowledge Service would be lifted up to an equal status, a status that the National Socialists had not conceded it?

HEIDEGGER: There is no mention of pillars. If you read carefully, you will notice that although Knowledge Service is listed in third place, it is set in first place in terms of its meaning. One ought to consider that labor and defense are, like all human activities, grounded in knowledge and illuminated by it.

SPIEGEL: But we must (we are almost done with this dreadful quoting) mention one other statement here, one that we cannot imagine that you would still subscribe to today. "Do not let theorems and ideas be the rules of your being. The Führer himself and alone *is* the present and future German reality and its law."[9]

HEIDEGGER: These sentences are not to be found in the rectorial address, but only in the local Freiburg student newspaper, at the beginning of the winter semester 1933/34. When I took over the rectorate, it was clear to me that I would not get through it without making compromises. Today I would no longer write the sentences you cited. Even in 1934, I no longer said anything of the kind. But today, and today more resolutely than ever, I would repeat the speech on the "Self-Assertion of the German University," though admittedly without referring to nationalism. Society has taken the place of the nation [*Volk*]. However, the speech would be just as much of a waste of breath today as it was then.

SPIEGEL: May we interrupt you with a question again? It has become clear in the conversation up to now that your conduct in 1933 fluctuated between two poles. First, you had to say a number of things ad usum Delphini ["for the use of the Dauphin"; revised for public consumption—Tr.]. That was one pole. The other pole was, however, more positive. You expressed it like this: I had the feeling that here is something new, here is a new departure—the way you have said it.

HEIDEGGER: That's right.

SPIEGEL: Between these two poles—that is perfectly credible when considered from the point of view of the situation at the time. . . .

HEIDEGGER: Certainly. But I must emphasize that the expression *ad usum Delphini* says too little. I believed at the time that in the questioning confrontation with National Socialism a new path, the only one still possible, to a renewal might possibly open up.

SPIEGEL: You know that in this connection some accusations have been made against you that concern your cooperation with the National Socialist German Workers' Party [NSDAP] and its associations. These accusations are generally thought to be uncontradicted as yet. You have been accused, for instance, of having participated in book-burnings organized by the students or by the Hitler Youth.

HEIDEGGER: I forbade the book-burning that was planned to take place in front of the main university building.

SPIEGEL: You have also been accused of having books written by Jewish authors removed from the university library or from the philosophy department's library.

HEIDEGGER: As the director of the department, I was in charge of only its library. I did not comply with repeated demands to remove books by Jewish authors. Former participants in my seminars can testify today that not only were no books by Jewish authors removed, but that these authors, especially Husserl, were quoted and discussed just as they were before 1933.

SPIEGEL: We will take note of that. But how do you explain the origin of such rumors? Is it maliciousness?

HEIDEGGER: From what I know about the sources, I am inclined to believe that. But the motives for the slander lie deeper. Presumably my assumption of the rectorate was only a catalyst and not the determining cause. Therefore the polemics will probably always flare up again whenever there is a catalyst.

SPIEGEL: You had Jewish students after 1933, too. Your relationship to some, probably not to all, of these Jewish students was supposed to have been warm. Even after 1933?

HEIDEGGER: My attitude remained unchanged after 1933. One of my oldest and most gifted students, Helene Weiss, who later emigrated to Scotland, received her doctorate from the University of Basel (after she was no longer able to receive it from the Freiburg faculty) with a very important dissertation on "Causality and Chance in the Philosophy of Aristotle," printed in Basel in 1942. At the end of the foreword the author writes: "The attempt at a phenomenological interpretation, whose first part we present here, was made possible by M. Heidegger's unpublished interpretations of Greek philosophy."

Here you see the copy with a handwritten dedication that the author sent me in 1948. I visited Dr. Weiss a number of times in Basel before her death.

SPIEGEL: You were friends with Jaspers for a long time. This relationship began to be strained after 1933. Rumor has it that this strain was connected to the fact that Jaspers had a Jewish wife. Would you like to comment on that?

HEIDEGGER: What you mention here is a lie. Jaspers and I had been friends since 1919. I visited him and his wife during the summer semester of 1933, when I delivered a lecture in Heidelberg. Karl Jaspers sent me all of his publications between 1934 and 1938—"with warm regards." Here, you can look at them.

SPIEGEL: It says here: "With warm regards." Well, the regards probably would not have been "warm" if there had previously been a strain in the relationship.[10] Another similar question: You were a student of Edmund Husserl, your Jewish predecessor in the chair of philosophy at the University of Freiburg. He recommended you to the faculty as his successor as professor. Your relationship to him cannot have been without gratitude.

HEIDEGGER: You know the dedication in *Being and Time.*

SPIEGEL: Of course.

HEIDEGGER: In 1929 I edited the *festschrift* for his seventieth birthday, and at the celebration in his house I gave the speech, which was also printed in the *Akademische Mitteilungen* in May 1929.

SPIEGEL: Later, however, the relationship did become strained. Can you and would you like to tell us what this can be traced back to?

HEIDEGGER: Our differences of opinion on philosophical matters had intensified. In the beginning of the thirties, Husserl settled accounts with Max Scheler and me in public. The clarity of Husserl's statements left nothing to be desired. I could never find out what persuaded Husserl to set himself against my thinking in such a public manner.

SPIEGEL: On what occasion was this?

HEIDEGGER: Husserl spoke at the University of Berlin before an audience of sixteen hundred. Heinrich Mühsam reported in one of the big Berlin newspapers on a "kind of sports-palace atmosphere."

SPIEGEL: The argument as such is uninteresting in this context. It is only interesting that it was not an argument that has to do with the year 1933.

HEIDEGGER: Not in the least.

SPIEGEL: That has been our observation as well. Is it incorrect that you later left the dedication to Husserl out of *Being and Time*?

HEIDEGGER: No, that's true. I clarified the facts in my book *On the Way to Language.* The text reads: "To counter numerous, widely spread, incorrect allegations, let it be expressly stated here that the dedication to *Being and Time*, mentioned in the text of the dialogue on page 16, was also placed at the beginning of the book's fourth edition in 1935. When my publisher thought that the printing of the fifth edition in 1941 was endangered, and that the book might be banned, it was finally agreed, following Niemeyer's[11] proposal and wish, that the dedication should be left out of the fifth edition. My condition was that the footnote on page 38, in which the reasons for the dedication are actually given, should remain. It reads: "If the following investigation has taken any steps forward in disclosing the 'things themselves,' the author must first thank E. Husserl, who, by providing his own incisive personal guidance and by freely turning over his unpublished investigations, familiarized the author with the most diverse areas of phenomenological research during his student years in Freiburg.' "[12]

SPIEGEL: Then we hardly need to ask whether it is true that you, as rector of the University of Freiburg, forbade the emeritus professor Husserl to enter or to use the university library or the philosophy department's library.

HEIDEGGER: That is slander.

SPIEGEL: And there is no letter in which this prohibition against Husserl is expressed? How did this rumor get started?

HEIDEGGER: I don't know either; I don't have an explanation for it. I can demonstrate the impossibility of this whole matter to you through the following example, something that is also unknown. The governmental ministry had demanded that the director of the medical clinic, Professor Thannhauser,[13] and von Hevesy,[14] professor of physical chemistry and future Nobel Prize winner— both Jewish—be dismissed. During my rectorate I was able to retain these two men by meeting with the minister. The idea that I would retain them and simultaneously take action against Husserl, an emeritus professor and my own teacher, in the rumored fashion is absurd. Moreover I prevented a demonstration against Professor Thannhauser that students and lecturers had planned to take place in front of his clinic. In the obituary that the Thannhauser family published in the local newspaper, it says: "Until 1934 he was the honored director of the university's medical clinic in Freiburg im Breisgau. Brookline, Mass., 12.18.1962." The *Freiburger Universitätsblätter* reported in February 1966 on Professor von Hevesy: "During the years 1926–1934, von Hevesy was the head of the Physical-Chemical Institute of the University of Freiburg im Breisgau." After I resigned from the rectorate, both directors were removed from their offices. At the time, there were unsalaried lecturers who had been stuck in their positions for a while and left behind, and they then thought: Now the time has come to move up. When these people came to talk to me, I turned them all away.

SPIEGEL: You did not attend Husserl's funeral in 1938. Why not?

HEIDEGGER: Let me say the following about that: The accusation that I had broken off my relationship to Husserl is unfounded. My wife wrote a letter in both our names to Frau Husserl in May 1933. In it we expressed our "unchanged gratitude," and we sent the letter with a bouquet of flowers to their house. Frau Husserl answered briefly in a formal thank-you note and wrote that the relations between our families were broken off. It was a human failure that I did not once again attest to my gratitude and my admiration at Husserl's sickbed and after his death. I apologized for it later in a letter to Frau Husserl.

SPIEGEL: Husserl died in 1938. You had already resigned from the rectorate in February 1934. How did that come about?

HEIDEGGER: I will have to expand somewhat on that. My intention at the time was to overcome the technical organization of the university; that is, to renew the faculties from the inside, from the point of view of their scholarly tasks. With this intention in mind, I proposed that younger colleagues and especially colleagues distinguished in their fields should be appointed deans of the individual faculties for the winter semester 1933/34, without regard for their positions in the Party. Thus Professor Erik Wolf became dean of the law school, Professor Schadewaldt dean of the faculty of philosophy, Professor Soergel dean of the faculty of natural sciences, Professor von Möllendorff, who had been dismissed as rector in the spring, dean of the medical school. But around Christmas 1933 it was already clear to me that I would not be able to carry out my intention of renewing the university against the opposition of both colleagues and the Party. My colleagues were not pleased, for example, that I included students in responsible positions in the administration of the university— exactly as the case is today. One day I was called to Karlsruhe, where the minister demanded, through his senior assistant and in the presence of the Gau student leader, that I replace the deans of the law school and the medical school with other members of the faculty who would be acceptable to the Party. I refused to do this, and said I would resign from the rectorate if the minister insisted on his demand. That is what happened in February 1934. I resigned after only ten months in office, whereas the rectors at the time spent two or more years in office. While the domestic and foreign press commented on the assumption of office in various ways, they was silent about my resignation.

SPIEGEL: Did you negotiate with [Reich Minister of Education, Bernhard] Rust at the time?

HEIDEGGER: At what time?

SPIEGEL: In 1933, Rust made a trip here to Freiburg that is still talked about.

HEIDEGGER: We are dealing with two different events. On the occasion of a commemoration at Schlageter's grave[15] in his hometown, Schönau im Wiesental, I greeted the minister briefly and formally. Otherwise the minister took no notice of me. At that point I did not try to have a conversation with him. Schlageter had been a student at the University of Freiburg and a member of a Catholic fraternity. The conversation took place in November 1933 on the occasion of a rectorial conference in Berlin. I presented my views on science and the possible structure of the faculties to the minister. He listened so attentively to everything that I harbored the hope that what I had presented might have an effect. But nothing happened. I do not see why I am reproached for this discussion with the Reich Minister of Education while at the same time all the foreign governments rushed to recognize Hitler and to show him the customary international courtesies.

SPIEGEL: How did your relationship to the NSDAP develop after you had resigned as rector?

HEIDEGGER: After I resigned from the rectorate, I retreated back to my task as teacher. In the summer semester 1934 I lectured on "Logic." In the following semester, 1934/35, I gave the first lecture on Hölderlin. The lectures on Nietzsche began in 1936. All of those who could hear heard that this was a confrontation with National Socialism.

SPIEGEL: How did the transfer of office take place? You didn't participate in the celebration?

HEIDEGGER: Yes, I refused to take part in the ceremony of the change of rectors.

SPIEGEL: Was your successor a committed Party member?

HEIDEGGER: He was a member of the law school. The Party newspaper *Der Alemanne* announced his appointment as rector with the banner headline: "The First National Socialist Rector of the University."[16]

SPIEGEL: Did you have difficulties with the Party afterward, or what happened?

HEIDEGGER: I was constantly under surveillance.

SPIEGEL: Do you have an example of that?

HEIDEGGER: Yes, the case of Dr. Hancke.

SPIEGEL: How did you find out about that?

HEIDEGGER: Because he came to me himself. He had already received his doctorate and was a participant in my advanced seminar in the winter semester of 1936/37 and in the summer semester of 1937. He had been sent here [to Freiburg] by the SD [*Sicherheitsdienst*; Security Service] to keep me under surveillance.

SPIEGEL: Why did he suddenly come to you?

HEIDEGGER: Because of my seminar on Nietszche in the summer semester of 1937 and because of the way in which work was done in the seminar, he confessed to me that he could not continue with the task of surveillance assigned to him. He wanted to inform me of this situation in view of my future activity as a teacher.

SPIEGEL: Otherwise you had no difficulties with the Party?

HEIDEGGER: I only knew that my works were not allowed to be discussed, for example the essay "Plato's Theory of Truth." The lecture I gave on Hölderlin in the Germanic Institute in Rome in the spring of 1936 was attacked in the Hitler Youth magazine *Wille und Macht* in a most unpleasant way. Those who are interested should read the polemics against me that started up in the summer of 1934 in E. Krieck's[17] magazine *Volk im Werden*. I neither belonged to the German delegation to the international philosophy conference in Prague in 1934 nor was I even invited to participate. I was also supposed to have been excluded from the international Descartes conference in Paris in 1937. This seemed so strange to those in Paris that the head of the conference (Professor Brèhier at the Sorbonne) asked me why I did not belong to the German delegation. I answered that the organizers of the conference should inquire at the Reich Ministry of Education about this case. After a while, I received an invitation from Berlin to belatedly join the delegation. I refused. The lectures "What Is Metaphysics?" and "On the Essence of Truth" were sold under the counter in dust jackets without titles. Shortly after 1934, the rectorial address was taken off the market at the instigation of the Party. It was only allowed to be discussed in National Socialist teachers' camps[18] as a subject for the Party's political polemics.

SPIEGEL: In 1939, when the war . . .

HEIDEGGER: In the last year of the war, five hundred of the most eminent scholars and artists were exempted from any kind of military service.[19] I was not one of those who were exempted. On the contrary, in the summer of 1944 I was ordered to dig trenches over near the Rhine, on the Kaiserstuhl.

SPIEGEL: On the other side, the Swiss side, Karl Barth dug trenches.

HEIDEGGER: The way in which it happened is interesting. The rector had called all the faculty into Lecture Hall 5. He gave a short speech to the effect that what he would now say was in agreement with the National Socialist district leader and the National Socialist Gau leader. He would now divide the entire faculty into three groups: first those who were completely dispensable, second those who were partially dispensable, and third those who were indispensable. First on the list of the completely dispensable came Heidegger, later G. Ritter.[20] In the winter semester 1944/45, after I had finished work on the trenches near the Rhine, I gave a lecture course entitled "Poetry and Thinking" [*Dichten und Denken*], in a certain sense a continuation of my Nietzsche seminar, that is to say, of the confrontation with National Socialism. After the second class, I was conscripted into the Volkssturm,[21] the oldest member of the faculty to be called for service.

SPIEGEL: I don't think we have to hear Professor Heidegger on the subject of the course of events until he actually, or should we say legally, received an emeritus status. It is well known.

HEIDEGGER: Actually, the events themselves are not known. It is not a very nice affair.

SPIEGEL: Unless you would like to say something about them.

HEIDEGGER: No.

SPIEGEL: Perhaps we might summarize. As an unpolitical person, in its narrow sense, not in its broader sense, you got caught up in the politics of this supposed new departure in 1933 ...

HEIDEGGER: ... by way of the university ...

SPIEGEL: ... by way of the university in the politics of this supposed new departure. After about a year, you gave up the function again that you had assumed in this process. But in a lecture in 1935, which was published in 1953 as "An Introduction to Metaphysics," you said: "The works that are being offered around today," today being 1935 "as the philosophy of National Socialism, but have nothing to do with the inner truth and greatness of this movement (namely with the encounter of planetarily determined technology and modern human beings), are fishing for big catches in the murky waters of 'values' and 'wholes.' "[22] Did you add the words in parentheses in 1953, when it was printed—perhaps to explain to the readers of 1953 what you thought of as the "inner truth and greatness of this movement," that is, of National Socialism, in 1935—or was this parenthetical remark already there in 1935?

HEIDEGGER: It was in my manuscript and corresponded exactly to my conception of technology at the time, but not yet to my later interpretation of the essence of technology as con-struct [*Gestell*].[23] The reason I did not read that passage aloud was because I was convinced my audience would understand me correctly. The stupid ones and the spies and the snoopers understood it differently—and might as well have, too.

SPIEGEL: Surely you would classify the Communist movement in that way as well?

HEIDEGGER: Yes, absolutely, as determined by planetary technology.

SPIEGEL: Perhaps you would classify the sum of American endeavors in that way, too?

HEIDEGGER: I would say that as well. During the past thirty years, it should meanwhile have become clearer that the planetary movement of modern technology is a power whose great role in determining history can hardly be overestimated. A decisive question for me today is how a political system can be assigned to today's technological age at all, and which political system would that be? I have no answer to this question. I am not convinced that it is democracy.

SPIEGEL: *Democracy* is merely a collective term that can encompass very different conceptions. The question is whether a transformation of this political form is still possible. After 1945 you gave your opinions on the political aspirations of the Western world and in the process you also spoke about democracy, about the political expression of the Christian worldview, and also about the constitutional state—and you called all these aspirations "halves."

HEIDEGGER: Let me first ask you where I spoke about democracy and all the other things you mentioned. I would indeed describe them as halves because I don't think they genuinely confront the technological world. I think that behind them there is an idea that technology is in its essence something human beings have under their control. In my opinion, that is not possible. Technology is in its essence something that human beings cannot master of their own accord.

SPIEGEL: Which of the political trends just outlined do you consider to be the most appropriate to our time?

HEIDEGGER: That I don't see. But I do see a decisive question here. First we would have to clarify what you mean by "appropriate to our time," what *time* means here. It is even more important to ask whether appropriateness to our time is the measure for the "inner truth" of human actions, or whether "thinking and writing poetry" [*Denken und Dichten*], despite all censure of this phrase, are not the actions that most provide us with a measure.

SPIEGEL: It is striking that throughout time human beings have been unable to master their tools; look at the magician's apprentice. Is it not somewhat too pessimistic to say that we will not be able to master this certainly much greater tool of modern technology?

HEIDEGGER: Pessimism, no. Pessimism and optimism are positions that fall too short of the realm we are attempting to reflect upon here. But above all modern technology is not a "tool," and it no longer has anything to do with tools.

SPIEGEL: Why should we be so overpowered by technology ... ?

HEIDEGGER: I do not say overpowered. I say we have no path that corresponds to the essence of technology as of yet.

SPIEGEL: One could naïvely object: What do we have to come to terms with here? Everything functions. More and more electric power plants are being built. Production is flourishing. People in the highly technological parts of the earth are well provided for. We live in prosperity. What is really missing here?

HEIDEGGER: Everything functions. That is exactly what is uncanny. Everything functions and the functioning drives us further and further to more functioning, and technology tears people away and uproots them from the earth more and more. I don't know if you are scared; I was certainly scared when I recently saw the photographs of the earth taken from the moon. We don't need an atom bomb at all; the uprooting of human beings is already taking place. We only have purely technological conditions left. It is no longer an earth on which human beings live today. I recently had a long conversation with René Char in Provence— as you know, the poet and Resistance fighter. Rocket bases are being built in Provence, and the country is being devastated in an incredible way. The poet, who certainly cannot be suspected of sentimentality or a glorification of the idyllic, said to me that the uprooting of human beings which is going on now is the end if thinking and poetry do not acquire nonviolent power once again.

SPIEGEL: Now, we must say that although we prefer to be here on earth, and we probably will not have to leave it during our lifetime, who knows whether it is human beings' destiny to be on this earth? It is conceivable that human beings have no destiny at all. But at any rate a possibility for human beings could be seen in that they reach out from this earth to other planets. It will certainly not happen for a long time. But where is it written that human beings' place is here?

HEIDEGGER: From our human experience and history, at least as far as I am informed, I know that everything essential and great has only emerged when human beings had a home and were rooted in a tradition. Today's literature is, for instance, largely destructive.

SPIEGEL: We are bothered by the word *destructive* here because the word *nihilistic* received a very broad context of meaning precisely through you and your philosophy. It astonishes us to hear the word *destructive* in connection with literature you could or ought to see as a part of this nihilism.

HEIDEGGER: I would like to say that the literature I meant is not nihilistic in the way that I defined nihilism.[24]

SPIEGEL: You apparently see, so you have expressed it, a world movement that either brings about or has already brought about the absolute technological state?

HEIDEGGER: Yes! But it is precisely the technological state that least corresponds to the world and society determined by the essence of technology. The technological state would be the most obsequious and blind servant in the face of the power of technology.

SPIEGEL: Fine. But now the question of course poses itself: Can the individual still influence this network of inevitabilities at all, or can philosophy influence it, or can they both influence it together in that philosophy leads one individual or several individuals to a certain action?

HEIDEGGER: Those questions bring us back to the beginning of our conversation. If I may answer quickly and perhaps somewhat vehemently, but from long reflection: Philosophy will not be able to bring about a direct change of the present state of the world. This is true not only of philosophy but of all merely human meditations and endeavors. Only a god can still save us. I think the only possibility of salvation left to us is to prepare readiness, through thinking and poetry, for the appearance of the god or for the absence of the god during the decline; so that we do not, simply put, die meaningless deaths, but that when we decline, we decline in the face of the absent god.

SPIEGEL: Is there a connection between your thinking and the emergence of this god? Is there, as you see it, a causal connection? Do you think we can get this god to come by thinking?

HEIDEGGER: We cannot get him to come by thinking. At best we can prepare the readiness of expectation.

SPIEGEL: But can we help?

HEIDEGGER: The preparation of readiness could be the first step. The world cannot be what and how it is through human beings, but neither can it be so without human beings. In my opinion that is connected to the fact that what I call "Being," using a traditional, ambiguous, and now worn-out word, needs human beings. Being is not Being without humans being needed for its revelation, protection, and structuring. I see the essence of technology in what I call the *con-struct.* This name, on first hearing easily misunderstood, points, if it is properly considered, back into the innermost history of metaphysics, which still determines our existence [*Dasein*] today. The workings of the con-struct mean: Human beings are caught [*gestellt*], claimed, and challenged by a power that is revealed in the essence of technology. The experience that humans are structured [*gestellt*] by something that they are not themselves and that they cannot control themselves is precisely the experience that may show them the possibility of the insight that humans are needed by Being. The possibility of experience, of being needed, and of being prepared for these new possibilities is concealed in what makes up what is most modern technology's own. Thinking can do nothing more than to help humans to this insight, and philosophy is at an end.

SPIEGEL: In earlier times—and not only in earlier times—it was thought that philosophy was indirectly very effective (seldom directly), that it helped new currents to emerge. Just thinking of Germans, great names like Kant, Hegel, up to Nietzsche, not to mention Marx, it can be proved that philosophy has had, in roundabout ways, an enormous effect. Do you think this effectiveness of philosophy is at an end? And when you say philosophy is dead, that it no longer exists are you including the idea that the effectiveness of philosophy (if indeed it ever existed) today, at least, no longer exists?

HEIDEGGER: I just said that an indirect, but not a direct, effect is possible through another kind of thinking. Thus thinking can, as it were, causally change the condition of the world.

SPIEGEL: Please excuse us; we do not want to philosophize (we are not up to that), but here we have the link between politics and philosophy, so please forgive us for pushing you into such a conversation. You just said philosophy and the individual can do nothing except...

HEIDEGGER: ... this preparation of readiness for keeping oneself open to the arrival or absence of the god. The experience of this absence is not nothing, but rather a liberation of human beings from what I called the "fallenness into beings" in *Being and Time*. A contemplation of what *is* today is a part of a preparation of the readiness we have been talking about.

SPIEGEL: But then there really would have to be the famous impetus from outside, from a god or whomever. So thinking, of its own accord and self-sufficiently, can no longer be effective today? It was, in the opinion of people in the past, and even, I believe, in our opinion.

HEIDEGGER: But not directly.

SPIEGEL: We have already named Kant, Hegel, and Marx as great movers. But impulses came from Leibniz, too—for the development of modern physics and therefore for the origin of the modern world in general. We believe you said just now that you do not expect such an effect today any more.

HEIDEGGER: No longer in the sense of philosophy. The role philosophy has played up to now has been taken over by the sciences today. To sufficiently clarify the "effect" of thinking, we must have a more in-depth discussion of what effect and effecting can mean here. For this, careful differentiations need to be made between cause, impulse, support, assistance, hindrance, and co-operation. But we can only gain the appropriate dimension to make these differentiations if we have sufficiently discussed the principle of sufficient reason. Philosophy dissolves into the individual sciences: psychology, logic, political science.

SPIEGEL: And what takes the place of philosophy now?

HEIDEGGER: Cybernetics.

SPIEGEL: Or the pious one who remains open?

HEIDEGGER: But that is no longer philosophy.

SPIEGEL: What is it then?

HEIDEGGER: I call it the other thinking.

SPIEGEL: You call it the other thinking. Would you like to formulate that a little more clearly?

HEIDEGGER: Were you thinking of the sentence with which I conclude my lecture on "The Question Concerning Technology": "For questioning is the piety of thinking"?[25]

SPIEGEL: We found a statement in your lectures on Nietzsche that seems to us appropriate. You say there: "Because the greatest possible bond prevails in philosophical thinking, all great thinkers think the same thing. However this sameness is so essential and rich that no one individual can exhaust it, but rather everyone binds everyone else more rigorously." It appears, however, that in your opinion this philosophical structure has come to a certain end.

HEIDEGGER: Has ended but has not become for us invalid; rather it is again present in conversation. My whole work in lectures and seminars during the past thirty years has been mainly simply an interpretation of Western philosophy. The way back into the historical foundations of thinking, thinking through the questions that have not been asked since Greek philosophy—this is not breaking away from tradition. But I say that traditional metaphysics' way of thinking, which ends with Nietzsche, no longer offers us any possibility to experience the fundamental characteristics of the technological age, an age that is only beginning, through thinking.

SPIEGEL: In a conversation with a Buddhist monk approximately two years ago, you spoke about "a completely new method of thinking" and said that "for the time being only very few people can execute" this new method of thinking. Do you mean to say that only very few people can have the insights that are, in your opinion, possible and necessary?

HEIDEGGER: "Have" in its very primordial sense, that they can, in a way, "say" them.

SPIEGEL: Yes, but in the conversation with the Buddhist, you did not clearly describe how it can be realized.

HEIDEGGER: I cannot make it clear. I know nothing about how this thinking is "effective." It could also be that the path of thinking today leads toward silence, so that thinking may be protected from being thrown out within a year. It could also be that it takes three hundred years to become "effective."

SPIEGEL: We understand that very well. But because we do not live three hundred years from now, but here and now, we are denied silence. We, politicians, semi-politicians, citizens, journalists, et cetera, we constantly have to make some sort of decision or other. We must adapt ourselves to the system under which we live, must try to change it, must watch for the narrow door to reform and for the still narrower door to revolution. We expect help from the philosopher, even if, of course, only indirect help, help in roundabout ways. And now we hear: I cannot help you.

HEIDEGGER: I cannot.

SPIEGEL: That has to discourage the nonphilosopher.

HEIDEGGER: I cannot because the questions are so difficult that it would be contrary to the meaning of this task of thinking to make public appearances, to preach, and to distribute moral grades. Perhaps I may risk this statement: The secret of the planetary predominance of the unthought essence of technology corresponds to the preliminariness and inconspiciousness of the thinking that attempts to reflect upon this unthought essence.

SPIEGEL: You do not count yourself among those who, if they would only be heard, could point out a path?

HEIDEGGER: No! I know of no path toward a direct change of the present state of the world, assuming that such a change is at all humanly possible. But it seems to me that the attempted thinking could awaken, clarify, and fortify the readiness we have already mentioned.

SPIEGEL: A clear answer—but can and may a thinker say: Just wait, something will occur to us in the next three hundred years?

HEIDEGGER: It is not a matter of simply waiting until something occurs to human beings after three hundred years have gone by; it is about thinking ahead, without prophetic claims, into the coming time from the standpoint of the fundamental characteristics of the present age, which have hardly been thought through. Thinking is not inactivity, but in itself the action that has a dialogue with the world's destiny. It seems to me that the distinction, stemming from metaphysics, made between theory and praxis, and the conception of a transmission between the two, obstructs the path toward insight into what I understand to be thinking. Perhaps I may refer here to my lectures that were published in 1954 with the title *What Is Called Thinking?*[26] This piece is the least read of all my publications, and perhaps this, too, is a sign of our times.

SPIEGEL: It has, of course, always been a misunderstanding of philosophy to think that the philosopher should have some direct effect with his philosophy. Let us return to the beginning. Is it not conceivable that National Socialism can be seen on the one hand as a realization of that "planetary encounter" and on the other as the last, most horrible, strongest, and, at the same time, most helpless protest against this encounter of "planetarily determined technology" and modern human beings? Apparently, you are dealing with opposites in your own person that are such that many by-products of your activities can only really be explained in that you, with different parts of your being that do not touch the philosophical core, cling to many things about which you as a philosopher know that they have no continuity—for instance to concepts like "home" [*Heimat*], "rootedness," and similar things. How do planetary technology and "home" fit together?

HEIDEGGER: I would not say that. It seems to me that you take technology too absolutely. I do not think the situation of human beings in the world of planetary technology is an inextricable and inescapable disastrous fate; rather I think that the task of thinking is precisely to help, within its bounds, human beings to attain an adequate relationship to the essence of technology at all. Although National Socialism went in that direction, those people were much too limited in their thinking to gain a really explicit relationship to what is happening today and what has been under way for three centuries.

SPIEGEL: This explicit relationship, do the Americans have it today?

HEIDEGGER: They do not have it either. They are still entangled in a thinking, pragmatism, that fosters technological operating and manipulating but simultaneously blocks the path toward a contemplation of what is characteristic of modern technology. In the meantime, attempts to break away from pragmatic-positivistic thinking are being made here and there in the USA. And which of us can say whether one day in Russia and in China age-old traditions of a "thinking" will not awaken that will assist human beings in making a free relationship to the technological world possible?

SPIEGEL: If no one has one and the philosopher cannot give one to them . . .

HEIDEGGER: It is not for me to decide how far I will get with my attempt at thinking and in which way it will be received and productively transformed in the future. In 1957 I gave a lecture entitled "The Principle of Identity" for the anniversary of the University of Freiburg. In it I last risked showing, in a few steps of thought, the extent to which a thinking experience of what is most characteristic of modern technology can go. I attempted to show that it may go so far as opening up the possibility that human beings of the technological age experience the relationship to a demand that they can not only hear but to which they also belong. My thinking has an essential connection to Hölderlin's poetry. But I do not think Hölderlin is just any poet, whose work is a subject, among many others, for literary historians. I think Hölderlin is the poet who points toward the future, who expects the god, and who therefore cannot remain simply a subject for Hölderlin research in the literary historical imagination.

SPIEGEL: Talking about Hölderlin (we apologize that we will quote once again), in your lectures on Nietzsche you said that the "differently understood conflict between the dionysian and the apollonian, the holy passion and the sober account, is a concealed stylistic law of the historical destiny of the Germans, and one day it must find us ready and prepared for its structuring. This opposition is not a formula with the help of which we can merely describe 'culture.' With this conflict, Hölderlin and Nietzsche have set a question mark before the Germans' task to find their essence historically. Will we be able to understand this sign, this question mark? One thing is certain: If we do not understand it, history will take its revenge on us." We do not know what year you wrote this. We estimate that it was 1935.

HEIDEGGER: The quotation probably belongs to the course on Nietzsche entitled "The Will to Power as Art" in 1936/37. It could also have been said in the years that followed.

SPIEGEL: Would you like to explain that a little more? It leads us away from generalities to a specific destiny of the Germans.

HEIDEGGER: I could put what is said in the quotation this way: I am convinced that a change can only be prepared from the same place in the world where the modern technological world originated. It cannot come about by the adoption of Zen Buddhism or other Eastern experiences of the world. The help of the European tradition and a new appropriation of that tradition are needed for a change in thinking. Thinking will only be transformed by a thinking that has the same origin and destiny.

SPIEGEL: At exactly the spot where the technological world originated, it must, you think . . .

HEIDEGGER: . . . be transcended [*aufgehoben*] in the Hegelian sense, not removed, transcended, but not by human beings alone.

SPIEGEL: Do you allocate a special task specifically to the Germans?

HEIDEGGER: Yes, in that sense, in dialogue with Hölderlin.

SPIEGEL: Do you think that the Germans have a specific qualification for this change?

HEIDEGGER: I am thinking of the special inner relationship between the German language and the language and thinking of the Greeks. This has been confirmed to me again and again today by the French. When they begin to think they speak German. They insist that they could not get through with their own language.

SPIEGEL: Is that how you would explain the very strong effect you have had in the Romance countries, particularly in France?

HEIDEGGER: Because they see that they cannot get through today's world with all their rationality when they are attempting to understand it in the origin of its essence. Thinking can be translated as little as poetry can. At best it can be paraphrased. As soon as a literal translation is attempted, everything is transformed.

SPIEGEL: A disquieting thought.

HEIDEGGER: It would be good if this disquiet would be taken seriously on a large scale and if it would finally be considered what a momentous transformation Greek thinking suffered when it was translated into Roman Latin, an event that still bars our way today to sufficient reflection on the fundamental words of Greek thinking.

SPIEGEL: Professor, we would actually always optimistically assume that something can be communicated and even translated, because if this optimism that contents of thinking can be communicated despite language barriers ceases, then provincialism threatens.

HEIDEGGER: Would you call Greek thinking provincial in contrast to the mode of ideas of the Roman Empire? Business letters can be translated into all languages. The sciences (today *science* already means the natural sciences, with mathematical physics as the basic science) can be translated into all the world's languages. Put more correctly, they are not translated, but rather the same mathematical language is spoken. We are touching here on an area that is broad and hard to cover.

SPIEGEL: Perhaps this belongs to this topic, too: At present there is, without exaggerating, a crisis of the democratic-parliamentary system. There has been one for a long time. There is one particularly in Germany, but not only in Germany. There is one in the classical countries of democracy, in England and America. In France it is not even a crisis any more. Now, a question: Can thinkers not give advice, even as by-products of thinking, that either this system must be replaced by a new one, and what it should look like, or that reform must be possible, and advice on how reform could be possible? Otherwise, the philosophically unschooled person—and that will normally be the person who has things in hand (although he does not determine them) and who is in the hands of things—this person will keep on reaching false conclusions, perhaps even terribly rash conclusions. So: Should the philosopher not be ready to think about how human beings can arrange living together in this world, which they have technologized themselves and which has perhaps overpowered them? Is it not rightly expected of the philosopher that he give advice on what he considers possible ways of living? Does the philosopher not fall short of a part, even if it is a small part, of his profession and his calling if he communicates nothing about it?

HEIDEGGER: As far as I can see, an individual is incapable of comprehending the world as a whole through thinking to the extent that he could give practical instructions, particularly in the face of the task of first finding a base for thinking itself again. As long as it takes itself seriously with view to the great tradition, thinking is overtaxed if it must prepare itself to give instructions. On what authority could this happen? In the realm of thinking, there are no authoritative statements. The only stipulation for thinking comes from the matter that is to be thought. This is, however, what is above all worthy of questioning. To make this state of affairs understandable, a discussion of the relationship between philosophy and the sciences, whose technical-practical successes make thinking in a philosophical sense seem more and more superfluous, is needed. The difficult situation in which thinking is placed with view to its own task thus corresponds to an alienation, fed by the powerful position of the sciences, from a thinking that must deny itself answering practical and ideological questions demanded by the day.

SPIEGEL: Professor, in the realm of thinking there are no authoritative statements. Thus it cannot really be surprising that modern art has a difficult time making authoritative statements, too. Nevertheless, you call it "destructive." Modern art often thinks of itself as experimental art. Its works are attempts...

HEIDEGGER: I will gladly be taught.

SPIEGEL: ... attempts made out of the isolated situation of human beings and artists, and out of every one hundred attempts, there is now and then one that hits the mark.

HEIDEGGER: That is the big question. Where does art stand? What place does it occupy?

SPIEGEL: Fine, but here you are demanding something of art that you no longer demand of thinking.

HEIDEGGER: I do not demand anything of art. I only say that it is a question of what place art occupies.

SPIEGEL: If art does not know its place, does that mean it is destructive?

HEIDEGGER: Fine, cross it out. I would like to state, however, that I do not think modern art points out a path, particularly as it remains unclear where it sees or at least looks for what is most characteristic of art.

SPIEGEL: The artist, too, lacks commitment to tradition. He might find it beautiful, and he can say: Yes, that is the way one could paint six hundred years ago or three hundred years ago or even thirty years ago. But he can no longer do it. Even if he wanted to, he could not. The greatest artist would then be the ingenious forger Hans van Meegeren, who would then paint "better" than the others. But it just does not work any more. Therefore the artist, writer, poet is in a similar situation to the thinker. How often we must say Close your eyes.

HEIDEGGER: If the "culture industry" is taken as the framework for the classification of art and poetry and philosophy, then the parity is justified. However, if not only the industry but also what is called culture becomes questionable, then the contemplation of this questionableness also belongs to thinking's realm of responsibility, and thinking's plight is barely imaginable. But thinking's greatest affliction is that today, as far as I can see, no thinker yet speaks who is great enough to place thinking, directly and formatively, before its subject matter and therefore on its path. The greatness of what is to be thought is too great for us today. Perhaps we can struggle with building narrow and not very far-reaching footbridges for a crossing.

SPIEGEL: Professor Heidegger, we thank you for this conversation.

[Comments by Dr. Hermann Heidegger, Martin Heidegger's executor, on the edition of the *Spiegel* interview published on 31 May 1976 can be found among the appendices.]

Afterthoughts on the Spiegel Interview

HEINRICH W. PETZET

THE REEMERGENCE OF Heidegger, a man tainted with the political stain of his support of National Socialism, in public life in Germany again awakened journalists' suspicion as well as the protest of old opponents who had thought him eliminated. Cultural functionaries were not at all happy that the "hopelessly provincial Heidegger" (as Hühnerfeld said)[1] dared to load the lightly built ships of postwar hopes with the onerous freight of his thoughts. They would have been glad to be rid of him again, before his thinking began to gain a foothold and to stir up trouble in a new generation.

A swelling hate arose against Heidegger's inconvenient call for a change in thinking and for a new beginning, a hate that was evident in numerous attacks, misinterpretations, even personal slights that were directed against the thinker in the fifties and on into the sixties. They did not even stop at offending his honor. This hostility was constantly spurred on by Heidegger's silence. All efforts to coax statements out of him, then to be pounced on again, were unsuccessful.[2] It was practically impossible to have an objective discussion in such an atmosphere. The discussion only began when the storms finally died down—and people began, moreover, to be ashamed when faced with the philosopher's foreign ad-

Source: *Heinrich W. Petzet.* Auf einen Stern zugehen. Begegnungen mit Martin Heidegger 1929–1976 (*Frankfurt: Societäts-Verlag, 1983*), pp. 97–105. *Reprinted with the kind permission of the author.*

mirers. Even the loudest throats will scream themselves hoarse against someone who is silent.

People often wonder why Heidegger never (except for a short rectification in *Der Spiegel*) defended himself. His best friends suffered most. Although they could counter with their own arguments, they could not reply with corrections in the attacked man's own words. Heidegger was frequently reproached for this. He was urged and beseeched to take a stand against insinuations that his supporters knew were completely unfounded. I myself experienced how a respected foreign paper refused to print a detailed, objectively "safe," response to a nasty attack with the explanation: We know better! Still Heidegger did not manage to say a word in an atmosphere so hostile to him. For a long time, therefore, he seemed to be agreeing that he had been in the wrong.

He was convinced, however, that only a fool would go onto this battlefield, a battlefield where one would always arrive too late. He did not read some of the awful things that were circulated about him, but he still heard about them somehow, or he asked his friends to tell him about them. Outwardly he appeared composed; nevertheless these things wounded and hurt him a great deal. "People were not nice to me," the eighty-year-old Heidegger still said to Richard Wisser, who interviewed him for the television program in honor of his birthday. No one knows how much he suffered under the injuries he received over the years. He did not have a "thick skin," and an unobjective or even personal reproof hurt him in a way we can no longer gauge.

What affected him most of all were the misrepresentations of his supposed conduct toward his former Jewish students. People wanted to brand him an antisemite. He was justifiably worked up about some statements made and events in connection with Karl Löwith's appointment to the University of Heidelberg after the war. I had drawn Heidegger's attention to an article called *"Heidegger-deutsch"* that had been published in the *Neue Zeitung*, not suspecting that my comment (mentioned together with a harsh essay against him that appeared in the *Neuer Rundschau*) would lead to such an angry outburst. Heidegger, who was lying sick in bed at the time, reveals all his bitterness in his response:

> It is not surprising that a man who is now 55 and who, after 1919, attended my lectures and seminars for all of nine years (and ran to our house in Marburg almost every second day to grill me with questions) can report things and make the

impression of an initiate on the army of today's unwitting. What the *N.R.* and the *N.Z.* do not say is that this same author, as an èmigrè, spread the most awful lies about me among the èmigrès in the USA, via Switzerland and Paris.—The horrible misuse of the word *turning*, an essential word for me, is painful to me.

In 1929, when Löwith was still the reddest Marxist (now he has "turned" to Christianity and will take a chair in philosophy as a full professor at the University of Heidelberg), he wrote that *Being and Time* was all "cleverly disguised theology." He later wrote that it was all atheism. Whatever the moment calls for. . . . L. also withholds from his readers that the genuine "turning" was mentioned for the first time in 1930 in a lecture on "The Essence of Truth." Herr L. heard that lecture at the time and received a typed transcript. He does not mention this. He also neglects to point out that for four hours each week in the lecture course I gave in 1927 (the year *Being and Time* was published) I dealt with the question of Being and not with subjectivity.

But I have already written too much—for we are dealing with very different matters here. Now that I am emerging again, the right man has been chosen to undermine everything in advance in the most cunning form through the most appropriate channels. There it stands printed in Herr Fischer's magazine what the opinion on Heidegger should be, and the *N.Z.* and the people behind it assist as needed. These people do not want to arrive at genuine questions and experiences at all. What they want is to keep the *upper hand* in the sphere of public discussions or to gain it again.

I ask myself again and again *why* these gentlemen do not do these things themselves and pose the questions and solve them, if they know so much about my thinking, apparently even better than I do myself. Soon the Greek thinkers will be put on trial because they "only" thought Greek, and not Egyptian, or Hebrew, or everything all at once.

You, too, have felt that we are only dealing with self-contented cleverness here. The author, who is only now beginning to develop his "effectiveness" in Germany, is arranging the literary industry with others of his kind. Now that such figures have turned up at the already questionable universities in the west of Germany, one should really refuse to step up to the lecterns of such institutions.—I am in the process of carefully considering this and other things. . . .

The letter shows the bitterness that almost threatened to gain hold of Heidegger in the fifties, despite the attention that he then received again from younger people. He finally even swallowed the slogan, invented by Löwith, "thinker in a destitute time,"[3] his deep skepticism confirmed: "Nothing came of that either." I do not know whether Heidegger and Löwith ever had a talk and reconciled themselves. (Heidegger regularly went to conferences of the Academy in Heidelberg.) Löwith later made a lengthy contribution to the television program in honor of Heidegger's eightieth birthday, but despite all the words of homage this was hardly enough to erase all that had happened before. . . . The journalistic hunters did not abandon their chase for years. "The rabble-rousing has a long way to go until it reaches its high point; that is, low point," Heidegger wrote to me once when the regrettable talk about him did not cease.

What he called the "literary industry" in the letter quoted above was detestable to him. Because after the war his thinking turned more and more toward language, devoting most space to poetry, he often had conflicts with philologists. It seems understandable that classical and modern linguists turned against him, since he was often in opposition to their sciences. He had already written to me in 1949 that the methods used in some articles were cheap. "But it seems that the literary type [Literat] is the necessary counterpart to technology." Nietzsche had already said what there is to say about this type in the 1880s: the literary type, "who actually is nothing, but represents everything, who plays and stands in for the expert, who also modestly takes it upon himself to be paid, honored, and celebrated in place of the expert."

He occasionally said that etymology would always get in the way of thinking as long as it was given priority over the essence of language and was considered to be the voice of the absolute. . . . He offended many specialists with such statements. It cannot be surprising that not only the "language of the specialities" but also the whole impoverished and abstracting way of modern language was in Heidegger's opinion determined by the workings and essence of the con-struct [Ge-stell].[4] This became clear enough in conversations; often his concern that human beings, who had evoked it all, would not be able to cope with it shimmered through. Heidegger did not conceal his criticism of the spirit of the West, which was so sure of its affairs. In September 1961 he wrote me from Todtnauberg that the whole hollow essence of the West was now coming to light. In the meantime, however, "one" did not notice it yet; the process of general stultification here would continue. One still did not understand that in the age of the "construct" a reshaping of all manners of *Dasein* must be demanded of human beings. Thinking, as Heidegger saw it, is no easy sinecure, as little as the conclusions that human beings should draw from it are.

We often came back to the unfortunate and degrading situation the philosopher saw himself in in his own university and department—even after he received the status of professor emeritus. He thought there was a "system" behind it; it had all been started to undermine things, to cause not only his own but also thinking's downfall. It was a great mistake to think that such "scribblings" would remain (beyond the momentary confusion) without effect. In the long term, admittedly, all this stuff would collapse. "People have hardly understood *Being and Time*. How can they begin to understand my later work?" That is why it was so difficult for him to lead readers and listeners toward the necessary constancy and cautiousness. He was always the teacher, concerned with true communication and so often disappointed. Nevertheless, Heidegger could not ignore that the attempts, both written and spoken, that he made in Germany at the time were often much more momentous and fertile than "the likes of us can survey."

Over the years, the more a new generation turned to Heidegger again, not least in foreign countries (France), the more those in his close circle suggested to him that he should remove the burden of these continually repeated accusations once and for all by making a kind of public "confession." Heidegger was deeply opposed to such things. He had a clear conscience and saw no reason to go on a humiliating penetential pilgrimage that would be a retrospective apology for his activities, especially for his thinking, and therefore an acknowledgment that they were wrong. Furthermore, he thought that such a step was unnecessary. In his opinion he had made it clear that he had never been a National Socialist[5] through his resignation of the rectorate in February 1934 and his whole intellectual position, which was evident in numerous statements that were well understood by those who attended his lectures or his seminars.

His insistence on such a position of conscience was not only a matter of pride; something very different kept him from making such a step. He knew only too well what a "commotion" such a gesture would cause: violent arguing for and against; things long buried being awakened again. He was afraid (probably rightly so) that his new productive work that was just beginning would again be destroyed. The work he had taken up again after 1949 would then have been in vain. It was this work, and its slowly attained products, that were most important to him during his old age. Apart from the fact that every "commotion" would not only harm but also might paralyze his own capacity for work for long periods of time, he believed that no one would benefit from the public being stirred up again by events of long ago. Young people, who had experienced the Third Reich as children and now stood at the gates of the universities, might put his books aside with irritation and suspicion. Then he would have to consider even the seeds he had sown in the furrows of his thinking endangered.

It had to be assumed at the time, in the mid sixties, that Heidegger would never publicly take a stand on the questions, statements, insults, and attempts at vindication. These had all already been discussed too much anyway and had become continually more unclear in the argument and counter argument. At the very earliest the truth would only be found out after his death.

This assumption proved correct. A few days after the philosopher's demise, the German weekly magazine *Der Spiegel* printed a conversation between Rudolf Augstein, the publisher, and Heidegger as a feature article. It had been recorded (as became clear from the editorial remarks) ten years before, on 23 September 1966, in Heidegger's house in Freiburg. The one nonnegotiable condition that the interviewee had for his participation was that it only be published after his death. The magazine complied with the condition and took care that the fact that the interview existed remained unknown—although the secret seems to have leaked a little. At any rate, its publication on 31 May 1976 created considerable excitement, particularly among those who had never suspected anything of the sort. The explosive nature of this "bomb" (to use appropriate jargon) had in no way lessened during its ten years of storage in a file safe—and *Der Spiegel*, known for its sensational stories, had provided one of the biggest surprises of its history.

The history of the interview is complicated, and it is hardly worth telling all its details. It amazed all those who knew Heidegger even a little bit that he would have chosen (if he decided to make this step at all) *Der Spiegel* to speak on these questions for posterity, for the journalism that *Der Spiegel* represented basically went against his grain. On the other hand, he knew (as a regular reader of *Der Spiegel* at the time) only too well that hardly any organ other than this magazine, which continually drew public attention, could reach such a diversified group of people. The posthumously published statements and words to the public printed in *Der Spiegel* would certainly be read—beyond the circle of genuine sympathizers—by the curious and the indifferent and even by opponents and contradictors.

I, taken relatively early into confidence (and strongly protesting at first), do not remember everything that happened during the preparation for the interview. There were complications, anger on both sides, new arrangements, and finally the procedure, the day, and the condition mentioned above were agreed upon. Heidegger asked me to be present at the interview, as a sort of second, since the other side would also consist of two. I still remember a visit to Hamburg, to *Der Spiegel*'s headquarters, to introduce myself to Georg Wolff, the philosophically trained second participant in the interview, and to discuss some questions. I first met Rudolf Augstein on the morning of the interview, when I picked up the gentlemen at the Colombi Hotel in Freiburg to bring them to Zähringen. Augstein, whom I had at first suspected to be a kind of "questioning hangman," wishing to bring about the master's downfall, won my complete sympathy within minutes, because he confessed from the depth of his heart that he was "scared stiff" of facing the "famous thinker."...

We were six: Augstein, Wolff, the photographer, a stenographer, a technician, and I. Frau Heidegger welcomed us at the door, and, following her sign, I escorted the small group upstairs, where Heidegger was waiting for us at the door of his study. I was a little startled when I looked at him and noticed how excessively tense he was. The photographs that were taken throughout the long morning (it started shortly after ten and ended close to one) clearly show this high tension: the swollen blood vessels on his temples and his forehead, the eyes slightly bulging in the excitement. These somewhat alarming signs nevertheless abated and dwindled in the course of the conversation. The photographer, Digne Meller Marcovicz, published most of her pictures in a beautiful volume—a book that is an amazing testimony to the ability of capturing nuances of expression, gestures, the important moments in conversation in a photograph. It was easy to completely forget Frau Meller Marcovicz's presence, and the camera was never for a moment bothersome, a beautiful testimony to human tact in the merciless service of technology.

The exciting process of the dialogue between Augstein and Heidegger, moving its two listeners as well, the continual increase of excitement from question to question, answer to answer, an excitement that hardly subsided, the intensifications and high points, will not be described here, since the conversation has appeared in a version that was checked by both sides and supplemented by Heidegger, according to his wishes, in a few places by hand. Here only a few words on the impression the whole event made will be added, an impression that cannot be described either by the written word or by the most vivid photographs, but that continues to have an effect on those of the participants who are still alive.

Because of that first tension (we got straight to business without many "preliminaries"), I was afraid that the seventy-six-year-old man would have an outburst of anger, after such long restraint and offenses that were hard to appease, now that he was offered the chance to speak his mind publicly for the first time. (Was he always aware that not only the few people in the room but also a world-wide circle was listening to him?) But he completely kept his composure. Only in the rumbling tone of some of his sentences could it be heard (particularly by those who knew him and knew what was behind those sentences!) that what had accumulated over the years was emerging. He refrained from swerving into the inessential, into anything that might look like a "private feud." A few times he took back what he had already said. The more the pettinesses of a political nature and personal rebukes disappeared from Augstein's tactful questions (in the course of the conversation, Augstein apparently thought that such things were inessential; what the hour demanded was an advance toward the authentic and the essential), the freer Heidegger's answers became and the more he imperceptibly gained control of the conversation. As they reached the interview's climax in the now-famous statement "Only a god can still save us," the questioner and responder had reached a level that left the actual reason for the interview far behind and that suffered no loss through the small controversies, like the one about the ability of modern art to make a statement. When finally that well-known stereotypical *Spiegel* last sentence had been said (which Augstein would have almost forgotten without my whispering to him), everyone breathed a sigh of relief. "Professor Heidegger—we thank you for this conversation!" was no mere phrase. We drank to each other with a wine from the Markgräfler Land—and then the door was opened to invite in Frau Heidegger, who had probably waited through the past three hours with a good deal of anxiety.

She remained with the small group that then—without the stenographer and the technician—started off, on Heidegger's invitation, toward Todtnauberg in Augstein's car. There they were introduced to the "cabin" the philosopher's other working place that had become just as important to him as the secluded room at his brother's home in Messkirch. This excursion, enhanced by the mild, sunny September weather, was also documented by the photographer. She later came back alone, unburdened by the official mission, to take a great number of especially successful pictures of life in and around the cabin. Heidegger first showed his guests his study, whose utter bareness (at the time not even the portrait of Schelling in old age hung on the wall) visibly startled them. No one had expected such an "icy" cell. But they quickly adjusted to the unusual surroundings. We were soon eating a small snack and sitting at the table by the windows in the corner of the bigger room, which had already witnessed quite a few conversations held at the most varying "altitudes." Heidegger had noticeably lost a heavy burden; his look told it to me, as someone who has known of this burden for a long time. How good his mood was could be discerned in that he soon took Hebel's poems and read aloud from them—as if he, in the sense of the *genius loci*, had to do something nice for his visitors. In the late afternoon and in a relaxed mood, we drove back to Freiburg.

The publication of the *Spiegel* interview with Heidegger had a clarifying effect, although it could not completely silence the accusations that had been raised for years. Many took no note of the interview at all. The thinker's unspoken hope that hostility would change to objective opposition has hardly been fulfilled since then. *It remains to be hoped that things will change in the future because of Heidegger's long-withheld (until 1983) explanation of questions of his rectorate, which has been referred to here various times.*[6]

Not everyone had the courage of the writer Rudolf Krämer-Badoni, who, although he decisively rejected Heidegger's understanding of art, was not afraid to publicly acknowledge his respect for Heidegger's philosophical as well as human positions. In a comment in a book published in 1980 that dismissed these theories of art, he wrote that he did not want to be understood as joining Heidegger's various unobjective opponents, or rather enemies. "I for my part expressly declare that I think Martin Heidegger is the most important contemporary philosopher. As far as the citizen Heidegger is concerned, his almost immediate turning away from a short political involvement should finally be seen for what it was: manfulness in the face of a dictator. . . ."

THE TELEVISION INTERVIEW

Introduction

RICHARD WISSER

MARTIN HEIDEGGER—few other names in the intellectual world carry such weight. Our age has plenty of great human beings, even plenty of people who think great thoughts, but it has no wealth of great thinkers.

When the word *thinking* comes to mind today, one thinks first of all of Martin Heidegger. No thinking person can avoid his thinking. For Heidegger, who has been called a "thinker in destitute times,"[1] thinking has become the matter of his life. He has freed the word *thinking* from the linguistic entanglements it is caught in as long as it is confused with mere cleverness or reflection in the service of planning and research. Despite the increasing thoughtlessness that is so much a part of today's world, he has kept awake awareness of the necessity of reflective, contemplative, composed thinking. Heidegger has shown that thinking can be a day's work without becoming everyday.

Whoever is unaware of the sacrifice that Heidegger, uninterested in his own personal self, has made to his work will not be able to grasp the solitude into which his thinking has led him for thinking's sake. From the experience of thinking, he once said: "In thinking all things become solitary and slow."[2] Throughout his life, Heidegger has known what it means to walk on a path that is far from the path chosen by those who are merely intellectually agile and those who are unable to distance themselves from what concerns them; it has meant to take a "step back"[3] so that the matter of his thinking might be served.

To characterize the work of his thinking, Heidegger himself

preferred the image of the path; he called one of his books "wood paths" [*Holzwege*][4] and another "path marks" [*Wegmarken*]. Far from the familiar tracks and routes where ordinary traffic goes, "wood paths" are paths in places never before walked in. "Wood paths" are also paths that lead into places where it is impossible to walk, but these paths must be walked if the wealth of the woods is to be saved. "Woodcutters and foresters know the paths. They know what it means to be on a wood path."[5] "Path marks" give an account of the direction. Neither the "new" nor the "old" concerns them. Heidegger looks for possibilities to keep the unconcealedness [*Unverborgenheit*], in which something reveals itself, from getting lost in the shrunken monosyllabism and the monotony of autocratic objectives and pressures. "Nothing," says Heidegger, "can be proved [*beweisen*] in this realm (of thinking), but some things can be pointed out [*weisen*]."[6]

Heidegger's work has pointed out the path to students and masters in many countries of the world. He has influenced the methods of many a science and has blocked long-familiar paths of thinking; he has moved the course of thinking.

The stimulus Heidegger provided can be seen in its impact. Therefore at least some of those for whom he was a point of departure, who joined him, who, however, also went their own paths will speak about what Heidegger means to them personally today. In their reflections, his effect comes to light. When absent, he becomes present in the recollection and the thoughtful reflection.

[Statements by Carl-Friedrich von Weizsäcker, Maurice de Gandillac, Medard Boss, Ernst Jünger, Kôichi Tsujimura, Emil Staiger, Leo Gabriel, Karl Löwith, Dolf Sternberger, Heinrich Ott, Karl Rahner, and Richard Wisser follow in the television program.]

Martin Heidegger in Conversation

with RICHARD WISSER

WISSER: Professor Heidegger! In our time more and more voices are being raised. The voices that are growing steadily louder are those voices that propagate a change of social conditions as the decisive task of the present and see it as the only approach that bears any promise for the future.

What is your opinion of such an orientation of the so-called Zeitgeist, for instance with regard to the reform of the university?

HEIDEGGER: I will only respond to the last question, because what you said before goes too far. And the answer that I will give you is the one I gave forty years ago in my inaugural lecture "What Is Metaphysics?" in Freiburg in 1929.

I quote a passage from it: "The fields of the sciences lie far apart. The ways they treat their subject matter are fundamentally different. This disintegrated multiplicity of disciplines is only held together today by the technical organization of the universities and their faculties and only retains some meaning because of the practical purposes set for the departments. However the roots of the sciences in their essential ground have died."[1] I believe *that* answer should be enough.

WISSER: Quite different motives have led to modern attempts to reorient objectives and "restructure" actual facts on a social and also an interpersonal level. It is clear that much philosophy is at play here, for better and for worse. Do you think philosophy has a social mission?

HEIDEGGER: No! One can't speak of a social mission in that sense! To answer that question, we must first ask: "What is society?" We have to consider that today's society is only modern *subjectivity* made absolute. A philosophy that has overcome a position of subjectivity therefore has no say in the matter.

Another question is to what extent we can speak of a *change* of society at all. The question of the demand for world change leads us back to Karl Marx's frequently quoted statement from his *Theses on Feuerbach.* I would like to quote it exactly and read out loud: "Philosophers have only *interpreted* the world differently; what matters is to *change* it." When this statement is cited *and* when it is followed, it is overlooked that changing the world presupposes a change in the *conception* of the world. A conception of the world can only be won by adequately *interpreting* the world.

That means: Marx's demand for a "change" is based on a very definite interpretation of the world, and therefore this statement is proved to be without foundation. It gives the impression that it speaks decisively against philosophy, whereas the second half of the statement presupposes, unspoken, a demand for philosophy.

WISSER: How can *your* philosophy become effective today, considering a definite society with its manifold tasks and concerns, needs and hopes? Or are those of your critics right who maintain that Martin Heidegger is concentrating so hard on Being that he has sacrificed the *conditio humana,* the being of *humans* in society and as persons?

HEIDEGGER: This criticism is a big misunderstanding! For the question of Being and the unfolding of this question presuppose an interpretation of *Dasein*; that is, a definition of the essence of human beings. And the fundamental thought of my thinking is precisely that Being, or the manifestation [*Offenbarkeit*] of Being, *needs* human beings and that, vice versa, human beings are only human beings if they are standing in the manifestation of Being.

With that answer, the question to what extent I have only been concerned with Being and have forgotten human beings should be settled. One cannot ask about Being without asking about the essence of human beings.

WISSER: Nietzsche once said: The philosopher is the bad conscience of his times. Let us leave open what Nietzsche meant by this. But in considering your attempt to unmask the previous history of philosophy as a history of decline with regard to Being and therefore to "destroy" it, some are perhaps tempted to call Martin Heidegger the bad conscience of Western philosophy.

What do you consider the most characteristic feature of what you call "forgetfulness of Being" [*Seinsvergessenheit*] or "abandonment by Being" [*Seinsverlassenheit*]?

HEIDEGGER: If you speak about the "history of decline," I must first correct one aspect of your question. "History of decline" is *not* meant *negatively*!

I do not talk about a history of decline but only about the fate of Being inasmuch as it withdraws more and more, compared to the manifestation of Being the Greeks knew; later, Being was unfolded as mere objectivity for science, and today, it is mere material [*Bestand*] for the technological mastery of the world. Therefore it is not a history of decline but a *withdrawal of Being* in which we stand.

As far as I can see, the most characteristic feature for the forgetfulness of Being (and here forgetfulness should *always* be considered from the Greek λήϑη; that is, from the self-concealing, from the self-withdrawing of Being), the characteristic feature of *our* destiny is the fact that the *question of Being*, which I pose, has not been *understood* yet.

WISSER: There are two things that you continually call into question and render questionable: *science's claim to rule* and an understanding of *technology* that only sees it as a useful means of reaching a desired goal quicker. In our age, when most people have the highest hopes for science, and worldwide television broadcasts demonstrate to them that they can achieve whatever they intend through technology, your thoughts on science and on the essence of technology are a headache for many. *First*, what do you mean when you maintain science does not think?

HEIDEGGER: To begin with that headache: I think it is very healthy! There are still too few "headaches" in the world today, and there is a great thoughtlessness that is connected to the forgetfulness of Being. And the sentence "Science does not think," which caused a lot of commotion when I said it in a lecture in Freiburg, means: *Science* does not move in the *dimension of philosophy*; but, without knowing it, science relies on this dimension.

For example: Physics moves in space and time and movement. What movement is, what space is, what time is cannot be decided by science as science. Therefore science does not *think*. With its methods, it *cannot* think at all in *this* sense.

I cannot say, for instance, what physics is, using the methods of physics. I can only think what physics is, using the methods of philosophical questioning. The sentence "Science does not think" is *not an accusation* but an *observation* of the inner structure of science. It is part of its essence that, on the one hand, it relies on what philosophy thinks and that, on the other, it forgets and does not pay heed to what is to be thought.

WISSER: And *second*, what do you mean when you say that the atom bomb is less dangerous for contemporary humanity than the law [*Ge-setz*] laid down by technology, the "construct" [*Ge-stell*],[2] as you call the fundamental trait of technology, "to reveal the real, in the mode of ordering, as available material,"[3] or, put differently, to make everything and everyone available at the push of a button?

HEIDEGGER: As far as technology is concerned, my definition of the essence of technology, which has not been picked up on anywhere as yet, is—to say it concretely—that modern natural science is based on the development of the essence of modern technology and not the reverse.

Now, let me say first of all that I am not *against* technology. I have never spoken *against* technology or against the so-called demonic in technology. Rather I am trying to understand the *essence* of technology.

When you quote these thoughts on the danger of the atom bomb and a still greater danger of technology, I think of developments today in the area of biophysics: in the foreseeable future we will be capable of *making* human beings; that is, to construct them purely in their organic essence just the way they are needed: skilled and unskilled, clever and—stupid. It will happen some day! The *technical* possibilities are already available, and they were talked about by Nobel prize winners at a conference in Lindau, which I pointed out years ago in a speech in Messkirch.

Therefore above all the *misunderstanding* that I am *against* technology is to be rejected.

In technology, namely in its essence, I see that human beings are subject to a power that challenges them and in the face of which they are no longer free. I see that something announces itself here, namely a relation of Being to human beings and that this relation, concealed in the *essence* of technology, will perhaps one day, in its unconcealedness [*Unverborgenheit*], step into the light.

I do not know whether it will happen! But in the essence of technology I see the first shimmer of a much deeper secret that I call the "happening" [*Ereignis*]. From this you can see that there can be no question of a resistance to or a condemnation of technology; rather, I am concerned with understanding the *essence* of technology and the technological world. In my opinion it will not happen as long as philosophy remains concerned with a subject–object relationship. That means that *Marxism* cannot help us to understand the *essence of technology*.

WISSER: All your reflections are based on and lead to the question that is the fundamental question of your philosophy: the "question of Being." You have pointed out again and again that you do not want to add a new theory of Being to previous theories. Because Being has been defined so differently, for instance as property, as possibility and reality, as truth, even as God, you ask for a comprehensible accord, not in the sense of a supersynthesis but as the question of the meaning of Being.

In which direction does your thinking head toward an answer to the question: Why are there beings [*Seiendes*] and not rather nothing?

HEIDEGGER: There are two questions I will have to answer here. First: the clarification of the question of Being. I think that there is a certain lack of clarity in the formulation of your question. The title "question of Being" is ambiguous. On the one hand, the question of Being means the question of beings insofar as they are. And in this question it is determined what beings are. The determination of Being will give an answer to this question.

On the other hand, the question of Being can also be understood in another sense. What is every answer to the question about beings based on; that is, what is the unconcealedness of Being really based on? To give an example: The Greeks determine Being as the presence of what is present. In presence the present speaks. The present is a moment of time, and therefore the determination of Being as a presence refers to time. If I now try to determine presence from the vantage point of time, and if I look into the history of thinking to see what has been said about time, I find that, starting with Aristotle, the essence of time is determined by an already *determined* being. Therefore the traditional concept of time cannot be used. And *that* is why in *Being and Time* I tried to develop a new concept of time and temporality in the sense of ecstatic openness.

The other question is a question that Leibniz already posed and that is taken up again by Schelling and that I repeat verbatim at the end of my previously mentioned lecture, "What Is Metaphysics?" But this question has an entirely different meaning for me. The usual metaphysical conception of what is asked in the question is: Why are there *beings* at all and not rather nothing? That means: Where is the *cause* or the *reason* for there being *beings* and not nothing? I ask instead: Why are there beings at all and not *rather nothing*? Why do beings have priority, why is nothing not thought as identical with Being? That means: Why does the forgetfulness of Being rule, and where does it come from? It is thus an entirely different question than the *metaphysical* question. That means: I ask "What *is* metaphysics?" I do not ask a *metaphysical* question but ask about the *essence* of metaphysics.

As you can see, these questions are all unusually difficult and basically inaccessible to common understanding. A long "headache" and a really critical confrontation with the great *tradition* are needed. One of the great dangers of our thinking today is precisely that thinking—in the sense of philosophical thinking—no longer has a real, primordial relation to the tradition.

WISSER: It is clear that what matters to you is the dismantling of subjectivity and not the concepts that are important today, the anthropological and the anthropocentric, not the idea that human beings have already comprehended their essence through the knowledge they have of themselves and through their doings. You instruct human beings to look, instead, at the experience of *Da-sein* [being-there] in which human beings recognize themselves as beings open to Being and where Being shows itself to them as un-concealedness. Your whole work is dedicated to proving the necessity of such a transformation, out of the experience of *Da-sein*, of being human. Do you see signs that what you have thought to be necessary will become real?

HEIDEGGER: No one knows what the fate of thinking will look like. In a lecture in Paris in 1964, which I did not give myself but was presented in a French translation, I spoke under the title: "The End of Philosophy and the Task of Thinking." I thus make a *distinction* between philosophy, that is metaphysics, and thinking as I understand it. The thinking that I contrast with philosophy in this lecture—which is principally done by an attempt to clarify the essence of the Greek ἀλήθεια [*aletheia*]—this thinking is, compared to metaphysical thinking, much simpler than philosophy, but precisely because of its simplicity it is much more difficult to carry out. And it calls for new care with language, not the invention of new terms, as I once thought, but a return to the primordial content of our own language, which is, however, constantly in the process of dying off.

A coming thinker, who will perhaps be faced with the task of really taking over this thinking that I am attempting to *prepare*, will have to obey a sentence Heinrich von Kleist once wrote, and that reads "I step back before one who is not yet here, and bow, a millennium before him, to his spirit."

Afterthoughts and Gratitude

RICHARD WISSER

FRIDAY AFTERNOON, 15 August 1969. A call from the head of the cultural division of the German television network ZDF.[1] Martin Heidegger's eightieth birthday was coming up on the twenty-sixth of September. Another television network, ARD, was planning a program. Heidegger had, however, refused to grant ARD an interview. ZDF had made some attempts to convince him that had also failed. It was unclear what was behind his refusal. It was probably not only connected to a certain timidity regarding this new medium but also to bad previous experiences. "Why don't you try to persuade Heidegger to give an interview?" the voice over the telephone asked.

My response: Why should I succeed where others have failed? And anyway, after the refusals received already, such a suggestion was, to put it mildly, impertinent to Heidegger and an unreasonable demand of me.

On 24 September 1969, ZDF actually broadcast a television interview. To the great surprise of all insiders, Heidegger had cooperated. The response in the press was considerable. The *Süddeutsche Zeitung* praised it, for instance, because "the viewer of this program had the unique fortune to see one of the world's great thinkers and to hear him speak,"[2] and the *Evangelische Pressedienst, Kirche und Fernsehen* [Protestant Press Service, Church and Television] counted it "among the most remarkable television programs in recent time" because it "gave not only Heidegger's disci-

89

ples but particularly his critics the opportunity to measure and correct their picture of Heidegger, determined in part by emotions and in part by simple misunderstanding, against reality."³

Six years later, one day after Heidegger's death, ZDF again showed the pictorial document to hundreds of thousands of viewers. It had been emphatically proposed to me that I should speak—as after Karl Jaspers' death—an obituary on the television screen, but, out of a sense of decency, I did not comply with the wish. I did, however, write the text for the introduction. Reinhart Hoffmeister, who had directed the cutting of the Heidegger film, read it, fittingly and with understanding.

Martin Heidegger, who—like no other German philosopher of this century—met with recognition and criticism in his own country and in the entire world, died yesterday at the age of eighty-six.

Heidegger helped human beings, who are, throughout the world, in danger today of becoming absorbed by the realm ruled by economic processes and ideological practices, to come to the realization that they are more than the object of machinations. Because his contemplative thinking, his much praised thinking-after [*Nach-denklichkeit*], asked about the meaning of things and the being of humans, Heidegger succeeded in exposing the extent to which human beings have oriented themselves—in history and at present—toward the superficially factual and the practical. At the same time Heidegger could make it clear, as few philosophers before him have, that human beings are capable of experiencing and of letting be that which reveals itself of its own accord.

Such an understanding of Being is not based on what can be proved, as objectively oriented science is, but remains under way in the unconcealedness [*Unverborgenheit*] of Being. Heidegger may inquire about what seems to be useless in the eyes of the usual busy and everyday understanding of the world. However, in asking about Being as the primordial horizon within which beings [*Seiende*] can be at all, he reveals to human beings what has priority.

Only one television interview with Martin Heidegger exists; he was extremely cautious about the television medium. On the eve of his eightieth birthday, he was interviewed by Richard Wisser, professor of philosophy at the University of Mainz. In the interview, Heidegger consciously speaks an epilogue to his philosophy. We are rebroadcasting this ZDF program in the conviction that, despite the many statements and comments on Heidegger, Heidegger himself knows best how to express what concerned him throughout his life.

How did I succeed in winning over Heidegger? My plan was simple: People who knew Heidegger should give accounts and testimonies. How could Heidegger fail to respond? I developed the concept for Heidegger in a letter. On 15 September his message arrived: "I have just returned from a lengthy trip and have found your letter. If time still allows it, I would be willing to do a very short interview with you [underlined] and be filmed briefly. Please call me to let me know when you might come . . ." (Freiburg im Breisgau-Zähringen, 14 September 1969). I called the same day. We agreed on September 17 at 3:00 P.M. for filming. As I hurried to get all the necessary things going, I got a call, much to my surprise, from a member of the editorial staff of *Der Spiegel.*

It had been heard, the editor from *Der Spiegel* said, that Heidegger had declared himself willing to give an interview on television, which was surprising, given his previous attitude. Quite perplexed, I mumbled something like "Thanks for the good news." I did not disguise my surprise, however, and asked how *Der Spiegel* had found out about the fact so quickly when only very few knew about it yet. "Oh, we have our connections. But more importantly, we want to be at the interview." He then suggested I should bring an editor from *Der Spiegel* with me into Heidegger's house and let him listen to the interview. I referred to Heidegger's letter to me, could see no reason to smuggle someone in who did not belong to the film team, thereby betraying Heidegger's trust, and so I rejected the suggestion. "But," the editor went on, "you could bring the tape to my car right in front of the house and give it to me or just let me listen to it." The whole discussion began to infuriate me. I would not do that either.

He became noticeably more conciliatory and, confidentially, told me the reason for his insistence: "An interview Heidegger gave to Rudolf Augstein in September 1966 is in a safe of ours. We have agreed, however, not to publish the discussion until after Heidegger's death." The subject, he insinuates, is primarily Heidegger's conduct during the Third Reich. "You must understand. . . ."

Yes, I understood. Only then did I understand at all. And we spoke extensively about the way in which I planned to structure the ZDF program, and I learned details about how ARD had constructed its film. We ended the conversation cordially, especially since my telephone partner had meanwhile identified himself as a student of a philosopher highly esteemed by both of us. I complied with his request to call *Der Spiegel* in Hamburg following my visit with Heidegger. Two days before the ZDF broadcast, on September 22, the following appeared in *Der Spiegel*'s preview of upcoming television programs: "What others did not succeed in obtaining, what was thought to be impossible, was achieved by the author Richard Wisser from Worms: a television interview with Heidegger; for 20 minutes the thinker responded."[4]

The situation was "somewhat uncomfortable" for *Der Spiegel*. *Der Spiegel* was understandably curious about whether or not Heidegger had thereby "finally broken his principle not to comment on his work publicly." My interview with Heidegger was thought to be the "beginning of a philosophical breakthrough toward publicity." Another reason for *Der Spiegel* to suspect that Heidegger was finally interested in publicity was an alleged extensive interview published in the French news magazine *L'Express*,[5] in which it was claimed that Heidegger had granted the interview to two editors.

Der Spiegel editors succeeded in proving that the text characterized by *L'Express* as a "document," as "l'entretien que Martin Heidegger a bien voulu accorder ... à notre collaborateur," and therefore as a conversation, which had, in good faith, been called an "interview" and a "discussion" by the newspaper *Die Welt*,[6] was in fact "a compilation of comments that are not protocoled, not recorded on tape, evidently not even cited verbatim, and were not submitted to Heidegger before printing or even sent to him after printing." The bubble had burst. *Der Spiegel* referred to two letters that Heidegger had written to them on the subject. Quoting from one of these letters, *Der Spiegel* drew attention (for the first time publicly) to an interview that was "hidden at *Der Spiegel* and shall only be published after my death."[7]

A letter to the editor from the secretary-general of *L'Express*, who read the *Spiegel* article "that questions the authenticity of the interview ... with amazement," was printed in *Der Spiegel* on 19 January 1970. In the same edition, a statement by Martin Heidegger was published, from which it became clear (1) that Heidegger "had refused to give an interview that would be recorded on tape," and (2) that the *L'Express* text "is a compilation, for which the authors are responsible, of thoughts and statements I expressed during occasional visits—especially during the last."[8] And so the

Spiegel interview remained hidden away until after Heidegger's death in 1976, when it was published under the title "Only a God can still save us."[9] According to a note in *Der Spiegel*, the interview was meant to serve as a "contribution to the 'resolution of my case'" as Heidegger had wanted, and, as *Der Spiegel* intended, to fulfill Heidegger's wish "to respond to accusations made about his position during the Third Reich."[10]

At a philosophy conference in Stuttgart in 1955 I had met the French philosopher Maurice de Gandillac from the Sorbonne in Paris, whose book on Nicholas of Cusanus had been published a year before in German translation. In discussions and letters we attempted to settle questions that arose from difficulties he had had in translating a story by Gertrud von le Fort, "The Magdeburgian Wedding," into French. Following lectures he gave in Mainz and Worms, common interests and friendliness led him to send me a written invitation to a "rencontre philosophique" at the Château de Cerisy-la-Salle in Normandy, where "philosophers of many countries will gather to hear Heidegger lecture on the concept of philosophy (in general)" (Neuilly sur Seine, 16 June 1955).

In the letter he had enclosed a prospectus that gave information on the various meetings taking place there, characterized in detail the themes of four other "rencontres," and named the authorities who would lead the respective discussions. It surprised me that the information on the "rencontre philosophique" were of an unsurpassed brevity. Just the time and the topic of the conversations were announced: QU'EST-CE QUE LA PHILOSOPHIE?, and nothing else. There is a handwritten note from de Gandillac for me: "Participation assurée de M. Heidegger et de G. Marcel." According to his letter of invitation, the reason for the very sketchy announcement was the strong reactions that Heidegger's name aroused in some sectors of the French public.

The year of Heidegger's trips to Provence had not yet arrived, not to mention the period in which Heidegger held his three famous seminars in Le Thor (Provence).[11] The trip to Cerisy-la-Salle in August 1955 was Heidegger's first trip to France, and there he gave the opening address, published by Günther Neske, as an introduction to a discussion: "What is that—philosophy?"[12]

It goes without saying that I gladly and gratefully accepted the invitation from de Gandillac, who belonged to the comité de honneur. I learned of the "colossal difficulties with some of the members of the Cerisy committee" in another informative letter. This was further explanation why the announcement in the pamphlet had to remain short and anonymous and only hinting. It was also mentioned that Heidegger, together with Beaufret, had "ordered" the "short list" of German philosophers "with whom he would like to discuss. We had more freedom with the French and other foreigners." He, de Gandillac, had talked about my participation with Gabriel Marcel, Birot, Beaufret, and Madame Herjon-Desjardin. "And they all agree with me that your personal attendance should be regarded as welcome . . . and perhaps your fiancée as well." This last was in parentheses. In order to get a grant for traveling expenses, de Gandillac suggested that I, using him as a reference, contact the French lecturer at the University of Freiburg, Gilbert Kahn, who was quite close to Heidegger and very involved with the meeting in Cerisy. I followed up on this suggestion and found out from Kahn that there would most likely be no subsidies. I was much more interested in something else, however: which Germans were going to Cerisy. The answer was evasive.

On July 31 I received a letter from Kahn that clarified for me the extent of what I had gotten myself involved in. "Tant bien que mal," I was—without Professor de Gandillac's knowledge—advised against participating in the philosophical "rencontre" in Cerisy. "Your person is naturally completely innocent." Heidegger had, however, very rapidly become aware of the special conditions of this meeting. He was therefore especially interested in direct contact with young French people. "This is not philosophical debate as confrontation between solidly occupied positions. Heidegger is not a man of debate. But neither does he care for people mediating his thought, such as his colleagues here, for example."

Heidegger had even (another broad hint) suggested to a German student, who was to have accompanied him as an assistant and secretary, that his presence was not imperative, so that this student probably had to choose another opportunity to become acquainted with France and the French. "Under these conditions I fear that regardless of your personal qualities and in spite of the interest I trust you have for Heideggerian thought, your position as the sole German might seem a little bit false next to Heidegger. It is true that I was forgetting Biemel, who for several years had German nationality. But Biemel is an old friend of Heidegger's, a sort of family member. You kind sir, whatever your own views, will "objectively" be, if I may say so, the eye of the German university on the meeting in Cerisy between Heidegger and his French interlocutors!" (Fribourg-Brisgau).

What these lines express in their delicately tortuous way; what is, despite their charming politeness, their definite goal; and what could be read "between the lines" persuaded me to respond to Kahn that, "with inner regrets," I would write the organizers of the conference, I would not come because "under the given circumstances, of which I had no previous knowledge, I would be out of place." I would be very sorry "if Heidegger could not achieve the effect that he quite simply has." My answer to Gilbert Kahn, the mediator and conveyor, was difficult for me. Perhaps that is why it turned out so polite. My negative reply to the kind hosts of the conference was much more difficult.

On 10 August and 11 September, I promptly received responses from the hosts that were extremely frank. Only one point will be documented here: "I am personally as disappointed as I am offended. Of course you would have participated as freely in the philosophical discussions and conversations as every French, Belgian, or Spanish participant. It is really foolish to regard you as an "observer" from the German universities (and from Prof. von Rintelen).[13] Heidegger has declared every possible German witness, with the exception of Herr Biemel, unwelcome. Unbelievable, but a fact!" On April 26 of the following year, the event was still talked about and its repercussions on the "conversations" were mentioned.

Despite my disappointment, it had already dawned on me at the time that such an occurrence should not be judged only by what can be seen up front but rather in view of its background. It becomes comprehensible only when the burdens Heidegger then had to bear are examined: they can, at least, explain how such a "misunderstanding" could have happened. However odd it might seem, my relationship to Heidegger's work and, later, to his person remained unburdened, although not unaffected, by this first, if indirect, memory of Heidegger. I felt a compassion toward him that never left me, compassion toward a man badgered by foes and "friends," by intrusiveness and ingratiation, as well as by polemics and tests of strength. A "closeness" develops where there is little air to breathe and where short-windedness can easily rob one of the ability to really think or, at the very least, of a true understanding. It is a closeness that is more of a confinement than a true closeness; it is false because it induces compulsory behavior. Others might blow their tops when confined in such a way. It was probably not easy for Heidegger and was not an escape when he tried to protect himself from such "closeness." And so I studied his work intently, while I considered his person with restraint but not detachment. Although Heidegger initiated contact with me in 1958, and I had since received letters and offprints from him, I met him only once in my life—on 17 September 1969.

The following are excerpts from a record I wrote from memory on 18 September 1969, directly after the television interview and a long, detailed conversation that followed.

My appointment is for 3:00 P.M. The camera team is not there yet. What should I do? I had strongly urged those responsible to send off the convoy of cars on time.

I want to be punctual, walk between the tall hedges that shield the house a bit from sight, through the simple, slightly crooked gate, over paving stones to the house. Covered with shingles on the side toward the street, it seems to me to be disguised and probably for that reason a little like a gingerbread house. I climb up the stairs to the wooden door. The two doorbells are curious: one says "Dr. Dipl. Ing. H.,"[14] the other, above it, "Martin Heidegger." They are accompanied by typewritten notes on how to ring. On the right is an old, small mailbox with Heidegger's unmistakable handwriting on a piece of paper. I ring, glancing at the blessing above the door: "Keep thy heart with all diligence; for out of it are the issues of life" (Proverbs 4:23). The door opens: Heidegger himself, small, surprisingly small—that greatness can be so small—waiting, an old man—although only the calendar says he is eighty—a host welcoming an expected guest.

The greeting is a bit lost in the mutual shaking of hands and in the expression of his quite perceptible attentiveness and my pleasure at finally meeting him personally. From the right, out of the kitchen of the house that seems on the whole small and slightly bare and woody, Frau Heidegger appears, lively, spontaneous, attentive.

Heidegger now, as he will do again later when he accompanies me, keeps a bit in the background. Measured, waiting, directing, letting me go ahead, offering a drink. He seems almost like a cavalier of the old school, but without affectation, not really like a peasant, as he is sometimes described. He possesses a composed casualness that is paired with tact and kindness. I climb, he wishes it, before him up the narrow, winding, steep stairs. I cannot help thinking of the danger, dangerous at his age. On the top floor I remain in the hall, turn to Heidegger who is slowly coming up the stairs—the "circulation problems of old age" [*Greislaufstörungen*] his funny, witty brother had written in his "birthday letter" for

Heidegger's eightieth[15]—and wait for him, although the door to his study is open.

I apologize for the people from television who have not yet arrived and perhaps have lost time in a traffic jam on the highway. Heidegger listens but dismisses it and shows me the way to the study, offers me a seat. I look around while he brings a tray with a bottle of Cinzano and two small liqueur glasses, prepared somewhere, and places it on the desk. He has also prepared two new publications, *Zur Sache des Denkens*[16] and the little book published by his hometown Messkirch for his birthday, which he gives to me. In both a dedication has been written: "For Richard Wisser with thanks Martin Heidegger." Thanks?

The room is rectangular with a continuous bookshelf on the long side of a wall. I am aware of much Heidegger. In front of the desk, toward the corner window, manuscript pages lie in separate piles next to each other, sorted, with covers. There is a lot of space behind the desk where he works with a view out the corner window. There is a small aisle on the right side of the desk, where there is a low leather armchair and a sofa with a blanket and an excessively highly placed headrest, and above that the only picture that dominates the room, probably in pastel, probably Titisee, a Black Forest landscape with shades of white. There are two or three other, smaller pictures. One is a drawing of Hölderlin; I cannot tell if it is an original. Heidegger asks me to have a seat in the armchair.

"Now, let's have a welcome drink first." It strikes me about the way Heidegger intonates the sentence that what has been said creates space and is aiming for time. Some of his later sentences begin without really ending, as if there were three dots at the end. They conclude less than they open. They finish in anticipation of an answer. Heidegger himself, although I offer to do it myself, pours out our drinks carefully and generously. The surprise of the first moment still lasts. We calmly put our glasses down simultaneously. He has drunk half of his, I have only sipped mine. I mention again how concerned I am that the technicians have not arrived punctually. Heidegger smiles at "technicians," I emphasize "punctually."

I quickly head toward my goal. I explain to Heidegger how I thought the interview could be done. Because he has agreed only to a short conversation, nothing should be left to chance, no time wasted.

We agree to go through the questions one by one. I read aloud.

Heidegger reads along with me, using the original I had handed him. He reads the text very attentively but also listens. I read aloud intentionally, because I hope that a real voice will help to convince him. I notice that he is sometimes behind me in his own reading and slow the flow of my words. He nods. "In our time more and more voices are being raised. The voices that are growing steadily louder are those voices that propagate a change of social conditions as the decisive task of the present and that see it as the only approach that bears any promise for the future. What is your opinion, Professor Heidegger, of such an orientation of the so-called Zeitgeist?" Heidegger had obviously expected something else. What, I do not know. That it is so, I can sense. "That's very general. What can I say about that?" Restraint and resistance can be felt, even a little unwillingness to get dragged into the usual, into the aggressive eloquence of self-satisfied slogans. Although he only hints at it, Heidegger leaves no doubt what his assessment of the "general" is. I nevertheless clarify my objective once again, using the key phrases: "change of social conditions," "orientation," "Zeitgeist." Heidegger does not respond. I therefore go on to the next question, which is connected to the first: "Quite different motives have led to modern attempts to reorient objectives and restructure actual facts on a social and also on an interpersonal level. It is clear that much philosophy is at play here, for better and for worse. Do you think philosophy has a social mission?" Heidegger makes a movement of the head that is, as I will later note, characteristic: first bent down and to one side, the head is then raised, with a clear, reciprocative look in his widened eyes. "No! I don't think so!" "Then say so! Say why you don't think so! Say what a good many others just swallow today! Why don't you clarify the misunderstanding that philosophy is equal to social philosophy?" "I would have to bring in so much, there is Marx, and you know . . ." Again I notice the three dots. "Well, that's exactly what we should tackle, because it's exactly Marx whom people refer to today. And I have deliberately worded my question—'reorientation,' 'restructuring,' 'actual facts'—to reflect today's doctrinaire jargon by which people communicate as if using passwords." "You are right. Yes, I have noticed it. The connection to the first question, too. You mean well. But there would be so much to say . . ."

I search for a way to save the two questions, which I believe many people expect me to ask, because I think it is becoming increasingly clear to Heidegger what venture he has gotten himself into. "Could we perhaps specify the first question? Perhaps by referring to the reform of the university, which is talked about so much today, is fought for, and was, after all, once your task, too!" I am thinking of a question I would like to pose Heidegger later. At least the ground for it will have been prepared. "Yes, that will do. I can say something about that which I already said a long time ago. Here old is new, and new is stylish." (I stick to our agreement later during the interview and add to my first question: "What is your opinion on such an orientation of the so-called Zeitgeist, for instance with regard to the reform of the university?" and get a slap on the wrist for the "general" part of my question. "I will only respond to the last question, because what you said before goes too far." The answer Heidegger gives is a quotation from his inaugural lecture held in Freiburg in 1929. It therefore lies exactly forty years back and—ahead!)

"But I would like to pose the second question on the social mission of philosophy, too. It is important to me, as I'm sure you realize, that you are brought into contact, that your thinking is not left standing alone, and to show that your thinking says something about what is going on and that one is referred to this thinking, because it has consequences that can be proved by transposing, indeed by applying, it." "Oh, the time hasn't come for that yet. It's all not understood." Is it resignation? I am reminded of Karl Jaspers. The spirit is powerless, but still Jaspers, that ill man, pounced on his opponents and the intolerable. Heidegger withdraws. I have no sense of reproach, because such behavior is based on experience. Heidegger withdraws, leans back in his chair, looks at me with smaller, narrow eyes. It seems to me that he is setting up distance, watching from a fortress, putting space around him, between us.

He speaks single sentences connected by pauses, pauses in which he recalls how things are and why they are so and, "because today to alter [*ändern*] means to change [*verändern*]," pushes what is so away from him. Suddenly his eyes are wide again, and while Heidegger, putting the manuscript aside, speaks, he seems great to me for the first time, this small man at his desk in the house in Zähringen on Rötebuck No. 47. He is fighting against experiences that burden him and that he hints at while speaking. He speaks openly, but leaves no doubt that he will not say such things in front of the camera. I nevertheless try to bring him back to my second question again. "It is precisely the question of philosophy's social mission that could allow you to speak about the concept of philosophy on which such a question is based. Why don't you contrast it with your own concept?" "Yes, but what is happening today has nothing to do with philosophy. It is sociology." Again the raising of the head and the look that attacks not me but the times. After Heidegger has broken some of his reserve, I add fuel to the fire that has flared up. "Why don't you say so? You should now prepare for what I would like to ask you about later: your thinking!"

We come to the third question, which I also read aloud. Heidegger turns to his desk again, picks up the original text, and reads with resistance—it seems to me—along with me. "Karl Jaspers has made a statement that points out the interdependence of philosophy and politics: 'A philosophy reveals what it is in its political appearance.' For that reason Jaspers, especially during the last years of his life, 'went public.' He took a stand, when asked and when not asked. He experienced approval and disapproval. But he spoke. Why are you silent?"

Heidegger does not speak Jaspers' name aloud. I notice that the questions are beginning to bother him. (After Jaspers' death, I had been informed about some aspects of the relationship between Jaspers and Heidegger by Hans Saner, Jaspers' assistant of many years and the editor of his posthumously published works. I know from him that although Jaspers had not arrived at a definitive picture of Heidegger's thought and person, in the end, he had still rejected Heidegger's way of thinking, just as Heidegger, conversely, had written almost devastatingly on Jaspers' *Psychology of World Views*. In the meantime the previously omitted chapter on Heidegger has been published in the new edition of Jaspers' *Philosophical Autobiography*. Hans Saner published Jaspers' *Notes on Martin Heidegger* in 1978. At present Saner is working with Walter Biemel on the correspondence.[17]) But I cannot bring Heidegger to speak about his "silence" in front of the camera; that is, to break it. Heidegger seems rejective. I have no other alternative: "We can cross out this question, if you would like." "Yes, let's do that. It . . . it is all so difficult for me . . . I have had quite a few experiences. I've alluded to some to you . . . We'll cross it out." I cross out the question with a pencil in my manuscript. Heidegger reaches for a felt-tip pen and crosses it, in red ink, carefully out. Relieved? He crosses it out almost gently; the matter has been settled.

Question 4 and half of Question 5 are likewise crossed out after a long discussion. Question 4: "It is well known and has been pointed out again and again that at one point in your life you did not avoid political engagement, as it is called today. It is less well known and has been pointed out less frequently that you had already resigned your position as rector following the winter semester 1933/34 after a ten-month period in office, in part because of the increasing difficulties you had in performing your office, and that you demonstratively stayed away from the public inauguration of your successor, who had been appointed by the governmental ministry. How do you yourself judge your short-lived hope that what was happening then could be the start of a national [*Volk*] "will to self-responsibility" as a "law of cooperation between nations?"[18] The background of the question is crossed out: "It is revealing that at the moment when the hope for a common [*gleichgerichtetes*] undertaking became unfounded and, put differently, when your philosophy was to have been forced into line [*gleichschalten*], you drew the consequences. There are witnesses that you told those listening to your lectures—at least those listeners who really listened—some things that went as far as it was then possible to go." Summarizing the quite unproductive conversation, Heidegger concludes: "That has no point. It will start a discussion again. People will not understand today what I say now. Self-justification, it is said, and already everything is twisted to mean its opposite . . . No . . ." It is again, however, not a dictatorial no, not a rejecting no, but the no of a man who is hurt by all this, who feels a burden, who makes almost tender gestures of the hand as if to wipe away, to remove what oppresses him.

Nevertheless I persist. I hope he can feel something fond, something loving in it. Explain. The discussion could finally be concluded by a statement. "I don't want to push you, push you toward something impossible, but I do want to use this chance to achieve something. A statement, not a clarifying or an explanatory statement, but a statement. A statement on this matter! I have tried to balance the formulation of my question and have consciously quoted you . . ." Heidegger interrupts my own statement that was to have persuaded him. "You mean so well, dear Herr Wisser. But I can't talk about that. Not now! Strictly in confidence, *Der Spiegel* has an explanation from me that will be published in due course . . . After my death . . . A clarifying conversation . . . As far as that is possible . . . In it I have said what you would like me to say now. I cannot say it now." I am glad that I have already been informed by *Der Spiegel*. I say nothing because I had assured confidentiality. Say nothing although Heidegger is obviously interested in the effect that this declaration, this divulgence, will have on me. If the event had been unknown to me, I would certainly have asked: Why *Der Spiegel*? Heidegger attempts to read my thoughts and says: "It was fair to me. I am fair to it."

Even if I do understand this, I persist, because only very few people know anything about the *Spiegel* interview. "It is important that you say something, because, as it is said, it is expected. Who knows anything about the interview and about what you said then, as it will only be made public in due course? It is also expected of me that I pose such a question. All right, perhaps my persistence is reason enough for you to accuse me of a lack of understanding." Heidegger, without harshness but with emphasis: "Dear Herr Wisser, you are really going all out ..." "For your sake, for the sake of your philosophy ..." Two veins on Heidegger's forehead are swollen. He is excited. Later, during the interview, it happens again. He is inwardly more moved than is meant to be outwardly visible, self-controlled, not controlling.

I stood up a while ago, am standing next to him at his desk since he has turned to it again, am bending down, close. Now I sit in the armchair again. We cross out. Heidegger is paler. I do not want to give up the second half of the fifth question, the direct question: "How could your philosophy then and how can it today become effective, considering a concrete society with its manifold tasks and concerns, needs and hopes? Or are those of your critics right who maintain that Martin Heidegger has concentrated so much on 'Being' that he has sacrificed the *conditio humana*, the being of humans in society and as persons?" I therefore say: "I would like to pose the direct question even if we cross out the reference to that earlier time. It contains an accusation against what you see as your task, to think about the 'meaning of Being' and what 'Being' is called and what it 'is'." Heidegger looks at me with wide eyes. A kind of defense? Approval? A practiced acceptance of "his" formulations, of appreciation, respect, approval, admiration, all of which are probably often bestowed upon him by visitors to his house?

I repeatedly have the impression that the interview is endangered. I say to myself: You have got to stay completely natural. I say what I think, my only goal being to carry through with the interview, though the carefully planned sequence of its questions has been broken up. A number of times it has crossed my mind to ask whether we should do without my plan for the interview. But what would be gained in doing that? Judging by all that had happened already, it would seem that then certainly nothing would be accomplished. Anyway, my biggest worry is that the mood will change and he will refuse. It seems to me that Heidegger is close to saying: Oh, we'd better forget it. I therefore explain my reasons for asking the question and remind Heidegger of the program and of the participant's statements. "My questions don't come from nowhere. They pick up on thoughts expressed by the congratulators, their praise and their reproach, reproach as their personal reaction to you.[19] Dolf Sternberger, for instance, accused you of sacrificing the actual human being, the person, history, through your thinking." "But that is nonsense! Without human beings there is no Being, but there are human beings for the sake of Being. It is for precisely that reason that human beings are so important to me. But they aren't all." "Sternberger is thinking of this or that human being, and it would be good, I think, if you yourself would describe how your thinking can benefit concrete human beings. That is precisely what I hoped to do with the other, the political, the 'sociological' questions."

While speaking, I get back up again from the low armchair, too low for me. I warm up, but still do not talk at Heidegger, but genuinely to him, hope to convince him. "The application is imperative, up to and including a social and individual application." "Very few understand what my thinking is. The others don't reach it." "It must be possible. It is so worthwhile." Heidegger smiles and smiles, much wisdom in his look, sympathy but also disappointment. About me, too? About how I talk just like those who think the great problem of our time is bringing Heidegger and the concrete human being, even "the social," together? Heidegger has taken back his smile. He has had, as one says and he says, his experiences. "People have made things very difficult for me and not at all nice," he had said in connection with the fourth and fifth questions. I am reminded of it again, as I see how he withdraws, leaning back in his simple desk chair. And yet he has an unusual certainty. Heidegger knows what he thinks and that he thinks. That is what it is about, not about mere understanding. It is about wanting to be understood but no longer, not yet, about understanding. He no longer believes in it.

My five questions have shrunk to two and a half. Heidegger accepts the questions that are actually philosophical, at least the next three, quicker, even quickly ("Martin Heidegger, the bad conscience of Western philosophy?"; "First, what do you mean when you maintain that science does not think?"; "And what do you mean, secondly, when you say that the atom bomb is less dangerous for contemporary humanity than the law [*Ge-setz*] of technology, the construct [*Ge-stell*]?").[20]

An inward excitement at the next question that I had hoped to have prepared for by the introduction of the Heideggerian term *construct* and by the seemingly tortuous explanation, based on Heidegger's way of expressing himself. It is a question aimed at the nature of his language. "The nature of your language, which has, incidentally, even changed the language of French philosophy, is criticized from time to time in quite emphatic terms. The social philosopher Adorno called your language a 'jargon of authenticity.' And although Ernst Bloch characterized Adorno's own language as a 'jargon of the inauthenticity of the good,' he accuses your language of 'a curiously experiential play with concepts,' 'word-splitting with a constantly forced etymology.' What does language mean to you?"

Heidegger has pressed his eyes shut. The wrinkle on his forehead above the bridge of his nose has become more prominent. But he only follows up on the last question. "That is very difficult." Pause. A pause that becomes oppressive and does not, on his part, stem solely from reflection. I break the silence. "Is language everything to you?" Heidegger: "No, it isn't. But it is hard to say." I remind him of, or rather refer to, several of his own statements. He is unwilling. Is he unwilling because Adorno and Bloch were mentioned before? I must try to find out! "It is precisely Adorno and Bloch to whom we should refer. We should mention their criticism, which is repeated by so many others. Both of them, after all, had something in mind. In order to give the often-repeated phrase "jargon of authenticity"—it occurs to most people when they hear the names Heidegger and Jaspers—an appearance of objectivity, something many people pride themselves in, I have consciously used one of your formulations in the question about technology: 'to reveal the real, in the mode of ordering, as available material.'[21] That appears to be play with language, is interpreted that way, and criticized by those who do not notice that terminological work is being done here: object [Gegen*stand*—what *stands* against] to do away with the object [*Gegen*stand—what stands *against*], to make everything available material [Be*stand*], to *make*." Heidegger nods in agreement. I am already hoping to have won him over when he says firmly: "But I can't speak about language." We cross it out.

Yet we do talk together about the question, because Heidegger picks up on the comment that his language has influenced the language of French philosophy. Relaxed and in a good mood, almost with a feeling of well-being, he talks for a longer amount of time about his experiences with the French and the French spirit. "The French respect the spirit! The Germans don't know what it is." "Yes, many have no respect for the spirit but sometimes *have* spirit." We speak about the age of German idealism, when Germans had a relationship to the spirit that could almost be called natural. Heidegger gains more color. He nods, agrees, listens, reflects, speaks, points out.

I had labored hard on the next question as I had tried to work out the sequence of questions late at night. "All your reflections are based on the question that is the fundamental question of your philosophy: the 'question of Being.' You have pointed out again and again that you do not want to add a new theory of Being to the previous theories. Because Being has been defined quite differently, for instance as property, as possibility and reality, as truth, even as God, you ask for a comprehensible accord, not in the sense of a supersynthesis but as the question of the meaning of Being. In which direction does your thinking lead us toward an answer to the question: Why are there beings [*Seiendes*] and not rather nothing?" I had hoped that this question—following the now-omitted discussion of language—would prompt Heidegger to speak on the "question of Being." At the same time it would give him an opportunity to discuss the difference between the expressions "beings" and "Being" and "nothing."

Heidegger corrects me immediately and says that the question contains two different aspects. I say openly what I had intended, and that my question has a catch that is meant to get him to correct it. When the question is concerned with the heart of his thinking, it is important to have a vital, not an oracular, response. "Fine! First one question, my question, and then the completely different question that Schelling poses." "Yes!"

The next question asks whether there are signs of a realization of the human being as a being [*Wesen*] open to Being and not as anthropocentric self-awareness. It remains, and it becomes the last question because Heidegger rejects the one with which I had planned to conclude the interview. I read aloud: "You, Professor Heidegger, live in an awareness of fate according to which it is your task to reawaken the sense for the possible destiny of Being in human beings. Your thinking has always stemmed from an awareness of the highest responsibility for Being. In your works you have sacrificed the personal, which is just what sometimes makes other philosophers' writings so attractive, to this responsibility. You do not try to lead people to the matter of thinking by way of Martin Heidegger as human being and as person, but to commit them to thinking by way of what has been thought. Do you feel lonely, and what do human beings and God mean to you on your eightieth birthday?" Heidegger's answer is abrupt, decisive, succinct: "That question is a slap in your own face!" Silence. I am affected, hurt, am reminded of the perplexing answers of Zen Buddhist masters. This is "rèsponse," retort, not "correspondance," it seems to me. I am silent, consciously, with emphasis, not only because I am reflecting. I had decided to ask this question not because I was doing a little socioeconomical groveling in "society," not to invade "inwardness," not out of tactlessness in the face of supposed "private affairs," but because I wanted to question the closeness to what is distant and yet hits close.

Heidegger himself breaks the silence. Almost mild, without a trace of whining, thoughtfully reminding, turned toward me almost solicitously, he looks me in the eye and, despite his composure, says seriously and with emotion: "Loneliness and human beings and God are all connected . . . Yes, that is the problem . . . I am lonely, how lonely you don't know, or yes, you ask me because you think you know, but exactly for that reason . . . I can't answer that here." I apologize, make an attempt. "It is probably tactless to ask so intrusively. I didn't want to step too close, not to come too close, wanted closeness . . ." This time *I* end my sentence with three dots. Heidegger: "No, that isn't it. It really is the question. But not *the* question, not my question. And if I talk about human beings and God, then people will take it . . . and the misunderstanding . . . and they have something . . . but loneliness?" "Fine, the second-to-last question also gives you a chance to come to an appropriate end, please don't misunderstand me, a highpoint of the interview."

I nevertheless try once again to persuade Heidegger to answer a part of the question. "I have consciously used a passage, the passage 'destiny of Being,' that Löwith uses." Heidegger starts, jolts: "Löwith? Is he taking part in this, too? You didn't write me that." Heidegger stands up, wants to reach for my letter, which has meanwhile been placed far away on one side of the desk. I remember that I had, in fact, not included Löwith in the list of congratulators, although only because he had not responded by the time I wrote my letter to Heidegger. I am baffled by Heidegger's reaction but nevertheless say, very naturally and without resorting to feigned composure: "When I wrote, there was probably no mention of him yet. But in the meantime he has been interviewed." Is there an obstacle here? In order to get over this dangerous moment, perhaps the suspicion that a new name had been smuggled in, I read to Heidegger from a prepared list of already filmed statements and the dates of those still to be filmed. It is once again clear to me how presumptuous it was to try to cajole me into taking a *Spiegel* editor with me into Heidegger's house and letting him listen.

Heidegger has sat down again. We talk about the key phrase "destiny of Being." He repeatedly emphasizes: "That is difficult. No one will understand if I say something about that." I point out that the interview will be a unique document, and add: "Disregarding *Der Spiegel.*" And Heidegger smiles. "But one that the viewers will not understand. It will sound like Chinese to them." "Then we'll just have to learn Chinese." Heidegger is still smiling his fine smile. "That will take a while." But he gives up a resistance that is not directed at me but at the "success" that I seem to expect and that, in his eyes, will obviously not occur. In any case Heidegger yields: "I will say something on the destiny of thinking, nothing final, that can't be. But how I categorize my own thinking." "Then I will call the technicians." They have long since arrived.

I hurry, because I do not want to risk a breakdown, another refusal, at this stage. A quick greeting. A reproachful question, worried, why they did not arrive on time? Someone mumbles: "We were only allowed to drive after twelve. That has to do with union regulations. Either before twelve or after twelve." I urgently request them to film as much as possible, even what appears unimportant to them, and to be discreet. They do not comply, at least not with the first request, the most urgent.

The setting up of the floodlights, the laying out of the cables, the search for sockets, the arrangement for recording the sound transform the house into an anthill. Nevertheless, or perhaps for that reason, everything goes smoothly. While he is testing the focus of the camera, Herr von Armin, the head cameraman, almost trips twice over objects, tripods, which are lying around. Heidegger: "No need to get excited." He would like to sit at his desk. Herr von Armin, as experienced in dealing with the Viet Cong as in positioning well-known politicians, unobtrusively but resolutely pushes Heidegger to where the conditions for filming, on the whole quite bad, are best. Like a doctor who must operate, he places the "patient," who resists inwardly but has already put himself into his hands, in the desired position on the "operating table." Heidegger reconciles himself to it, keeps his composure during the preparations. I am positioned with my back to the desk, next to me the camera that is filming Heidegger. Diagonally behind Heidegger is a second camera that is aimed at me.

I try to ease the paradoxical situation, the establishment of communication while the atmosphere that promotes it is being dissolved, try to make it more human in the web of cables and between tripods and equipment. Not exactly with success. Heidegger stands up, runs a careful slalom course around the busy technicians, who are positioning themselves and calling to each other, gets the Kröner edition of Karl Marx's *Early Writings*, asks me, because I am closer, to pass him a black notebook, heads for the bookshelves, and pulls his book *Wegmarken* [*Path Marks*] out of the row of books. Papers, which he can only fit in the cracks above the rows of books in the bookrack with an effort. *Wegmarken* falls down. Heidegger bends down, I am quicker. Heidegger opens to the page he intends to read. Now the book can be shoved into the crack.

The television people are still tinkering. They are disagreeing about something. Heidegger reaches for a manuscript. "This is the handwritten manuscript of *Being and Time*." "Would you show it to me later?" Heidegger promises. And he actually remembers it later of his own accord. The lights flare, spotlights, glaring, merciless. The light is metered. The microphones are placed on us. We are fettered. I apologize for the activity [*Umtrieb*] and the glaring spotlights. Heidegger: "They are blinding." He does not say "me." "But that doesn't matter at all. I don't mind the commotion [*Betrieb*]." He glances at me mischievously. One of the technicians, apparently the last one to bring in equipment or something, comes into the room, goes straight to Heidegger, beams at him with a friendly face, and shakes the hand of the seated Heidegger, who is caught in the beam of the spotlights: "Well, hello, Professor. So how are you doing?" He knows Heidegger will be eighty. Heidegger is puzzled. But only for a second. I say: "The people from Mainz are very natural when dealing with everyman." "That's good," Heidegger chuckles happily. With an impish look in his eyes, he twinkles at me. The mood has distinctly improved.

We begin filming. Strain, the confinement, this pressure, the theatricality. It is difficult for me to concentrate. For other reasons I have long since given up my intention to squeeze in more questions during the interview. We look at each other almost continually. I have to check myself, cannot give in to my inclination to voice an agreement with an interlocutor or to vocalize a disagreement, am not allowed to jump in when it seems necessary to me, to intervene, interrupt, conclude the sentence of another in his own sense more quickly. I am no interviewer. What is called "interview discipline" by television people does not suit me, although I understand the optical and acoustic reasons for it. The course of the interview, which has lost its systematic form anyhow, goes against my nature. But I keep to the agreed sequence of steps.

Just as Heidegger is talking about his thinking, in the middle of a sentence, the roll of film is at an end. Heidegger keeps on speaking, does not notice the technical failure at first despite the calls: "Cut," "Stop," "That won't be on film any more." The time is bridged over until the new film is loaded. Jutta Szostak, without whom the statements would never have come about and who has taken over the clapperboard, says from the sofa to Heidegger: "Start from where you left off." I intervene, not meaning to be schoolmasterly to her (as a psychology student, she had attended my lectures on philosophy) but to signalize understanding to the eighty-year-old man. "It's not that simple. Professor Heidegger was just getting to something important." "Yes, so I was. But it doesn't matter. You can just add what I say now. But please, be careful about it." I promise that that can be taken for granted. "Where was it that I wanted to say something about Marx? It wasn't after this, was it?" "You said something when I asked you about the social mission of philosophy. But because we have interrupted the filming anyway and will have to edit, you could begin by saying it again." Heidegger agrees, says this important passage, waits and begins to speak again almost at the point where he had had to leave off, continuing his train of thought.

We are interrupted again. This time the tape is finished. This will give us the chance to separate a long passage of Heidegger's, in which he has combined two of my questions, one on science and one on technology, and thus given quite a long answer. There will be quite a bit of editing to do, and not only because we have to unite two synchronous films, one of him and one of me. What is most important is that we have gotten Heidegger to speak. He complies with what he had promised for the last question, the second-to-last question as far as I am concerned. He finishes with a quote from Heinrich von Kleist—Heidegger reads it aloud from his black notebook. A touching look at me. "That's enough now." We do not have the impression that a king is giving up his throne, but that Heidegger the thinker is withdrawing.

Spotlights out. It is almost unbearably hot in the crammed, tight room. Loading up, packing in, confusion. Disentangling the knots. Some things do not work the first time around. Forward and backward, back and forth. What had been moved out of the room is brought back in. Heidegger, lost, as if absent, tired but composed. The others, self-important. The battlefield is vacated, the task is done. Things are put in order again. Heidegger: "Oh, just leave it." I nevertheless put his desk chair back in its old place. We bring book and notebook back to their proper places. Heidegger himself goes over to the narrow bookrack opposite the bookshelves, near the door. He has to stretch a little to put Karl Marx back onto the shelf. "Look," he shows me the edition, "this is by Landshut. Also a student. But in the second edition he left out his foreward to the first edition." "Why?" "It was probably too Heideggerian." "So?" "It wasn't opportune any more (in 1953)!" The room becomes austere again. The severity, almost reminiscent of impoverished days as a student, returns, as does the grandfatherly look of the furnishings. It is only now that I notice the climbing plant that has wound itself around the corner window. Leaf for leaf it sprouts up, following the frame of the window.

I ask Heidegger to put himself at our disposal, as he had promised, for a few shots in the garden. He does not want to. I try to persuade him: "In his congratulatory remarks for your birthday, Ernst Jünger walks with a bouncy, still lively military step through his garden. You should, too." Heidegger has fun: "Yes, Jünger is younger. He is sprightly. He has a beautiful garden. Jünger makes hard work of thinking. I mean, doesn't make it easy for himself. He does it." I finally urge Heidegger, almost taking him with me.

We need material for the opening moments of the film and for a possible ending. Heidegger, hesitating, remains standing at the top of the stairs. I worry whether he will follow me. "As I was about to drive to your house, our eight-year-old son Andreas wanted to come with me. 'You can't come,' I said to him, 'I have to visit an important philosopher.' 'Yes, Papa, but you said that he is a grandpa, so that means he has children I can play with.' " "Yes, five grandchildren." Heidegger enjoys the topic and the idea. "You should have brought him, yes, yes. Volkmann-Schluck's little son was in Todtnauberg at the cabin and said: 'Papa, is that the philosopher who knows what Being is?' " Heidegger is amused, enjoys what lies behind the question, and willingly goes down the stairs with me.

I prompt the second cameraman, who has positioned himself in the garden, but leaves get in the way of the filming. And I am in the picture. I want Heidegger to come out of the door and walk through the garden alone. Heidegger is standing around undecidedly. "So what should I do now?" The head cameraman, Herr von Armin: "You see, Professor, you go out the door, down the stairs, along the path through the lawn, turn halfway down the path, and head toward the chestnut tree, where I will be filming." Heidegger seems upset, almost alarmed: "But that's a walnut tree!" Heidegger appears disturbed, as if he is thinking about something, perhaps about how a walnut tree could be mistaken for a chestnut tree. At any rate, he does not have the stage directions in mind, because he asks me: "Now what should I do? Please show me." I walk, as he watches, down the path he should take, even walk it twice. Each time, however, the leaves of the walnut tree, under which von Armin has positioned himself, brush against my face. Will Heidegger be able to walk under it? Von Armin must know what he is doing: Heidegger's back, departure, disappearance?

Later: "The cameraman would like you to walk in the direction of the forested mountain. He thinks that will make a good picture. Expanse, distance, outlook." "It is now obstructed by buildings . . . For years, for a long time, the view was free. Now it has been obstructed." Regrets on both sides. But then von Armin calls: "Come toward me!" Heidegger is standing in front of the door to his house. Von Armin: "No, go back once more, Professor. You shouldn't be seen at first. You should be stepping out of the door, not just standing around." I move Heidegger to the right position, push him back. He goes into the house. Comes. Walks. He walks with a somewhat uncertain step on the staggered paving stones. There he goes, a solitary, old man, walks through his garden because camera people, people from television, have asked him to. He goes at the bidding of people who want to capture him, who hope to soon have him on film. Von Armin makes Heidegger walk once more. Heidegger does it. Finally it is all over.

The camera people say goodbye. I ask Jutta Szostak to wait, and then I walk back with Heidegger. He must be tired after all this. But he invites me to stay. We talk together for another hour and a half. Several times I make moves to go, but just then Heidegger always pronouncedly asks something new. It is like the offering of a hand. I have to talk a lot. It thus seems to me that he is interested in information. From the start I have taken care to be natural, physiological in the Greek sense. Has more than vitality or vivacity come across? Every now and then I felt quite "literary" compared to

Heidegger. I did not want to let the thread break. Perhaps I experienced the silence and the pauses too musically.

With "I think the interview will be good," I introduce a new phase in the conversation. "Yes, it could be. But please be careful that nothing gets mixed up." It seems to me that Heidegger honestly thinks that the matter, or, more correctly, the whole affair, has turned out better than he had originally expected. "Precisely by 'masterfully' correcting the implications of my questions and by going into what could be suspected behind them, could lie hidden behind them, you spoke vitally." "What I said about the history of decline occurred to me while reading," he said almost apologetically. I had been interested in Heidegger's method of "destruction" of the previous history of Western philosophy.

Suddenly: "At the end comes the beginning." Heidegger reaches for the promised manuscript of *Being and Time*. I do not have to voice my own request any more. He shows it gladly. Now he seems a little bit like a peasant to me, too, a peasant like the one Jünger describes in his statement, a peasant who shows his possessions. But even now I cannot put my finger on what it is that makes him seem like a peasant, even rustic, to me. Despite his hardness, despite the aggressiveness bordering on anger that revealed itself in the discussion in several places, he appears gentle, so careful in his movements. His beautiful German script is clear, without mistakes, the pages are structured, the handwriting of this thinker is a joy. "The manuscript went to the typesetter just like this."

We talk about what Heidegger intends to do with the manuscript. "It is the third fair copy. I don't exactly know yet. It will work itself out." Because I had heard about it, I mention that there are supposed to have been plans to sell it to an American buyer, but that it would now probably go to the Schiller Archive in Marbach. I indicate, however, that I understand that what is valuable to us should also be of some use to him. He is silent. Then: "We will see."

We look at the rough draft of the beautifully legible manuscript of *Being and Time*; it is hard to read, written in such small letters one almost needs a magnifying glass. Heidegger gets another manuscript, a lecture on Schelling's piece "On the Essence of Human Freedom,"[22] to which Heidegger obviously attaches special importance. Heidegger reaches for another carton, which is in a row of similarly shaped boxes containing Heidegger's lectures and manuscripts. What did I say: peasant? It seems to me he is more like a bee, peaceful but with a sting, and the bookshelves are a honeycomb.

"All unpublished. Look," he points to the piles of pages on the table near the window, "but there's time. The time has to be right." I am not satisfied, am perhaps also being a bit pompous: "Agreed. But even though I have not read your dissertation or your postdoctoral thesis [*Habilitationsschrift*], there are other people who are very interested in new publications of yours." Heidegger looks at me with a smile, but then gets harsh: "Only new publications count today. And they only count as long as a newer new publication doesn't push the older new publication into oblivion. Like the ... publisher. But that isn't a publisher, that is a catastrophe." His openness leaves me speechless. I feel that it should be the reverse.

After this outburst, Heidegger returns to our topic of conversation. "People, I know you meant it differently, people always want something new. And they haven't read the old yet, not really read it." "But 'people' don't count. Of course 'people' want new publications, which they don't read, which they see, buy, want to have because they will then feel up-to-date. But your friends and your opponents, the serious ones, are trying to explore your thinking, where it comes from, how it progresses, want to go along with you or look for paths that wander afield and for . . ." I want to say "paths that lead astray" but Heidegger interrupts me, curt, dangerously quiet: "Not even what has been published is understood. If those who write on my thinking—not to mention those who talk about it—had at least read the most important of my publications, then thinking would be in a better way." Noticing that I look a little amazed, which is not because I think he is wrong but because I feel a little found out myself, Heidegger adds: "Not only *my* thinking." It occurs to me that I actually had for a moment uncritically equated Heidegger's thinking with *thinking*, as if I had forgotten what Heidegger had said shortly before at the end of the interview in and through the quotation from Kleist.

Later, on 26 March 1971, I read a review in *Publik* written by someone who "is carefully thinking about the dangerous quotation with which Heidegger ends the interview with Wisser." Heidegger

speaks of a "coming thinker" who may "perhaps be faced with the task" of "really taking over" the thinking that he, Heidegger, is trying to "prepare." This "coming thinker," as it is said in the diction of positive apocalyptic thought or of mere dialectical thought, "will have to obey" a sentence written by Heinrich von Kleist that goes as follows: "I step back before one who is not here yet, and bow, a millennium before him,

to his spirit." Aside from it not being clear what is meant by
this thinker, envisioned as a redeemer, having to "obey a
sentence," an exegesis of this quotation gets caught in a
dilemma: Does Heidegger understand himself to be the
precursor who is already "bowing" to the coming thinker, or
is it only the coming thinker who will once again point—"a
millennium"—ahead to one who will come then? Whatever the
answer, this chiliasm offers no comfort, no hope . . . it is, one
has to admit, elitist, gnostic, and disastrously apolitical and
asocial. It is an expression of that German excessiveness, the
dèmesure des minuit, as Albert Camus has called it so astutely
and passionately, and to which he has opposed the thought of
the midi, his philosophy of limit and measure, inspired by the
Greeks.[23]

And then the eighty-year-old leans back in his chair, retreats, not
to widen the distance but, as I will soon see, to impress upon me
something that is important to him, and speaks very personally and
directly to me: "Thinking, dear Herr Wisser, thinking takes time, *its*
time and its *time*. It *has* time, lots of time . . ."
How different, it flashes through my mind, the relationship of
great philosophers to time and to "their" time is. I have to think of
Karl Jaspers. Jaspers, who was originally, as he characterized himself, "apolitical," entered the political arena with breathtaking
speed during the last years of his life, much to the dismay of some
politicians. That was what I had wanted to show Heidegger
through the question we crossed out. "A philosophy reveals what it
is in its political appearance," Jaspers had ultimately said, and he
had even acted accordingly. He had taken a stand, invited or unin-
vited, asked or unasked. In the letters I received from Jaspers, it
became increasingly clear that he wanted to use the time he had
left to do what needed to be done, which is why he repeatedly
emphasized how important the political was for him. "You know
how glad I always am that you also take an interest in my political
books. You are almost the only one" (Basel, 20 May 1967). For us it
must read: "Take an interest . . . right away."
In the face of another of Heidegger's handwritten manuscripts, I
feel like a manuscript enthusiast who cannot find either the words
or the closeness to deal with them, to really read, because Heidegger is standing there, thus paradoxically "standing in the way."
Heidegger leafs through them himself. He shows me. I cannot leaf
through them, could perhaps do so, but prefer to keep away be-

cause I cannot become engrossed in them and do not want to just nibble at them. I therefore ask him—because I am silent, Heidegger has already stowed away the manuscript and has stepped aside—whether he would sign his name in the copy of *Being and Time* that I worked through as a student. A bit too late, because Heidegger has already brought a publication, the printed transcript of a rèunion in France, *Thor Seminar—August 30—September 8 1968. Seminar taught by Professor Martin Heidegger on Hegel's Differenzschrift.* (Exemplaire 36). I recapitulate a bit of philosophical history, one of my own advanced seminars, "Fichte and Schelling as seen by Hegel and from Heidegger's perspective," and am very interested. "I would like to give you this work. It is not available in bookstores." It is the third of the visit. Heidegger prepares his fountain pen carefully, writes, and hands me the publication with its uncut pages. I spot a sentence in German at the end of the French text, "Only unfolded Being itself makes God-being possible," and read the dedication: "For Richard Wisser as a remembrance Martin Heidegger." Is he alluding to my last, crossed-out question? He keeps my copy of *Being and Time* lying in front of him.

We talk together, talk about my time as a prisoner of war, my extradition to the French, the difference between American and French prison camps. He tells me about his two sons, who—if I remember correctly—spent three and five years in Russian prison camps and still feel the effects of it today. Then he talks about the circle around Beaufret. He says it is a pleasure to be together and to speak with them. Twice he talks about Beaufret, that "intellectually awake human being," with warmth. Before he puts his slow handwriting in *Being and Time*, he looks over at me: "The first piece of yours I read was an article in the *Frankfurter Allgemeine Zeitung*. You wrote on the record Neske had persuaded me to make, 'The Principle of Identity,' the lecture for the five hundredth anniversary celebration of the University of Freiburg. Do you remember the title of your description?" Although I remember the event well, I do not have the exact title in mind and say: "The Thinking Voice and Its Thought." Heidegger: "Yes, that was on target ..." A longer pause for ruminating, for pondering, for remembering, for reflecting. I do not know all that is going on behind his forehead, but he has a friendly smile, kind, almost a little grateful.

At the time, I had hoped to make it clear that Heidegger's voice offered effective help in interpreting what had been thought, what had been said.[24] Does Heidegger remember what he wrote me then in his first letter? "My thanks for your essay 'The Thinking Voice and Its Thought' are already too late because your work is so excellent that I have never before had the chance to read anything like it. You have brought something to light that I had previously simply carried out without knowing it. But the knowledge of it that you have imparted to me and to the readers and listeners suits the matter so well that it cannot confuse or lead astray. You could fulfill a true wish of mine if you would let me know more about your work and about yourself. Such a free treatment of a subject as your essay manifests has become rare today . . ." (Freiburg, 27 May 1958).

More than eleven years have since passed. Heidegger looks *at* me for a long time, not merely *over* to where I sit again in the low armchair, and then he writes, sets down the fountain pen, and gives me my copy of *Being and Time*, his book: "For Richard Wisser as a remembrance of the television interview on 17 September 1969 Martin Heidegger." Many still think it a mystery that Heidegger granted me of all people the television interview that "others did not succeed in obtaining and that was thought to be impossible," as *Der Spiegel* had written, but that mystery should be solved now.

As I read, Heidegger hesitatingly reaches over to a small photograph standing next to others on the desk. Without sentimentality: "This is a lonely man, too." Silence. Then: "Rudolf Bultmann."[25] I react soberly, register, precisely because I sense the personal: "His birthday was recently, too." Heidegger, in what seems to me a completely unprompted comment: "Yes, the students. It's a difficult matter. They all want to 'overcome' Martin Heidegger. They think they owe it to themselves to 'overcome.'" I recall a sentence Heidegger once wrote me: "Students are a mysterious matter" (Messkirch, 28 May 1959). But how does he get from Bultmann to his own students? Suddenly, how dense I can be, it is clear to me that Heidegger is alluding to loneliness, to my last, crossed-out question. "What do you attribute that to?" "There are many reasons for it. I don't know. But some think they must do it. Swimming with the tide?" "Don't you think it could possibly be a sort of self-defense? They have all learned and received from you. They would be poor if they didn't act as if they also had something to offer. And haven't some of them offered something and don't some of them still have something to offer?" "But many of them just follow fashion and write what people want to hear . . . And many haven't understood a thing . . ."

From time to time, I have the impression that Heidegger has a lot of a prankster about him, not the shrewdness of a peasant. There is mistrust in him, the kind of mistrust that is a part of common sense and will not let anyone get the better of it. Perhaps that accounts for his suspicion of apples that do not fall far from the tree or of birds that leave the nest to fly in their own other, narrower circles. There are rejective traits in his character that cannot be overlooked either. Rejection that is not directed against objections and does not in the least fear them, no, rejection of what is for him philosophy in name only and not thinking "hard to the wind of the matter."[26]

I ask Heidegger about his own relationship to the university. "I have no connection to the university any more." Heidegger stops. Gives me the opportunity to gauge what it means to him. Again one of his pauses, spaces that allow what has been intimated to unfold. He leaves it to the other to react, to take a stand. I say: "Even if this seems to be the fate of the emeriti, it doesn't and probably shouldn't have to happen that way." "People haven't been very nice to me!" Heidegger hints at only some of what has happened. Why should he say more? He draws a line, not because he is done with it but because it hurts. [. . .]

We talk about Adorno. I report on experiences I have had when dealing with students of Adorno on the editorial staff of radio stations and newspapers, and on how it is not always easy these days to express certain thoughts that are not simply "reflections of a critical awareness" without being torn apart. Heidegger: "When Adorno came back to Germany, he said, I was told: 'In five years, I'll have cut Heidegger to size.' You see what kind of man he is." I: "A small statement but a great feeling of power. He was certainly mistaken in the matter, but there are many signs that the impact he has does not help to further the reception of your thinking." In order to check this actual or only rumored flexing of the muscles, I tell Heidegger about a meeting I had with the philosopher Julius Ebbinghaus from the University of Marburg, who, when Karl Jaspers was mentioned, cut me short: "With one tiny speck of logic I would explode Jaspers!" But Heidegger sticks with Adorno. He is evidently alluding to the answer he still owes me to another of my crossed-out questions: "I have never read anything of his. Hermann Mörchen[27] once tried to convince me to read Adorno. I didn't."

In the conversation I deliberately use the expression "negative dialectic" as a key phrase for Adorno's way of thinking. "What does he mean by that—really?" Heidegger mischievously stretches the controversial adverb. I suggest that he understands his dialectic, in contrast to the positive Hegelian dialectic, to be a "denunciation" and a critique of what is for the sake of that about it which it is not and which is not allowed to be *that* way. I speak at length, perhaps too long, because I have recently published a review of Adorno's *Negative Dialectic.*[28] "One reacts critically." Heidegger's commentary: "So he *is* a sociologist and not a philosopher." "But one who has more success with our 'revolutionary' students than almost everyone else today. He practically causes critical protest, opposition. By reading him, it is possible to gain a philosophically supported position that is essentially a position of negation and that allows one to stand out, be different, act in reaction, agitate. Philosophical questioning in your sense is lost." Heidegger's response irritates me: "With whom did Adorno study?" I cannot answer this question and point instead to his origin as I interpret it; that is, to his publications. Heidegger does not go into it or into my comments on Adorno's *Minima Moralia.* He listens and then returns to his question that had only been postponed, not answered, by my discussion: "No, has he really studied with someone?" "I don't know!"

Heidegger asks about Adorno's language and thus comes back to another one of the omitted questions. The expression "Adornoizing imitators" is used in the conversation, which causes me to mention "heideggerizing re-verers." "I find some of Adorno's publications literarily complex, others brilliant, associatively delicate, others I find to be manneristic gesticulations of thought. Therefore I find that they differ in (I am imitating Adorno's manner of speech) 'kuality.' " I do, however, also emphasize my approval of Adorno's works on aesthetics and of his love of music, which we both share. I remind him of Thomas Mann's *Dr. Faustus.* Musical listening can also be a means of access to many areas. I talk about the sharp, almost cutting tone in Jünger's statement, since Heidegger, although he listened attentively, seems to have had enough of my attacks for and against Adorno. He picks up the welcome cue "Jünger" and uses the opportunity to change the subject.

"When will the program be televised? I'd like to write it down. My brother Fritz has a television set and might like to watch it." "You won't watch it?" "No!" When Heidegger notices my amazement, he adds: "We don't have a television set." "Wouldn't you like to have one?" Heidegger's look at me is almost as crazy as my question evidently seems to him. Only his dismissive gestures answer, answer more than no. Still I wonder whether Professor Holzamer, the director of ZDF who is carefully following our project, should not give him the "pleasure" of a television set for his birthday. I recall what Ms. Szostak had told me: Ernst Jünger had only recently acquired one, and it had been purchased by his wife against his own bitter resistance. Now Jünger watches it quite often. But precisely this, it crosses my mind, would be a sin against Heidegger's remaining lifetime. "A pleasure?" Heidegger, the withdrawn thinker, in an armchair in front of the television? The entertainment he needs is of a different sort. The enjoyment one would offer him would be, if he were to allow himself to be persuaded at all, perhaps via his wife, perhaps for her, an outrageous seduction. On the other hand it would let him see a world, even if it is very different from the one thought by him and sighted by Husserl.

Unprompted, Heidegger talks about the filming ARD had done at his house and about the circumstances and his evaluation of it. Then spontaneously: "I liked your plan to get friends and former students to talk. It recalls so many things, what happened then and how things are today, what they say today, and what they consider something special." I am glad about Heidegger's approval and tell him in detail, since I now know that he will not see the program but will only read the statements, how it will all take place. First he, absent-present, will be made to "appear" and then he himself, speaking-thinking, will be seen. "Yes, that sounds reasonable."

We also talk about the situation of those who are at the beginning of their university careers. It surprises me that he practically interrogates me. His own judgment is sharp but not unkind, exposes weaknesses but does not open wounds. I notice that, although aware of the concerns of younger colleagues, he primarily interprets the conformity demanded by the Zeitgeist as a renunciation of the task of thinking. "Many want to become someone, and they do become someone by losing themselves in the process." Then, as if Heidegger were consistently moving backward through the questions he rejected: "The 'social.'—You asked me about that! Those people who tear everything to pieces should think about it. They always know everything better.—It's always possible to know everything better, and no one really discusses the matter at issue.—They coat everything, things and human beings, with their talk. They have narrow-minded answers at hand and forget so much about everything. . . . When will someone tell the sociologists what 'the social' is? Definitions aren't enough, and actions alone don't suffice. The social is an interpretation. That's what they should first figure out and comprehend. But they determine what the 'spirit' is. . . ."

We talk about professors and universities, reputations and appointments, his evaluations, and the like.

When Heidegger leans back in his desk chair once more, I take it as a sign that it is time to leave. He agrees, concerned that now I will get home in the dark. I ask to say goodbye to his wife, too. Heidegger gets her from the kitchen, and we say a warm and friendly goodbye. Heidegger accompanies me to the door. "I only hope that this visit was not the last." Encouragement from Heidegger. He accompanies me to the garden gate. There we see the waiting car, which I had completely forgotten. Heidegger: "You had to wait the whole time? We didn't want that to happen!" Another goodbye. He goes back into the house.

A solitary, old man but certain in his thinking and convinced of his task. "In thinking all things become solitary and slow."[29]

Immediately after broadcasting, it was suggested that the program be documented. Conversations with Dr. Meinolf Wewel from the publishing house Alber quickly lead to a small volume with the allusive title *Martin Heidegger in Conversation*, which was distributed before Christmas 1969 and soon thereafter appeared in Italian, Spanish, and Japanese editions, followed by English, Swedish, Portuguese, and French translations. Hans Kimmel, himself a cameraman, alludes to the dual meaning of the title when he writes in his review in *Hochland*:

> A television program that interested, as measurements showed, about 1 percent of the German viewers. . . .
>
> One percent of the households with televisions in the Federal Republic of Germany—that late in the evening, that is perhaps 250,000 people. In a single moment more people than the number of people who had the chance to actually see Heidegger speak during his entire lifetime. . . .[30]

Heidegger asked me for a list of the participants' addresses so that he could thank each one personally. In his thanks to me, he had added a correction ("Correction necessary") that speaks for itself. In my presentation I had said that Heidegger had "grown roots in his Alemannic home" and: "It has been tried, often with bad intentions, to push Heidegger into a corner because of this, as it is said, 'naïve rootedness,' which is confused with an anachronistic attachment to nature and description of landscapes. He draws strength for his work from this radicalism. It is his most personal."[31] In using the word *Alemannic* I had been taken in by a characterization that made me think of his critics' accusations and not of geography. Heidegger accurately called to my attention: "Messkirch belongs to Upper Swabia; the dialect is Swabian. All of my ancestors were born there. The 'Alemannic' comes from the cabin in Todtnauberg, where, since 1922 and even during our time in Marburg, we have spent all our weeks of vacation, including Christmas; we got the little tree ourselves from the frequently very snowy forest." To make the "geographic and demographical [*landsmannschaftliche*] orientation" easier for me, Heidegger enclosed a pamphlet that had been sent to him "recently by the mayor of Messkirch."

I leafed through the pamphlet. On the border of the picture of the Wildenstein castle is noted carefully and in red ink: "Below the castle is the ancestral home of the Heideggers. Grandfather Martin H. born there in 1801." On the map at the end of the pamphlet, the Heideggers' ancestral farm and the "mother's home" west of Krauchenwies are drawn in. Next to nearby Kreenheinstetten it is noted: "Birthplace of Abraham a.S. Clara." Heidegger dedicated one of his perhaps most beautiful, as it is one of the simplest, speeches to him (on the occasion of a school reunion in 1964). The Messkirch student to the Messkirch student, whose path is "a sign of the loyalty and rigidity with which Abraham a Santa Clara followed his destiny. If we pay heed to this, then we will not only have met a former student of a school in Messkirch here at our reunion but also a teacher for our lives and a master of language."[32]

As a sign of his thanks for the television work, Heidegger also encloses a handwritten page of a manuscript with a dedication in his letter. He notes on it: "Preparatory text for the interpretation of Hölderlin's poem 'Remembrance' for the commemorative publication in 1943." The page has been carefully chosen; I particularly respect this about Heidegger and have other documentation of such attentiveness on Heidegger's part. Its text is analogous to what I had developed and remembered in the program. On this page, Heidegger tries to protect Hölderlin against the misunderstanding that the poem "Remembrance" is concerned with a "feeling for nature" or a "personal condition." "The n.e. [north-east] wind is preferred to all the other winds . . . the 'dearest' because it turns the speaker in the direction of his innermost and only essence. . . . The poem says nothing of the 'personal experiences' of the 'human being' H."

Today I ask myself whether there is not a sign that transcends time in this and in Heidegger's acknowledgement ("Both your texts," Heidegger means the 'Introduction' and the statement 'On the Responsibility of Thinking' in *Martin Heidegger in Conversation*, "speak a restrained language that does indeed fit the condition of M.H.'s thinking ..." [Freiburg im Breisgau, 18 December 1969].). Could it not be a sign to leave it, in a certain sense and in view of the memoir the publisher Neske had asked me to write, as, in fact and literally, a "personal" and not-to-be-published memory? Had Heidegger not dedicated an essay in his *Comments on Hölderlin's Poetry* to the poem "Remembrance," in which he makes it clear how little unambiguous reports of what happened, memories of the poet's life, and personal experiences matter? Had he not shown that what matters is the poetry of the essence of "remembrance"? When we recall Hölderlin's distich "Know! Apollo has become the God of writers for newspapers, / And his Man is anyone who faithfully tells him the Fact" (III, 6), must we not either be silent or, if we could, write a poem, or realize that human beings can be brought together or pulled apart by the human and all-too-human, but that they can only be committed to thinking by way of what has been thought? Is the opening of chests and archives anything more than gossip? Diogenes Laertius' *Lives, Teachings and Sayings of Famous Philosophers*, or Xenophon's *Memorobilia*? What's the point? Anecdotes, common experiences, photographs, things understood, misunderstood, some things in focus, others out of focus, and always the embarrassing reference to one's own person, because one has crossed the path of and has met the person who alone matters.

And yet, there are experiences that make one more experienced. And perhaps it is the experience I had gained that caused the publisher Günther Neske, prompted by Heidegger's upcoming eighty-fifth birthday, to try to win me over to his plan not to lose the chance of making a film during Heidegger's lifetime with Heidegger himself at the center. My experience told me that there would be little hope of getting Heidegger in front of the camera again. There are many reasons why, against Neske's expectations, no new filming of Heidegger was done. Walter Rüdel (Neske-Film) and I were forced to come up with a new concept. All the available material was checked for its usefulness and its usability. Heidegger's path was to be rendered visible by means of photographs and private films and by shots of important settings and stations of his journey through life. "Only image formed keeps the vision. / Yet image formed rests in the poem."[33] An appropriate text could make what can be seen, or, as Heidegger once called it, "seeing in thinking," transparent in what has been shown.

Günther Neske supported me in this and in my intention to not only combine information and citation in the text, but also to take criticism into account, to collect polemical statements, to awaken understanding, to expose misinterpretation. "Heidegger has been mocked as a 'sergeant of thinking' [*Denkwebel*], as an 'Alemannic stocking cap' [*alemannische Zipfelmütze*]. Critics who must be taken seriously accuse him of the uselessness of his thought with view to society, to 'open' and uniform society. Where usability and serving a purpose set the criteria, where reason only calculates, thinking withers. Heidegger is measured with measures one has set up oneself.—Heidegger does not challenge anyone's business, and his own vocation should not be underestimated. Although he may shortchange understanding, he lets reason come into its own.— Heidegger in Greece, at the Acropolis, on Cape Sounion, in the amphitheater at Delphi. Experienced in Greek possibilities by reading Hölderlin and Nietzsche, he is stubbornly trying, for the sake of the future, to take a 'step back'[34] in order to bring 'the earliness of what has been thought in the proximity of what needs to be thought.' Heidegger, a thinking human being, sees that, despite the gigantic amount of acumen spent on scientific theory and ideological critique, we are in danger of losing our senses and that thoughtlessness is 'an uncanny guest, who goes in and out all over today's world.' Heidegger teaches human beings, who are about to pounce on the whole of the earth and to subjugate humanity to their dictates, to recognize, despite all their power and will to dominate, what it means to be unable to simply say what is.—Heidegger's style of language has been said to be incapable of conveying information that enriches knowledge. He has been accused of hiding the triviality of his thinking with seemingly meaningful empty phrases and of trying to impress his readers by using vague-atmospheric-cosmic undertones. Heidegger's language does not establish meaning like the language of the poet. It wants to open up the relationship of human beings to Being and to awaken listening to the unheard-of in linguistic expression. For some, Heidegger is a tryst with questions, for others, with question marks."

Günther Neske and Dr. Paul Schlecht of Südwestfunk Baden-Baden stood by me, knowing that the response would be very divided. Some saw it as "hard to digest" (*Frankfurter Rundschau*, 25

September 1975), as "tough stuff" (*Evangelische Pressedienst, Kirche und Fernsehen*, 2 October 1975), as a film that "merely showed how dark what is only suspected remains" (*Frankfurter Allgemeine Zeitung*, 25 September 1975). Others thought it was the "first comprehensive film documentation to make it possible for a larger audience to once again establish a dialogue with the philosopher" (*Hannoversche Allgemeine Zeitung*, 25 September 1975), and that it was "unforgettable" in some passages and "exemplary" because the Neske film "had placed a thinking, which Heidegger himself understands to be an exercise in seeing, at the center" (*tv*, 4 October 1975). "Not a 'wrong path' [*Holzweg*]," said the *Funk-Korrespondenz* (2 October 1975), but it thought "the time has come to demand even more of Heidegger in a carefully prepared television series."

Heidegger himself wrote to me three days before broadcasting that it gave him "no pleasure" to know that a program was being put together. "Because, happily, we have no television, I can save myself from the annoyance of watching this program . . . I thank you, however, for making the best of the matter" (Freiburg im Breisgau/Zähringen, 20 September 1975). Heidegger thanked me two days after the program, however, after friends had reported "good things about the program," and as, "in many letters that reached me," he had been assured that "the 'best' was made of the matter." "Unfortunately other things—as usual—are brought up in public statements. I would have gladly avoided 'stepping into the limelight' once again . . ." (Freiburg im Breisgau/Zähringen, 25 September 1975).

One day after Heidegger's death, ARD turned to the Neske film "Martin Heidegger, On the Way in Thinking . . ." for a commemorative program. ". . . What Heidegger calls the 'turn' [*Kehre*] in thinking is neither Heidegger's turning back [*Umkehr*] nor his conversion [*Bekehrung*], but rather expresses that the path toward Being is always already a path issuing from Being." And Heidegger himself says: "No one knows what the fate of thinking will look like. . . . A coming thinker, who perhaps will be faced with the task of really taking over this thinking that I am attempting to *prepare*, will have to obey a sentence Heinrich von Kleist once wrote, and that reads: 'I step back before one who is not yet here, and bow, a millennium before him, to his spirit.' " The "end of philosophy" is reached when it is absorbed by science. Thinking continues. . . . Happy are the few who meet the precursor, who leads the way without the majority even noticing.

POSITIONS

Heidegger and Politics: Stages of a Discussion

EMIL KETTERING

SELDOM HAS A BOOK on a philosopher created such a stir in such a short time as the book *Heidegger and Nazism* by the Chilean Victor Farías. It was published in the fall of 1987 in France, where it started a sort of landslide among readers of Heidegger. It caused the French press to use headlines like "The book is a bomb" (*Le Monde*) or even "Heil Hitler!" (*Liberation*). It not only caused the sky of the philosophers to fall—as Hugo Ott said in his article in the *Neue Zürcher Zeitung*, reprinted in this volume—but went beyond that to kindle a wildfire that spread very quickly from France to Germany and was hotly discussed by the general public as well as in philosophical circles. For months, not a week went by without not only the important national but also local newspapers dealing with the topic "Heidegger and National Socialism." Even radio and television networks did not want to be left out. The extraordinary interest shown in Farías's book, which is still inflaming passions, is surprising to authorities on Heidegger for two reasons: on the one hand because Farías presents information that has long been known as if it were a novelty and on the other because his research and particularly his interpretation on the whole (as has meanwhile been demonstrated by various people) leave much to be desired and do not in the least satisfy the criteria of historical or hermeneutic scholarship.

For our purposes here I will neither be able to present the short-comings of Farías' book in detail nor investigate the question why such an unserious book could have such a great effect. Rather I will have to limit myself to giving a broad outline of the most important stages of the discussion of Heidegger and politics.

The attentive observer, when following the history of the discussion of Heidegger's relationship to National Socialism, will notice that it took place in several big clusters or waves. The triggering factor was usually a new revelation of facts or a claim of supposed facts of Heidegger's political engagement during the years 1933–1945, which would then ignite a controversial discussion of their plausibility. At least seven stages or phases may be discerned up to the present.

1. A first wave of discussion of the connection between politics and thinking in Heidegger was set off by an article by Karl Löwith, written in Japanese exile in 1939 and printed directly after the Second World War, in 1946, in the periodical *Les Temps Modernes*, edited by Jean-Paul Sartre. In it, Heidegger's former student emphasizes the "political implications of the existentialism" of his teacher. Löwith's accusatory revelations provoked a dispute with Alfonse de Waelhens and Eric Weil in the following issues of *Les Temps Modernes*.

2. A review in the *Frankfurter Allgemeine Zeitung* written by Jürgen Habermas, then a twenty-four-year-old philosophy student, on Heidegger's recently published lecture "Introduction to Metaphysics," given in the summer semester of 1935, initiated the first major discussion in Germany in 1953. The focus of Habermas's attacks, and the ensuing debate with Christian Lewalter, Karl Korn, and Egon Vietta, was Heidegger's easily misunderstood sentence in which he speaks of the "inner truth and greatness" of the National Socialist movement as an expression of the "encounter between planetarily determined technology and modern human beings," which has "nothing at all" to do with what is "offered around" today (that is, 1935) as "the philosophy of National Socialism."[1] The bitter argument about the sentence's correct interpretation finally caused Heidegger to send a letter to *Die Zeit* in which he calls Lewalter's interpretation "accurate in every respect."

3. The publication of Paul Hühnerfeld's polemic *On the Matter of Heidegger. An Attempt to Understand a German Genius* [*In Sachen Heidegger. Versuch über ein deutsches Genie*] (1959), Guido Schneeberger's *Texts on Martin Heidegger* [*Nachlese zu Martin Heidegger*] (1962), which collects shorter texts from

the National Socialist era, and Theodor W. Adorno's linguistically and ideologically critical study on *Jargon of Authenticity* (1964) evoked (again first in France) an extensive countercriticism by François Fédier, a student of Beaufret, in the periodical *Critique* in the mid sixties. Fédier's exposure, as detailed as it is savage, of the shortcomings of Hühnerfeld's, Schneeberger's, and Adorno's argumentation caused Robert Minder, Jean-Pierre Faye, and Aimi Patri, whom Fédier had also criticized in passing, to reply. Fédier, in turn, responded twice. The course and essential arguments of this discussion, concisely summarized, can be followed in Beda Allemann's essay "Martin Heidegger und die Politik."

4. In 1965 Alexander Schwan made a first attempt to determine a "political philosophy in Martin Heidegger's thinking." Schwan's study is already pleasantly different from the previous pieces, often merely polemical, in that it does not use Heidegger's activities as rector of the University of Freiburg in the years 1933/1934 but Heidegger's thinking itself as its point of departure. Starting from Heidegger's analysis of works in "The Origin of the Work of Art" (1935), Schwan attempts to determine the place of the political in Heidegger's thinking. Jean-Michel Palmier's book *Heidegger's Political Writings* [*Les ecrits politques de Heidegger*] was published in 1968 in France but had no noteworthy effect in Germany. Karl August Moehling's dissertation *Martin Heidegger and the Nazi Party* (1972) is even less well known, particularly as it is only available on microfiche. More interest was shown in Otto Pöggeler's investigation of the relationship between *Philosophy and Politics in Heidegger* [*Philosophie und Politik bei Heidegger*] (1972), which uses Heidegger's question on modern technology as its point of departure. The French sociologist Pierre Bourdieu's publication with the title *Martin Heidegger's Political Ontology* (1975), which focuses on linguistic criticism, seems to me a relapse of the uncritical polemics at the beginning of the sixites à la Adorno and Minder.

5. The publication of the *Spiegel* interview after Heidegger's death in 1976, the new edition of Karl Jaspers' *Philosophical Autobiography* [*Philosophische Autobiographie*] in 1977, supplemented by the chapter on Heidegger, and his posthumously published *Notes on Martin Heidegger* [*Notizen zu Martin Heidegger*] (1978) provided new topics for the discus-

sion of Heidegger's political error during the National Socialist era and of a possible causal connection between his thinking and political activities. In the discussion on the topic "Heidegger and Politics," the informative study by Heidegger's student Hermann Mörchen on *Power and Rule in the Thinking of Heidegger and Adorno [Macht und Herrschaft im Denken von Heidegger und Adorno]* (1980) has unfortunately been paid too little attention so far.

6. Heidegger's rectorial address "The Self-Assertion of the German University," long out of print and now supplemented by the notes on "The Rectorate 1933/34: Facts and Thoughts," recorded in 1945, was republished in 1983 by Hermann Heidegger, his son and executor. This and research by the Freiburg historian Hugo Ott on Heidegger's term as rector, published in numerous essays after 1983 and containing new source material, stimulated renewed interest. Ott's revelations prompted the publication of a collection of essays by the *Freiburger Universitätsblätter* called *Martin Heidegger: A Philosopher and Politics [Martin Heidegger. Ein Philosoph und die Politik]* (1986), in which Heidegger's contemporaries were given a chance to speak as witnesses and critics. In the fall of 1987, another collection on *Heidegger and Practical Philosophy [Heidegger und die praktische Philosophie]* (1986) followed; the title, according to the editors Annemarie Gethmann-Siefert and Otto Pöggeler, stands "for a knot of thoughts, actions, and events in the philosophical area that is difficult to untangle."[2]

7. The last phase so far was introduced by Farías' book, with which the fever of coming to terms with the past reached its peak and which provoked a number of subsequent publications in France and Germany. The studies by Philippe Lacoue-Labarthe and Jacques Derrida and François Fédier's book are, it seems to me, the most noteworthy. The German edition of Farías' book will soon be published by Fischer in Frankfurt. However, considerable changes are to be expected. Hugo Ott has also announced a compilation of his close studies of the sources in a book to appear at the end of this year.[3]

An interpretation of Heidegger's political views before, during, and after his 1933/1934 rectorate that is convincing and supported by facts seems to me impossible at present because of the very small amount of available texts. The nature of the consulted sources—diaries, letters from third persons who were not even in Freiburg at the time, reports written for specific purposes, and fragments of recollections written at a much later time—makes an accurate scholarly interpretation difficult. It is to be hoped that the publication of further original Heideggarian documents from this time, particularly his correspondence, will provide new information. It seems to me that more of a sense for history is desirable. This is missing in most of the publications on the "Heidegger case." It is unacceptable, for instance, that Heidegger's conduct in 1933/1934 be judged from the standpoint of our detailed knowledge today of the ideology and the atrocities of National Socialism. Rather we must attempt to assess Heidegger's actions from the situation at the time. Little consideration has been given so far (presumably because of a lack of knowledge of Heidegger's works) to Heidegger's partly open, partly concealed barbs at National Socialism in his lecture courses in Freiburg from 1933 to 1945, of which so far fourteen (of twenty) are available in the complete edition.[4]

Although I cannot give my own tentative statement on this subject here, I would still like to mention in conclusion one point that has almost always had a central position in discussions on Heidegger and politics and has led and still continually leads to fierce controversies: the interpretation of Heidegger's persistent silence on the topic "National Socialism" after 1945, despite numerous demands for a statement. Whereas some see this as an inexcusable mistake and unwillingness to admit his guilt, which would throw an expositive light on Heidegger's understanding of responsibility, others consider it an expression of his deep shock, which has, in a way, left him speechless, or they think of it (as Derrida does in his contribution to this volume) as a conscious refusal to speak in order not to settle the problems that are connected to the phenomenon "National Socialism" in one statement and then consider the case closed. Although such speculation may seem legitimate for heuristic reasons, they cannot satisfy the demands of careful hermeneutic interpretation. Bearing in mind that Heidegger himself interpreted silence to be a form of speaking, it seems to me that in this case neither his moral condemnation nor his vindication can be conclusively deduced from his silence. The commitment to one direction of interpretation, at any rate, robs the silence of its perhaps consciously intended provocative character. However, I am convinced, along with Derrida, Gadamer, and many others, that no matter how Heidegger's political conduct during the National Socialist era and a possible causal connection to his thinking are judged, we are not released from the task of carefully studying Heidegger's writings, from reflecting on the questions in which they intend to train us as well as from searching for an answer to the questions which they leave open, and from taking a critical position.

ment with the Third Reich (from the point of view of the French military government, this dismissal was final and without the possibility of appeal) yet, at the same time (after the fall of 1945), he was visited by French cultural officials and various envoys from French publishers and philosophical schools and was practically transferred to France with his thinking. He rose out of the ashes like a phoenix, transformed into the main authority for Jean-Paul Sartre's existentialism and the masters of postmodern thinking.

Heidegger's political past was disguised, minimized until it appeared insignificant, even glossed over with decorative epithets describing Heidegger's supposed attitude of resistance after the short episode of his rectorate 1933/1934. Had not Jean Beaufret, a member of the Resistance, been able to comprehend Heidegger? The "Letter on Humanism" written for Beaufret at the end of 1946 was more than Heidegger's thanks that Beaufret had quasi-included him in the "intellectual" Resistance—an action that was sanctioned by his friend, the poet René Char (Captain Alexandre in the Resistance). Whoever opposed Heidegger was branded mediocre by these Frenchmen and was seen to be operating as an agent of the conspiracy of mediocrity.

Much could be said about the method of apologia for Heidegger. It is masterful and has strategic features. It begins with Alfred (Frédéric) de Towarnicki's "Visite à Martin Heidegger," published in 1945 in the first volume of Sartre's *Les Temps Modernes* (opposing pictures, for instance by Karl Löwith, printed in the same periodical were virtually ignored) and leads, after a few stops in between, to the speedily arranged translation of the Freiburg philosopher's own account of his actions.[1] They were first published for the fiftieth anniversary of Hitler's seizure of power—posthumously, like the famous *Spiegel* interview (which had been predetermined down to its finest ramifications) he gave in 1966 and that was published the week after Heidegger's death (1976).[2]

Arguments raised against this touched-up, even false, picture fell into a void. Even serious studies were quickly relegated to the "enemy" or "hostile" camp, classed with the genre of anti-Heidegger books à la Hühnerfeld.[3] Jean Beaufret's line, continued by the loyal François Fédier, kept the upper hand in France. New insights that were, no doubt, reached objectively and showed the absurdity of Heidegger's account published in 1983, were simply ignored. They were irrelevant. Beaufret had determined in an interview "It is charitable not to deal with the matter any further," and this is the attitude that was in force. How else could it be explained that it was still possible to give a last, admittedly thin, rehash of all the Heidegger apologia that was strewn throughout the decades in the November 1986 issue of *magazine littéraire?*

A Heidegger "Pupil"

And this solid and stable house, in which the French intellect had comfortably settled itself, appears to have now become uninhabitable. The man who has ravaged it has even come dressed in the robe of a pupil of Heidegger; he was once a participant in the Heraclites seminar that Eugen Fink gave with Martin Heidegger in the winter semester 1966/1967 at the University of Freiburg. That is probably the only element of his "pupilage," since Farías received his doctorate in 1967, with Gerhart Schmidt (from the school of Eugen Fink) as his advisor, with a dissertation on Franz Brentano; there is little in the oeuvre that evokes Heidegger. That is, unless a statement Farías has now made numerous times in various media can be taken seriously: that Heidegger had once cured him of the idea of translating *Being and Time* into Spanish because he thought the Romance languages were inferior for his thinking. Did the philosophical disciple Farías suffer a trauma that might explain some of the approaches in his book on Heidegger? In any case, he soon took up Heidegger's trail, following in Guido Schneeberger's footsteps,[4] and hunted after him in a strictly inquisitorial fashion.

The manuscript was probably completed in 1985, since Farías did not use more recent literature and there have been quite a few new publications in the field. Many titles he did not take into account should be named, for instance Karl Löwith's *My Life in Germany* [*Mein Leben in Deutschland*] (1986). Farías' book is not up-to-date, although admittedly up-to-date enough for France. Some of the blunders could have been avoided. For example, Farías knows nothing about the background, the process, and the weight of the *Spiegel* interview, something about which we have been minutely informed since the correspondance between Martin Heidegger and Erhart Kästner was published in 1986.[5] Rather, he merely derides the fact that he was not allowed to compare the rough draft (in his opinion the more interesting and actually authentic version) to the published version.

Let us first establish what previously unused sources for the question "Heidegger and National Socialism" Farías was able to evaluate: the archival material in the state archives of the German Democratic Republic (inaccessible to citizens of the Federal Republic of Germany; not, it seems, to foreigners), for example the records of the Prussian Ministry of Culture and the Reich Ministry of Science, Art, and Education (in Merseburg and Potsdam respectively). Now we are able to determine what the exact nature of Heidegger's "political mission," connected to his second summons to Berlin in the fall of 1933, was. Namely, there was a plan to create a Reich academy with Heidegger as its president. Previously we only knew that he was to have headed a "Prussian academy for university teachers." We also knew that Heidegger's adversaries within the National Socialist Party, Jaensch (Heidegger's philosophical colleague of many years at the University of Marburg) and Krieck, vehemently opposed this plan and called in Rosenberg's office to intervene.[6] However, these are already questions of detail.

It captured our attention that Farías was said to have discovered the center of Heidegger's path of thinking and found the great circle: the beginning and the end. The spirit of Abraham a Santa Clara, the man Johann Ulrich Megerle from Kreenheinstetten (very close to Messkirch), barefoot Augustinian monk, powerful preacher in Vienna at the time of the war with the Turks, floats over it all. Abraham a Santa Clara was, according to Farías, an especially committed antisemite and xenophobe (against the Turks), evident in his spoken and written words. Martin Heidegger had, Farías goes on, identified with his famous fellow countryman early on, as is shown in the theology student Heidegger's piece (his first work) on the dedication of the monument to Abraham a Santa Clara in Kreenheinstetten in 1910, published in Armin Kausen's (and not Armin Krausen; Farías treats names with nonchalance in his book) *Allgemeiner Rundschau* in Munich. This weekly periodical for a sophisticated Catholic public was politically situated to the right of the Catholic Center Party and, therefore, was the appropriate organ for the twenty-one-year-old Messkircher! And Farías makes as many associations as he possibly can (incidentally, a peculiarity of method that runs throughout the entire book). Thus Adolf Hitler also already appears on the scene in 1910, because Martin Heidegger mentions the Viennese mayor Karl Lueger in the article, a man young Adolf Hitler had also admired.

One wonders why Martin Luther, former Augustinian monk, whom Heidegger had subsequently carefully studied, was not also called in as a main witness to attest to Heidegger's early antisemitism. Consider Luther's pieces against the Jews from the year 1543 or his pieces against the Turks. This list of witnesses could be continued.

The "Basis"

Farías considers the man from Kreenheinstetten to be the basis per se for comprehending the authentic Heidegger: determined in early youth by the factors antisemitism, national [*völkisch*] community thinking, antidemocracy, antiliberalism, xenophobia. It is possible that literary critics (Farías belongs to at least some extent to this guild) adhere to such a method; for a historian it is, at any rate, unacceptable. A detail, which seems very important to me, may show how work is done associatively here. For his description of Heidegger's time in high school and at the seminary in Constance (1903–1906), Farías uses a passage from the memoirs of Günther Dehn (formerly a professor of practical theology in the school of Protestant theology in Bonn).

Dehn had graduated from high school in 1900 in Constance and came from an educated, middle-class family—his father was a high imperial post office official and had been transferred from Köslin (Pomerania) to Constance in 1895. Dehn very subjectively characterizes the alumni of the seminary in Constance, mostly children of ordinary people destined for the profession of Catholic priest, and deals with the expression capons [*Kapauner*], as the seminarians were popularly called. He could not make heads or tails of it (although the matter is clear: capon, a castrated rooster): "I thought it must be in some way connected to Capuchins [*Kapuziner*]." Farías manipulates the text, suppresses "capon" and "capons" and translates it: "Without knowing where this expression came from, we called them 'les capucins.'" Why? Because a few lines later he presents Abraham a Santa Clara, this time in the version of the Capuchin preacher in Schiller's *Wallenstein*, and thus fully identifies the pupil Heidegger (Capuchin) with the (Capuchin) Abraham.

As soon as Farías starts to interpret, his work becomes problematic. His attempt (to come to a later level of interpretation) to connect Martin Heidegger to the head of the Storm Troopers, Ernst Röhm, whose political convictions Heidegger had, according to Farías, completely adopted, is downright fantastical. His proof of this is Heidegger's intimacy with a Dr. Stäbel, who was both the leader of the German students and the Reich leader of the NSDStB [National Socialist German Student Association] after the fall of 1934. Dr. Stäbel had been appointed Reich leader by Ernst Röhm, says Farías. It is admittedly somewhat difficult to understand the complicated organizational structure of the German student body at the beginning of the Third Reich. However, if a far-reaching conclusion is to be drawn, then the premises must be correct. The supreme SA leader Röhm had nothing to do with the appointment of the (double) student leader Stäbel. This was done on the one hand by the Reich Minister of the Interior and on the other by Hitler's representative, Rudolf Hess. The head of the Reich SA Office of Higher Education, appointed by Röhm, was a Dr. Bennecke. From my research I know that the rector Heidegger was more likely arguing with SA students toward the end of his rectorate. It is thus pure construct when Farías depicts 30 June 1934 (Röhm putsch)[7] as Heidegger's great political turning; Heidegger's revolutionary thinking, he writes, ran out along with the crushing of the SA.

Limits

Farías' contribution lies in his collection of new sources and their positivistic treatment. Many facts. However, he quickly reaches the limits of his abilities when he begins to interpret and especially in places where the connection between political practice and Heidegger's thinking should have been clarified. But that is precisely what one should be able to expect of a philosopher. He made an attempt in several approaches. However, these approaches are not convincing, for example the endeavor to correlate the Schlageter speech held in May 1933[8] with *Being and Time*.

The book is, for the most part, structured chronologically and is probably supposed to offer the reader a biographical framework. But the development of the early Heidegger, the stops he made in Freiburg, Marburg, and Freiburg again, are not well-founded enough. Too much is still missing, for example the relationship between Edmund Husserl and Martin Heidegger. Farías' fixation on the "ideologue" Abraham a Santa Clara is thus all the more serious. In his conclusion Farías even makes a trilogy of the Viennese baroque preacher and the concentration camps Sachsenhausen and Auschwitz. He extracted it from an incorrectly understood proverbial expression Heidegger drew from the sayings of the Kreenheinstettener at a talk given in Messkirch in 1964: War and peace are not further apart than Frankfurt and Sachsenhausen; that is, they can quickly change from one to the other. For Farías this town Sachsenhausen that lies directly across the Main River from the old free city of Frankfurt is, of course, the infamous concentration camp. And already Abraham and Heidegger are caught and interwoven with Hitler's genocidal guilt. But the concentration camp Sachsenhausen was in the district of Potsdam, county of Oranienburg, not far from where Victor Farías now works in Berlin.

Superficiality and Ignorance: On Victor Farías' Publication

HANS-GEORG GADAMER

THE SENSATION THAT Victor Farías' book on Heidegger and the Nazis caused in France is astonishing. So that's how little is known about the Third Reich there, even though the great thinker is read often and respectfully. Heidegger's admirers may have had a hand in this lack of knowledge by playing down the affair in defending Heidegger with the argument that he had "broken" with National Socialism after only a year of disappointing experiences as the Nazi rector of the University of Freiburg. How did they picture that break—a public statement, protest, leaving the Party, or however it would happen in a constitutional state?

Most of what Farías presents has long been known in German-speaking countries. His zealous work in archives has revealed more about bureaucratic procedures during the years after Hitler seized power than presented new points of view. No one in Germany should feign surprise that Heidegger did not "leave" the Party (since Farías' book was published, some people now talk about this fact as if it were new information).

Source: *A shortened French text appeared in* Nouvel Observateur *in December 1988. The German text was kindly supplied by Prof. Gadamer. First publication in German. The title was provided by the editors.*

The young generation in Germany also has difficulty imagining the way things happened here at that time, the wave of conformity, the pressure, the ideological indoctrination, unpredictable sanctions, etc. One is sometimes asked today: Why didn't you all cry out? The general human inclination toward conformity, which always finds new ways and means of self-deception, is especially underestimated. The most important means of self-deception was the question "Does the Führer know about this?" That is how we tried to play down things for ourselves in order not to stand completely on the outside. In the spring of 1934, the general opinion in academic circles, also among my Jewish friends, was that, for example, antisemitism had been a nasty campaign tactic that the "drummer" (as Hitler was called at the time) had used crudely enough. Papen's speech, written by Jung and given in Marburg in May 1934, was thought to be a hopeful sign that the revolution would end and there would be a return to the constitutional state.

Sometimes, in admiration for the great thinker, Heidegger's defenders declared that his political error had nothing to do with his philosophy. That they could pacify themselves with such an argument! They did not notice how insulting such a defense of such an important thinker was. And how did they hope to unite that with the fact that this same man had seen and said things in the fifties about the industrial revolution and about technology whose foresight truly amazes us today?

For the past fifty years, some of us have thought about what alarmed us at that time and what separated us from Heidegger for years. Thus it can hardly be expected that we will be surprised when we hear that he "believed" in Hitler in 1933—and many years before and how many years afterward? He was no mere opportunist. It would be better to call his political engagement not a political point of view but a political illusion that had less and less to do with political reality. Later, when he continued to dream his dream of a "national religion" despite all realities, he was naturally very disappointed in the course of events. But he still guarded his dream and was silent about it. In 1933 and 1934, he believed that he could follow his dream and fulfill his most authentic philosophical mission in revolutionizing the university from the bottom up. In order to attain this, he did things that horrified us at the time. He wanted to break the political influence of the church and the inertia of the academic bigwigs. He also placed Ernst Jünger's vision of *The Worker* next to his own ideas of overcoming the tradition of metaphysics from the standpoint of Being. He later outdid himself in the radical lecture he gave on the end of philosophy.[1] That was his revolution.

Because he expected nothing of the Weimar Republic, which was not held together by any fundamental attitude toward the state, and because he only experienced disappointments during his own political engagement, he later kept himself from in any way identifying with political events. Even after the end of the Thousand Year Reich, he saw his vision of the forgetfulness of Being [*Seinsvergessenheit*] in the age of technology confirmed. What did he have to retract? And did he recognize anything at all in the German university with its thirty thousand students?

We could pose the question: Did he not feel in any way responsible for the horrible consequences of Hitler's seizure of power, the new barbarity, the Nürnberg Laws, the terror, the sacrifice of humanity's blood in two world wars—and finally for the indelible ignominy of the extermination camps? The answer is clearly no. That was the corrupted revolution, not the great renewal from the spiritual and moral strength of the people that he dreamed of and that he longed for as the preparation for a new religion of humankind.

And now I am asked whether today, after Farías' revelations (which were not revelations for us at all), we can "still" concern ourselves with the philosophy of this man as we had previously done. "Still today?" Anyone who asks such a question has a lot of work to do. Heidegger's lifelong confrontation with the Greeks, with Hegel, and finally with Nietzsche was seen as a great intellectual renewal in Germany and in France and throughout the entire world. Is that all of a sudden wrong? Or have we long finished with that? Or do we perhaps believe that we no longer need to think at all, that we should follow an established ideological-political recipe or apply a collection of rules that have been worked out by the social sciences? The sad story of the failure of Heidegger's revolution of the university and of his entanglement in the cultural politics of the Third Reich, which we watched from the distance with trepidation, probably reminded some people of what happened to Plato in Syracuse. After Heidegger resigned from the rectorate, one of his Freiburg friends met him in the trolley and greeted him with "Back from Syracuse?"

It is regrettable that Farías' book, despite the trouble he took in studying the sources, completely lacks depth and is long outdated. Where he touches on philosophical topics, he is full of grotesque superficiality and ignorance.

It is not that easy to get around thinking. Those of us who kept our distance from Heidegger for years, troubled by Heidegger's political adventure, and who lived through the steadily darkening future of our own country until the end, would still not think of denying the philosophical inspiration we received from Heidegger early on and then again and again. The following that gathered around Heidegger in the twenties was not blind; and later developments caused us to search for our own paths of thinking all the more. Some things we did may have met with Heidegger's approval, like my own hermeneutic philosophy or my small book on Paul Celan entitled *Who am I and Who are You.* [*Wer bin ich und wer bist Du?*], which will soon be published in France. But certainly Heidegger remained true to himself to the extent that he was disappointed that we did not really continue on the paths of thinking that he had pointed out. It is possible that he thought those in France understood his thinking better. And yet Heidegger had experienced the fascination he inspired in the form of mere imitation long enough in Germany to not accept us.

Anyone who believes that we no longer need to concern ourselves with Heidegger has not at all realized how hard it was and will always be to concern oneself with him and not make a fool of oneself as soon as one acts superciliously.

Heidegger's Silence*

Excerpts from a talk given on 5 February 1988

JACQUES DERRIDA

IT IS OFTEN THOUGHT in Germany and sometimes also in France that Beaufret and his friends are the sole heirs to Heidegger's legacy. This is not the case. To use myself as an example, I studied after the war, from 1948 to 1952, wanted nothing to do with Beaufret, and was only interested in Heidegger from Sartre's and Merleau-Ponty's point of view. Then I started to read Heidegger himself and began to emancipate myself, still without Beaufret's help, from Sartre's and Mearleau-Ponty's understanding of Heidegger and Husserl.

Yet I also do not want it to be ignored that Beaufret (and I feel all the more free to say this as I myself was very critical of Beaufret's interpretation of Heidegger) at least studied Heidegger's work

---

* Editor's note. The original text of this piece, as published in the volume *Antwort: Martin Heidegger in Gesprach*, was not seen by Professor Derrida prior to publication in Germany. In this English-language version Professor Derrida has made slight alterations for points of clarification. It differs in no way essentially, however, from the German.

Source: *Excerpts from Derrida's spoken contributions to the colloquium "Heidegger—Portée philosophique et politique de sa pensée" held with Hans-Georg Gadamer and Philippe Lacoue-Labarthe in Heidelberg on 5 February 1988. Discussion leader, Reiner Wiehl. Translated into German by Philip Rinke. Excerpts were broadcast on the second station of Hesse radio in March 1988. The title was provided by the editors.*

word for word and was not interested in absorbing it quickly, in the style of Sartre or Merleau-Ponty; he worked at it with an attentiveness that cannot simply be called negative.

Then, in the past twenty-five years, methods of reading Heidegger were developed by Philippe Lacoue-Labarthe, by Jean-Luc Nancy, and also by myself that were not influenced by either Merleau-Ponty or Sartre or Beaufret. For those who understand how to read, there can be no doubt that these readings, in different ways, also express an interest in the political dimension of the text; they attest to an early concern without limiting themselves to non-philosophical documents, which we had, of course, already had at our disposal since 1960–1962. We were attempting to understand the way in which Heidegger's difficult work could fit together with what we knew of his political engagement. This is, indeed, no light matter. I believe we have made some steps in the right direction, but an enormous amount of work remains to be done.

But when I see that so many people in France are suddenly interested in Heidegger's National Socialism, that there is a public outcry, that they are accusing the philosophers of not telling them anything, passing sentence not only on Heidegger, who is dead, but also on living philosophers in France, then I am often tempted to ask them a very simple question: Have you read *Being and Time*? For anyone (like some of us) who has begun to read *Being and Time*, anyone who has examined it in a questioning and critical, not an orthodox, manner, knows very well that this book (like many others) is still waiting to be really read. There are still enormous reserves in Heidegger's text left for further interpretations. It is therefore justified to demand of those who want to draw hasty conclusions from Heidegger's political conduct about his philosophical work that they should at least begin to read.

Ever since the first week after the publication of Victor Farías' book in France, some have been very quick to say: "Heidegger is over with. It's not necessary to read him any more." They almost said: "Let's burn him." I believe that these people have not only supplied evidence of their political irresponsibility, which is, of course, combined with their good, antifascistic conscience, but also evidence of their sociological inexperience. For it is obvious that there is growing interest in Heidegger. And it is up to us to ensure that this interest does not do any damage. It is up to us to take care that in reading Heidegger's entire work, his rectorial address, the political texts, as well as all the other texts, as carefully and as responsibly as possible, we do not relinquish our own political responsibility. We must keep it and should attempt to define it in such a way that the questions Heidegger posed are taken into consideration.

I think everyone agrees (at least many of us do) that even if Heidegger's political engagement in 1933 and many of its consequences, which dragged on in the years that followed in a complicated and ambiguous way, could be understood, explained, and excused, what would still remain inexcusable, as Philippe Lacoue-Labarthe has put it, what would remain a wounding of thinking, in the words of Blanchot, is Heidegger's silence after the war with regard to Auschwitz and many other topics.

I, too, sense this wounding, and it is possible for me to think about it as Philippe Lacoue-Labarthe, Blanchot, and a few others have done, but I ask myself: What would have happened if Heidegger had said something, and what could he have said? What I express here is very hazardous, yet I do so as a hypothesis, and ask you to accompany me while I walk this hazardous path.

Let us assume that Heidegger had not only said about 1933 "I have made a very stupid mistake" but also "Auschwitz is the absolute horror; it is what I fundamentally condemn." Such a statement is familiar to all of us. What would have happened then? He would probably have immediately received an absolution. The files on Heidegger, on the connection between his thought and the events of so-called National Socialism, would have been closed. And with one statement, which would have been aiming for an unproblematic consensus, Heidegger would have finished the affair; it would not be necessary for us to ask today what affinities, synchronisms of thinking, and common roots Heidegger's thinking could have with National Socialism, which is still an "unthought" phenomenon.

If he had been tempted to make a statement, let us say a statement made as an immediate moral reaction or a manifestation of his horror or his nonforgiving and thus a statement that would not stem from his work of thinking, at the peak of all that he had already thought, I believe we would then be more likely to feel dismissed from the duty of doing the work we must do today. For we do have this work to do, I mean this legacy, Heidegger's horrible, perhaps inexcusable silence. There are very few statements we can make today about Heidegger's relation to National Socialism; this lack of statements leaves us with a legacy. It leaves us the commandment to think what he himself did not think.

I believe Philippe Lacoue-Labarthe said that Heidegger did not come to terms with National Socialism theoretically. At least Heidegger did not pretend to have understood what happened and to condemn it in a statement, something which would have been easy. Perhaps Heidegger thought: I can only voice a condemnation of National Socialism if it is possible for me to do so in a language not only at the peak of what I have already said, but also at the peak of what has happened here. He was incapable of doing this. And perhaps his silence is an honest form of admitting he was incapable of it.

This is a very hazardous hypothesis (as I said, I am speaking extemporaneously this evening). Without Heidegger's terrible silence, we would not be conscious of the commandment that addresses itself to our sense of responsibility and tells us of the necessity to read Heidegger the way he did not read himself. At least he did not claim it. Or perhaps he did claim it and wrapped himself in silence, as I suspect, because of it. Perhaps he claimed that in his own way, without being tempted to make effortless statements, he had already said what would necessarily corrupt itself in National Socialism. Anyone who wants to find something in his texts on the basis of which one could condemn not only the inner truth of this powerful movement [National Socialism] but also its fall and its ruin will be able to find it. He was unable to say anything more about it. It is up to us to say more than "Auschwitz is the absolute horror, one of the absolute horrors in the history of humanity." If we are able to say more, then we should say more. This commandment is, I believe, inscribed in the most horrible and yet perhaps most valuable chance in Heidegger's legacy.

I believe, and here I agree with what Philippe Lacoue-Labarthe has said, that a reading of Heidegger, not an orthodox or philological reading, but an active reading (so to speak) can help us to approach what we condemn and to know what it is that we condemn.

Admiration and Disappointment

A Conversation with Philippe Nemo*

EMMANUEL LÉVINAS

NEMO: When you went to Freiburg to attend Husserl's lectures [in 1928], you discovered a philosopher who, although previously unknown to you, was to have central significance in the development of your own thought: Martin Heidegger.

LÉVINAS: Indeed, I discovered *Being and Time*, a work that everyone around me was reading at the time. And very soon thereafter I began to admire this book greatly. It is one of the most beautiful books in the history of philosophy—I say this after several years of reflection. One of the most beautiful, among four or five others . . .

NEMO: Which others?

LÉVINAS: For example, Plato's *Phaedrus*, Kant's *Critique of Pure Reason*, Hegel's *Phenomenology of Mind*, and also Bergson's

* Source: *Emmanuel Lévinas*, Ethik und Unendliches. Gespräche mit Philippe Nemo (*Graz/Vienna: Böhlau, 1986*), *pp. 26–33.* (*Translation from the French* Ethique et Infini: Dialogues avec Philippe Nemo [*Paris: Fayard, 1982*] *by Dorothea Schmidt.*) *Reprinted with the kind permission of Prof. Lévinas. The title was provided by the editors. An English translation of all the conversations contained in* Ethique et Infini *are contained in the edition:* Ethics and Infinity: conversations with Philippe Nemo, *trans. by Richard A. Cohen (Pittsburgh: Duquesne University Press, 1985*).

Time and Free Will. My admiration for Heidegger is above all admiration for *Being and Time.* I have tried again and again to recapture the atmosphere of those lectures then, when 1933 was still inconceivable.

The word *being* (*être*) is normally talked about as if it were a noun, although it is the epitome of a verb. In French, one says *l'être* (*Being*) or *un être* (*a* being). Heidegger reawakened the "verbality" of the word *being*; that is, what constitutes the event [*Ereignis*], the "happening" ["*Geschehen*"], of Being in the word *being.* As if things and everything that is "have a certain way of Being," "practice a profession of Being." Heidegger accustomed us to the richness of these verbal tones. Although it might seem trite today, this reeducation of our listening is unforgettable! Consequently, philosophy would have been (although philosophy itself did not take this into account) an attempt to answer the question of the meaning of Being as verb. Whereas Husserl still proposed—or seemed to propose—a transcendental program for philosophy, Heidegger clearly defined philosophy, in comparison with other methods of cognition, as "fundamental ontology."

NEMO: What does *ontology* mean in this context?

LÉVINAS: It is precisely the understanding of the verb *being.* According to this definition, ontology would differ from all other disciplines that examine *what* is, namely beings (*êtres*), their nature, their relations, and forget that, when speaking of beings, they have already interpreted the meaning of the word *being*, without, however, having clearly formulated it. Those disciplines are not concerned with such an explicit formulation.

NEMO: *Being and Time* was published in 1927; was it an absolute novelty at the time to present the task of philosophy in such a way?

LÉVINAS: That is, at least, the impression that I still have of it. In the history of philosophy, it is certainly possible later to find tendencies that, in retrospect, seem to be advance signs of today's great innovations. But at the very least, these innovations consist of focusing on an issue that hasn't yet been brought up. A focus that demands genius and will involve a new language.

The work I did on the "theory of intuition" in Husserl's phenomenology[1] was thus influenced by *Being and Time* to the extent that I attempted to depict Husserl as someone who had seen the ontological problem of Being, and had seen it more in the question of the *state* [*Verfaßtheit*] of beings than in the question of their *whatness* [*Washeit*]. As I said at the time, in examining the constitution of what consciousness perceives as real, phenomenological analysis devotes itself less to the investigation of transcendental conditions in the idealistic sense of the word than it raises the question of the meaning of the Being of beings for the various realms of cognition.

In the analyses of anxiety, care, and Being-toward-death in *Being and Time*, we experience an expertly executed phenomenological exercise. This exercise is extremely brilliant and convincing. Its aim is to describe Being, or the existence, of human beings—not their nature. What has been called existentialism was certainly influenced by *Being and Time*. Heidegger didn't like it when his book was given this existential meaning; human existence interested him as the "scene" of fundamental ontology. But the way the analysis of existence is carried out in this book influenced and determined the analyses that were later described as existential.

NEMO: What especially affected you about Heidegger's phenomenological method?

LÉVINAS: The intentionality that stimulates *Dasein* [*l'exister*] itself, as well as a whole number of "psychological states" that were considered "blind," simple contents, before Heideggerean phenomenology; the passages on affects, on *state-of-mind* [*Befindlichkeit*] and, for instance, on anxiety. When superficially investigated, anxiety would seem to be an affective movement without cause or, put more precisely, "without object." In Heideggerian analysis, it is exactly the fact that it has no object that is of importance. Anxiety appears to be the authentic and appropriate access to nothing. Nothing could appear to the philosopher to be a derivative concept, the result of a negation, and perhaps, as Bergson sees it, illusory. Heidegger does not think one "arrives" at nothing by making a number of theoretical steps, but that there is an immediate and nondeducible access to nothing through anxiety. Existence itself becomes stimulated, as it does by the effect of an intentionality, by a meaning of prime importance, the ontological meaning of nothing. It does not stem from what one is able to know *about* the fate of human beings, *about* its causes, or *about* their goals; in anxiety, existence itself, as the event of existence, means nothing, as if the verb *to exist* had a direct object.

Being and Time has remained the actual model of ontology. The Heideggerian concepts finiteness, *Dasein*, Being-toward-death, etc. remain fundamental. Even if one has liberated oneself from the systematic rigidity of this thinking, one still has been influenced by the style itself of the analyses made in *Being and Time* as well as by the "cardinal points" referred to by "existential analysis." I know the homage I am paying here to *Being and Time* will seem pale to enthusiastic supporters of this great philosopher. But I think Heidegger's later work, which made no comparable impression on me, remains valid because of *Being and Time*. Not, as I'm sure you can imagine, that his later work was unimportant; it is just much less convincing. I am not saying this because of Heidegger's political engagement of a few years after *Being and Time*, although I have never forgotten that engagement and I think that Heidegger never freed himself from the guilt of his involvement in National Socialism.

NEMO: In what way are you disappointed in the second part of Heidegger's work?

LÉVINAS: Perhaps because the actual phenomenology disappears from it; because of the priority that the exegesis of Hölderlin's poetry and etymology begin to have in his analyses. Of course I know that etymology is not a part of his thinking by chance; he thinks that language contains wisdom that must be rendered explicit. But this way of thinking seems to me to be much less verifiable than the way of thinking in *Being and Time*, a book in which etymologies can actually already be found but are here subordinated and only serve to round off what constitutes the unusual strength in the actual analysis and in the phenomenology of existence.

NEMO: Don't you think language has this primordial importance?

LÉVINAS: Indeed, *what is said* does not matter as much to me as *saying* itself. It is not so much the informational content that makes saying important to me, but rather the fact that it is directed to an interlocutor. Despite these reservations, I think that anyone who attempts to philosophize in the twentieth century cannot avoid traversing Heidegger's philosophy, even if only to distance oneself from it. His thinking is one of the great events of our century. To philosophize without knowing Heidegger would contain something of the "naïveté" in Husserl's sense. Husserl thinks there are very worthy and reliable findings, scientific findings, that are still "naïve" to the extent that they disregard the problem of the status of the objectivity of the object by being totally preoccupied by it.

NEMO: If everything else were the same, would you say about Heidegger what Sartre said about Marxism: that he represents the unsurmountable horizon of our time?

LÉVINAS: There are many things I can't forgive Marx for, either . . . As far as Heidegger is concerned, fundamental ontology and its problems can, indeed, not be ignored.

NEMO: And yet there is a Heideggerian scholasticism today . . .

LÉVINAS: . . . that considers the unexpected turns in his path of thinking to be the very last points of reference for thinking.

I must emphasize another essential contribution Heidegger's thinking has made: a new way and means of reading the history of philosophy. Hegel had already liberated the philosophers of the past from their archaism. But they entered into "absolute thinking" as moments or as stages that had to be traversed; they were resolved [*aufgehoben*]; that is, completely destroyed and simultaneously preserved. Heidegger presents us with a new, direct way to have a dialogue with the philosophers and to take advantage of the great classics for the benefit of current knowledge. Of course the philosopher of the past does not offer us the possibility of a dialogue from the start; one must do a considerable amount of interpretive work in order to make the philosopher topical. But engaging in this hermeneutics does not consist of tinkering around with what is old; one directs what is unthought back to what has been thought and to saying.

RECOLLECTIONS

Last Meeting with Heidegger*

KARL LÖWITH

IN 1933, when I was last in Freiburg for two days, I attended Heidegger's lecture course. He was in the process of analyzing different ways of silence, something he was an expert in. He invited me to dinner at his house; his wife was not there. We avoided all delicate topics in our conversation and limited ourselves to the question of whether I should give up my position at the University of Marburg and take up a prospect in Istanbul. He offered me a bed in his house for the night and seemed a bit surprised when I did not accept his offer. I had a place to stay with a former university friend who was an assistant professor in the medical school. The next day I visited Husserl. Heidegger had completely broken with him and had not called on his "fatherly friend" (this had been the stereotypical form of address in his letters) since the radical change in government. Husserl was mild, composed, and absorbed in his work yet he was inwardly hurt by the behavior of his student, who was now the rector and the successor to his chair at the University of Freiburg. derlin in the Italian-German Culture Institute there.

In 1936, when I was in Rome, Heidegger gave a lecture on Hölderlin in the Italian-German Culture Institute there. Afterward he

---

* Translator's note. A translation by Richard Wolin of parts of this piece appeared with the title "My Last Meeting with Heidegger in Rome, 1936" in *New German Critique* 45 (Fall 1988) pp. 115–116.

Source: *Karl Löwith*, Mein Leben in Deutschland vor und nach 1933. Ein Bericht, *Reinhart Kosellek, ed. (Stuttgart: Metzler, 1986). Reprinted with the kind permission of the Metzler Verlag. The title was slightly changed by the editors.*

came back with me to our apartment and was visibly taken aback by the destitution of our furnishings. Above all, he missed my library, which was still in Germany. In the evening I accompanied him to his room in the Hertziana, where his wife greeted me with stiff but friendly restraint. It was probably embarrassing for her to remember how often I had previously been a guest in her house. The director of the Institute had invited us to the Osso Buco for dinner, and we avoided political topics.

The next day, my wife and I made an excursion to Frascati and Tusculum with Heidegger, his wife, and his two sons, whom I had often taken care of when they were younger. It was a brilliant day, and I was happy about this last get-together, despite inevitable reservations. Even on this occasion, Heidegger had not removed the Party insignia from his jacket. He wore it during his entire stay in Rome, and it had apparently not occurred to him that the swastika was out of place when spending a day with me. We talked about Italy, Freiburg, and Marburg and about philosophical things. He was friendly and attentive, yet avoided, as did his wife, every allusion to the situation in Germany and his views of it. On the way back, I wanted to get him to make an open comment on it. I turned the conversation to the controversy in the *Neue Zürcher Zeitung* and explained to him that I agreed neither with Barth's political attack [on Heidegger] nor with Staiger's defense,[1] because it was my opinion that a partisanship for National Socialism lay in the essence of his philosophy. Heidegger agreed with me without reservation and elucidated that his concept of "historicity" was the basis of his political "engagement." He also left no doubt about his belief in Hitler. According to him, Hitler had underestimated only two things: the vitality of the Christian churches and the obstacles to the Anschluss of Austria. He was still convinced that National Socialism was the path that was mapped out for Germany; one merely had to "hold out" long enough. Only the excessive organizing at the expense of vital energies seemed questionable to him. He did not notice the destructive radicalism of the entire movement and the petit bourgeois nature of all its "Strength through Joy" [*Kraft-durch-Freude*] institutions, because he himself was a radical petit bourgeois. He was silent at first in response to my comment that although I could understand many things about his behavior, there was one thing I could not; namely, that he could sit at one and the same table (in the Academy for German Law) with an individual like J. Streicher.[2] Finally the well-known justification reluctantly followed (K. Barth has compiled it very well in his *Theologische Existenz heute*). It boiled down to this: that everything would have been "much worse" if at least some of those with knowledge had not involved themselves. And with bitter resentment against the "intelligentsia," he concluded his explanation: "If those gentlemen had not thought themselves too fine to get involved, things would have been different, but instead I was all alone." To my response that one did not exactly have to be "fine" to refuse to work with Streicher, he replied: one need not waste any words over Streicher, the *Stürmer* was nothing but pornography. He could not understand why Hitler did not get rid of that character; he must be afraid of him. This response was typical, for nothing is easier for Germans than to be radical in their ideas and indifferent in everything actual. They somehow manage to ignore *all individual facts* in order to hold on to their *concept of the whole* all the more resolutely, to separate the "matter" from the "person."[3] In actuality, however, the program of that "pornography" was completely fulfilled and was a German reality in November 1938,[4] and no one can deny that Streicher and Hitler agree precisely on this point.

Later, when I sent him my book on Burckhardt and my book on Nietzsche, which had appeared a year before, I did not receive a word of thanks, let alone an objective comment. I wrote to Heidegger twice more from Japan: once because of a translation of *Being and Time* into Japanese and the other because of a few rare works that I had given him in Freiburg and now needed temporarily. He answered both letters with silence. Thus ended my relationship to the man who, in 1928, conferred upon me the qualification to teach at the university level. I was the first and only one of his students at the University of Marburg upon whom he conferred the Habilitation.

Husserl died in Freiburg in 1938. Heidegger attested his "admiration and friendship" (the terms with which he had dedicated *Being and Time* to Husserl in 1927) in that he risked no words of remembrance or condolence, neither publicly nor privately, neither spoken nor written on the occasion of his death. B. [Oskar Becker], who owed his whole philosophical "existence" to Husserl, likewise evaded this awkward situation by not reacting, for the "simple" reason that his teacher was a dismissed Jew and he was an Aryan with a permanent position. Since Hitler, this heroism had become typical behavior of Germans who owed their positions to a German Jew. But Heidegger and B. probably felt that their behavior was "honest" and "consistent." What else could they have done in such awkward situations?

The Power of Thinking

GEORG PICHT

WHEN I WAS AN eighteen-year-old student attending Heidegger's lecture course for the first time I felt, almost physically, that what was happening there was an attack against everything I loved and admired. After only the second week, I understood: If what this man is saying is true, then the culture I belong to is untrue, and the science I am being taught has no ground. My instinctive and vehement resistance to this struggled with an equally strong feeling that I could not evade it. I was afraid. When he came into the lecture hall I felt that the power of thinking was a force that was perceptible to the senses. His appearance made the meaning of the Greek word *deinos* clear to me. Because I had listened to Heidegger's criticism of science, I experienced Hitler's takeover of power as the catastrophe of a form of European thinking that had long betrayed its own fundamental principles. The German university's moral capitulation to the new rulers seemed to me to be the empirical confirmation of Heidegger's insight.

Because of the environment I grew up in, because of my love for my parents' Jewish friends, because of my passionate admiration for Brüning,[1] because of my nonecclesiastical form of Christian belief, and because of my personal circumstances, I was immune to the temptations of the "national uprising." The credit is not mine, however. Yet, under Heidegger's influence, I thought that the political and spiritual standpoints that opposed National Social-

Source: Erinnerung an Martin Heidegger, *Günther Neske, ed. (Pfullingen: Neske, 1977), pp. 197–205.*

ism seemed weak and implausible. Heidegger's criticique of the science restored after 1945 is still urgently evident to me today.

The year 1933 has receded as far away from us as the Middle Ages. Today it appears to us as the first year of a regime on which our verdict has been settled. This perspective, which can only be granted retrospectively, is also imposed on its beginning. It is forgotten that no one could have known then what era had just begun. Much of what happened was horrifying. I can still hear the song I heard for the first time on a Sunday morning on the main street in Freiburg, when an SA troop sang: *"Und wenn das Judenblut vom Messer spritzt, dann geht's noch mal so gut"* ["And when Jewish blood spurts from the knife, then things will be twice as good"]. But what National Socialism was and what it became only started to become apparent after the Röhm putsch[2] and was only clear in 1938. In the fall of 1933, I walked down the Kaiserstrasse with two members of Heidegger's seminar—on the right a beanpole of an SS man; on the left an SA man; I, the civilian, in the middle. Naturally we discussed politics. I said something about one of the most recent atrocities. The SS man thereupon shouted so loud that people on the other side of the street turned around: "There is one thing that is, of course, obvious to all of us. Now, in the first phase of the revolution, we are ruled by a gang of criminals." This was not uncharacteristic of the mood of that part of the student body who, under Heidegger's influence, was obsessed with the idea that the true revolution had to come from the university.

Heidegger's own conception of this revolution became clear to me on a memorable occasion. It had been ordered that every month a lecture for the purpose of political education would be given, obligatory for all students. No room in the university was big enough so the Paulus hall was rented. Heidegger, who was then rector, invited my mother's brother-in-law, Viktor von Weizsäcker, to speak at the first of these lectures. Everyone was at a loss to explain this, because they all knew that Weizsäcker was not a Nazi. But Heidegger's word was law. The student he had appointed head of the students in the philosophy department felt obliged to open the event with a programmatic speech on the National Socialist revolution. After a few minutes, Heidegger scraped his feet and shouted with a harsh voice, which cracked in his infuriation: "This jabber will stop immediately!" The student, totally destroyed, disappeared from the podium. He had to give up his office. Viktor von Weiszäcker, however, gave a flawless speech on his medical philosophy in which there was no mention of National Socialism and quite a bit of Sigmund Freud. In his conversation with Heidegger, in which I, as Weiszäcker's escort, participated, it became completely clear how close Weiszäcker's thinking touched Heidegger's conception of "revolution." I asked my uncle later if he could explain to me why Heidegger identified with National Socialism. He answered: "I am pretty sure that it is a misunderstanding— things like that have happened often in the history of philosophy. But there is one thing in which Heidegger is ahead of everyone else: He is aware that something is happening here of which the others haven't the slightest idea." Schadewaldt, who was close to Heidegger and whom I asked in complete bewilderment what I should really think of this National Socialist revolution, gave me the answer: "It is not always smart to talk about everything. But remember one thing: Whoever roars is afraid."

It was not easy to digest all this at twenty years of age. Today no one has any idea what confusion had then seized the most important minds. In March of 1933, no one less than Eugen Rosenstock-Huessy, the author of the great book on European revolutions, visited my grandfather. He asked to be permitted to read a supplementary chapter on the National Socialist revolution aloud. I cannot remember details, but I do remember how frightened I was by the hypothesis that the National Socialist revolution was the attempt of the Germans to fulfill Hölderlin's dream. When I was studying in Kiel during the summer semester, Felix Jacoby, a great scholar with an impeccable character, opened his lecture on Horace with the following words: "As a Jew, I am in a difficult situation. But as a historian, I have learned not to consider historical events from a personal perspective. I have voted for Adolf Hitler since 1927 and consider myself lucky to be able to give a lecture on Augustus' poet in the year of the national uprising. For Augustus is the only figure in world history who can be compared to Adolf Hitler." Jacoby later emigrated and went to Oxford. A friend who visited him there after the war told me that his German nationalism was completely unbroken.

In the midst of this confusion of the minds, Heidegger's unwavering consistency was very impressive. Despite his political error, he stood up to the rulers. This was hard for a young person to endure. His first lecture after he had resigned from the rectorate is unforgettable to me. By abandoning every unnecessary word and every gesture, he talked about the matter of philosophy with as-

cetic soberness—more austere and bare than before. I felt: This is
what intellectual resistance to National Socialism looks like when
it is done without self-pity.

In a lecture he gave in 1944, Heidegger could say that, seen from
the point of view of the history of metaphysics, Communism, Amer-
icanism, and National Socialism were identical. This characterizes
his political attitude during the second half of the war. I was not
astounded when I was called on by a younger man who said to me:
"Don't ask about my sources. You are exposing yourself to great
personal danger if you are seen with Professor Heidegger so often." I thanked him and added that he should not be surprised if it
stayed that way. Heidegger was one of the few people with whom I
could openly speak about politics at the time. When I resigned from
my position as teacher at the Birklehof school in 1942 because it
had been taken over by the SS, he took care, with the help of the
archeologist Schuchhardt, that I got a position as assistant in the
classics department, although I did not want to enter the Party. I
probably owe my life to this.

I first became Heidegger's student in 1940, after a few years
spent in Berlin, when I registered for his seminar, which my wife
had already participated in for quite a while. He invited me to visit
him one afternoon, and here I got to know a Heidegger that I had
previously been completely unaware of: the kind and patient
teacher, who was ready to explain everything one asked him, who
had understanding for every insecurity, and to whom one could
talk like an apprentice talks to a master craftsman. When I asked
him what I should read to learn about philosophy, he answered:
"Read *Logik* by Lotze." I obediently bought the book, but the longer
I struggled through it, the less I was able to understand what I
should learn about philosophy from it. I finally asked Heidegger
and received the answer: "I wanted it to become clear to you what I
have had to work my way through." What the analysis of Lotze
meant for the development of Heidegger's philosophy can now be
followed in the published version of his course on logic held in
Marburg in 1925/1926. In his seminar one semester later, he interpreted the first chapter of Book IV of Aristotles's *Metaphysics*. He
discussed the *analogia entis*. I wrote him a detailed letter in which I
tried, with considerable philological effort, to give reasons for a
different and, as I know today, incorrect interpretation. He did me
the unusual honor of going into my letter in depth at the beginning
of the next class and gently proving me wrong. After that he no
longer treated me as a student but as a young colleague. He asked

me to regularly read Plato through a number of semesters with members of his seminar. Because my parents' house was close to his house and he liked the hour-long walk home after the seminar, it became a habit that my wife and I accompanied him. Thus for four years we had partly casual, partly very intense conversations about philosophy and everything else that moved thinking human beings during those times of war. He entrusted me with a huge pile of manuscripts because of the danger of bombs and allowed me to study them.

Heidegger's lecture courses were masterfully staged and also rhetorically highly stylized performances. In his seminars, students participated in the way he himself worked. The now published Marburg lectures reproduce some of this atmosphere. One learned an immeasurable amount. But the incongruity between the sphere in which he moved and this small group of students' capacity for comprehension bordered on the absurd. Heidegger took the seminar very seriously. He was always surrounded by the pathos of the awareness: a new epoch of world history is beginning here and now, and you can say you were there. The greater the temporal distance becomes, the more I am inclined to think he might have been right. His style in the seminar was, as one would say today, "authoritarian." When he was tired, it could switch to the style of a schoolmaster. He became impatient, even angry, if the exact answer that was called for did not come. Whoever said something that he could not prove and give clear reasons for was rebuffed. He thought that saying the first unthought-out thing that came to mind, which is called "discussion" today, was empty chit-chat. Yet his teaching style, shaped by the old Catholic tradition, imparted a discipline of thinking of which I know no other example in the humanities. Heidegger is not without blame that some of his students developed a dogmatism and literalness that was an exact contradiction of what should have been thought. For he made his pupils afraid. A false dependency was unbearable to him. When a student once read aloud the minutes, peppered with Heidegger's own phraseology, he interrupted her: "We do not Heideggerize here! Let's move on to the matter at hand." I took this to heart. The openness of philosophical conversation that he allowed me became possible in that I tried to say, in my own language, nothing other that what I believed I had understood.

How can Heidegger the person be described? He lived in a thundery landscape. As we were taking a walk in Hinterzarten during a severe storm, a tree was uprooted ten meters in front of us. That touched me, as if I could then visualize what was going on inside him. The awareness of being smitten, as it were, with the mission of thinking, his monumental lucidity, and a great strategy of the intellect stood directly next to a defenselessness, a vulnerability, and a softness that could suddenly switch to the peasant's cryptic cunning and always alert mistrust. Wounds that life had inflicted upon him never healed. When he occasionally treated students, colleagues, and even friends in a manner that could not be justified, I explained it to myself as the defensive reaction of a person who knew himself to be incessantly threatened from the outside and from within. Above all, he was threatened by what he had to think. The history of Being could abruptly make its way into the personal, and the personal into what was to be thought. It deeply impressed and shaped me that his lucidity, self-discipline, and sovereignty still did not desert him and that he walked along his path with unwavering devotion. I am still grateful to him today for encouraging me with kind understanding to preserve my independence of him.

Shortly after the war, we took a walk in the forest above his house. I got up my courage and tried to explain to him why his interpretation of Plato's allegory of the cave did not convince me. This was a central point, because his entire interpretation of European metaphysics relied on it. I have never met another person who could listen the way Heidegger did. After posing, with restrained passion, a number of apt, exact questions, which I did not evade, he stood still and said: "I must say one thing to you: the structure of Platonic thinking is completely unclear to me." A long silence. "Now we had better turn around." On the way back, we only talked about everyday things, but I felt I had been pronounced capable of independent reflection and judgment. When I visited him again shortly thereafter, he urged me to get my qualification to teach at the university level [*habilitieren*] as soon as possible; he knew already that when the universities were opened again, the representatives of yesterday's schools would emerge from all their hiding places and would occupy all the influential positions. "Whoever thinks something new will not be let in any more then." I had not found my path yet and answered that I was in a philosophical aporia and did not feel myself entitled to raise my voice *in philosophicis* in this state. He looked at me from the side with an expression as if suddenly all the curtains had been pulled away, and said: "I have been at that point for almost the past twenty years."

As a point of departure for my own reflection, I have used

Heidegger's concluding question in *Being and Time*: "Does *time* itself manifest itself as the horizon of *Being*?" Our last philosophical conversation, which we had in 1952, reached the point where he said to me: "I have meanwhile forbidden myself the use of the word *horizon*." When I wanted to know why, I experienced for the first time that he was incapable of expressing what he thought. It would have been impertinent to press him with questions that he no longer needed to pose himself. The silence he had meanwhile entered seemed to me inviolable; a retreat to the conventional was not in keeping with our relationship. That is why I never visited him again. We occasionally exchanged greetings and had coincidental meetings of no significance. The last thing I received from him was a deeply moving letter on the death of my mother in 1972.

One night after dark in December 1944, our doorbell rang. Heidegger was standing outside with his daughter-in-law and his assistant. They were fleeing from Freiburg, which was bombed and threatened by the invasion of the Allies, and were on their way to Messkirch, but there was no means of transportation. They asked for beds for the night. We spent a quiet, relaxed evening. On Heidegger's request, my wife played Schubert's posthumously published sonata in B major. When the music faded away, he looked at me: "We cannot do that with philosophy." In our guest book, the entry is written: "Declining is something other than ending. Every decline remains contained in the ascent."

to 1974, I was a full professor of Arabic and Islamic studies at the University of Vienna, after which I retired.

Now to your commemorative book. Your choice of collaborators is excellent. If they are still alive, perhaps the following are missing: Wilhelm Szilasi, as an honorary professor Heidegger's successor after 1945 and a close friend of H. before 1933, and Günther Stern, the son of the Hamburg psychologist William Stern, who got his doctorate from either Husserl or Heidegger and emigrated to the USA in 1933, as did his parents. It is too bad that Karl Löwith and Hannah Arendt could not write anything any more; they would be an interesting counterbalance to Herbert Marcuse. For this one can now read Karl Jaspers' *Philosophische Autobiographie* with its chapter on Heidegger.

To the collaborators: Hans Georg Gadamer, whom I do not personally know, was thought to be the student of Richard Kroner, from whom I first heard his name, in Freiburg. Hermann Heimpel, an unsalaried instructor in Freiburg in the twenties, a student of Heinrich Finke, and his attractive wife often visited my parents' house and so I know them well; I met Heimpel again in the fifties in Vienna, where he gave a lecture. I also knew Wolfgang Schadewaldt and his wife quite well. He was the member of the Institute of Archeology in Berlin who had been there the longest when I was a student in Berlin, and even then he was thought to be the up-and-coming man. His position in 1933 was unclear; anyhow Eduard Fränkel, the famous Latin scholar and his closest colleague at the University of Freiburg, who later taught at Oxford, was outraged. If you want to collect more memories of Heidegger from the time after 1933, I would suggest that you ask the Indo-Germanic scholar Johannes Lohmann, who was close to H. throughout the years. He came to Freiburg in 1933, was a full professor until he retired in the sixties, and has since continued to live in Freiburg.

I only heard Heidegger speak publically twice: on the occasion of his inaugural lecture in the assembly hall of the University of Freiburg and a while later in a lecture on Plato's cave allegory in Lecture Room 5. In both cases, I was deeply impressed by his talk except that his interpretation of a Greek text seemed to me, as a classicist and student of Werner Jaeger, quite primitive. My father was, by the way, also present at his inaugural lecture and afterward walked home with the zoologist and Nobel Prize winner Hans Speemann; they both admired the lecture, although they did not agree with the content. In his manner of speaking and his appearance, he reminded me of the theologian Karl Barth; certainly no coincidence, they were both typical Alemanni. At the end of 1928 I visited Heinrich Rickert in Heidelberg and the conversation came around to Heidegger. Rickert: He visited me a while ago and assured me that he still only considers himself my student. Rickert seemed very happy about this and repeated this sentence several times. Heidegger had been drafted during the First World War but had not been on the battlefield and therefore had neither been promoted nor decorated. As far as I can remember, he was a shoveler. He also worked at the mail censorship office in Freiburg, where numerous "intellectual" figures congregated, like the art historian Friedländer, the poet Burte, and others, whereas Richard Kroner and Julius Ebbinghaus were officers on the battlefield. It might be that this fact later annoyed H. However, it did not lessen his effect on the students. Jaspers writes on the time after the First World War that is "hardly publically known and yet still the origin of a rumor about him [Heidegger]." After *Being and Time* was published, Heidegger became the epitome of the philosopher of his generation. He received a position in Berlin, which he refused, so he did not suffer from an inferiority complex like so many who became Nazis in 1933. He also did not belong to the nationalistic or reactionary wing of the Freiburg philosophical faculty, as did Ludwig Curtius and Ludwig Deubner. His close friendship with the Szilasis, especially his wife, with the Husserls, and with his many non-Aryan students show that he was also not thought to be an antisemite or racist.

Now to 1933/1934. The anatomist von Möllendorff was elected as rector by a vast majority. Only a small minority of (I believe) seventeen professors voted for Heidegger. Thus it was all the more surprising that Heidegger was willing to take over the rectorate on the order of the government. Herr von Möllendorff's reaction was to accept an appointment in Zürich a few months later, probably the only time a full professor at Freiburg did this. Heidegger behaved perfectly correctly as rector; for instance, he asked my father to continue to give lectures, when, after 1 April, my father offered to stop lecturing since he neither wanted any problems nor would he greet with the "Hitlergruss." Heidegger also tried to prevent avoidable antisemitic acts of violence by the students. When students came to him and asked for his permission to hang up an edict, "Jewish professors shall publish in Hebrew," he refused to give authorization with the comment: "Everyone makes a fool of himself as best he can." He also never forbade the use of the university library or made it more difficult for either my father or me. In June

1938, shortly before my move to England, I met him near the card catalogues. He greeted me very amiably and said so that everyone could hear: "It won't always stay like this." It was generally known and was understandable that his relationship to Husserl had become strained since he had taken over the rectorate. Husserl had, after all, made him his successor in 1928 and had always considered him "his" student. And the Husserl family was especially shaken by the "non-Aryan laws," since one son had been killed in the First World War, the second, Gerhard, professor of Roman law in Kiel, had been very badly wounded, and their daughter Elli had been a nurse throughout the war. We "Jewish Christians" were naturally very sensitive when former friends turned out to be Nazis in 1933 and made tactless statements.

But Heidegger's behavior in 1933 not only aroused the indignation and dismay of his colleagues; I have heard statements made by archbishop Conrad Gröber, who had supported Heidegger as a young boy, which are as harsh as they can possibly be. I will not repeat them as long as Frau Heidegger is still alive, because he quoted a remark she made about her husband. The judgment of the theologian Engelbert Krebs was no less harsh. But even the Nazi bigwigs were not very pleased with his election as rector, however useful he was as an advertisement for the "revolution of the third bandmasters"—one need only think of Wilhelm Fürtwangler or the physicist Philipp Lenard. Heidegger proved to be unsuitable for the administrative business of a rector and was replaced by the German Nationalist Kern, an expert in criminal law, in 1934. This was not a political demonstration by Heidegger but an end to an unworthy epoch, gladly accepted by the university with a gloating smile. Heidegger did not belong to the well-known Freiburg resistance group around Gerhart Ritter and Constantin von Dietze or the Catholic group around Engelbert Krebs and Dr. Gertrud Luckner later, either. Therefore he was not able to keep his position after 1945; instead Szilisi took his place. When I came back to Freiburg for the first time in 1949, I asked Leo Wohlleb, then the president of Southern Baden, the musicologist Willibald Gurlitt, and others about Heidegger and his behavior in the years 1938–1945. No one knew anything about a clear statement against the Thousand-Year Reich, its rulers, or its horrible deeds. I found this, and still find it today, regrettable, as does the theologian Bultmann; one would have expected it. I therefore avoided a meeting when he came to give a lecture in Vienna in 1958 so as to not stir up embarrassing memories. The sentence "He was given emeritus status in 1951" in his vita is incomprehensible; he was not in office any more after 1945, and therefore could not have been "given emeritus status" according to usual linguistic and legal usage. He was never forgiven the sentence "Labor Service is more important (for students) than Knowledge Service," probably rightly so, as Wohlleb said.

I will conclude with that. Meanwhile forty-five years have passed since the events of 1933, and the number of Freiburgers who remember or want to remember is getting steadily smaller. The conduct of the universities at the time was not worthy of their tradition, and many felt it then and later. My teacher Gotthelf Bergstrasser, the great Middle Eastern scholar in Munich, wrote to me on an open postcard: "I am ashamed of myself." And others thought the same way—like Paul Kahle, who later emigrated to England with his family, Enno Littmann in Tübingen, and also Hans Speemann, Engelbert Krebs in Freiburg, to name just a few. And so everyone regretted Heidegger's position all the more. And some who let themselves be carried away then later regretted their behavior.

Perhaps you, Herr Neske, have been interested in my comments, and perhaps they have shown you how much your book preoccupied me.

Respectfully yours,
Hans L. Gottschalk

Martin Heidegger:
A Philosopher and Politics: A Conversation*
MAX MÜLLER

On 1 May 1985 the philosopher Max Müller answered questions by Bernd Martin and Gottfried Schramm, two historians at the University of Freiburg. Müller received his doctorate in 1930 at the age of twenty-four with a dissertation entitled "On Basic Concepts of Philosophical Doctrine of Rules." His advisor was Martin Honecker; the second examiner was Heidegger. He finished his postdoctoral thesis [Habilitationsschrift] on "Truth and Reality: Systematic Examinations of the Problem of Reality in Thomistic Ontology" in Freiburg in 1937. After the end of the war, he was an assistant and then, from 1946 to 1960, full professor at the University of Freiburg im Breisgau. From 1960 to 1971, he was a professor at the University of Munich. After he retired, he moved back to Freiburg, where he was given the title of honorary professor by the theological faculty of the University of Freiburg.

SCHRAMM: In the past few months, new evidence about the most famous Freiburg philosopher of the twentieth century has come to light. Although some people dismiss the years 1933 to 1934 as a clouding of vision limited to those years, the new evidence urges

* Source: "Martin Heidegger. Ein Philosoph und die Politik," Freiburger Universitätsblätter, (June 1986); 13–31. Reprinted with the kind permission of the author.

us to take that segment of his political life seriously. They obviously made it too easy for themselves. We are glad that you are willing to answer our questions as an eyewitness who observed Heidegger from close by during those critical years.

MARTIN: Let us start by recalling several stations of Heidegger's life that can provide an orientational framework for our conversation. Martin Heidegger, born in the Upper Swabian town Messkirch in 1889, became an associate professor in 1923 and later a full professor at the University of Marburg, where he stayed until 1928. Then, after Edmund Husserl[1] was named professor emeritus and his chair became free, Heidegger accepted a position as full professor at the University of Freiburg. Even before the publication of *Being and Time*, thus before 1927, he was thought of as up-and-coming, as the rising star of German philosophy. Without the Party directly intervening, he was elected rector of the Albert Ludwig University on 21 April 1933. He joined the National Socialist Party on 1 May 1933. On 27 May 1933, he gave an address[2] on the occasion of the solemn assumption of the rectorate that was to bring him more criticism than any of his other statements. According to his own testimony, an amiable conversation in the Ministry for Higher Education in Karlsruhe caused him to resign from the rectorate in February, at the end of the winter semester 1933/1934. However, according to the records our colleague Hugo Ott[3] has found, Heidegger by no means had a falling out with the regime because he rejected Nazi radicality, but because he was radical in his own independent way, a way that soon became a nuisance to the National Socialists. He officially resigned from the rectorate on 23 April 1934. Thus he was at the head of our university for exactly a year. We would like to clarify the political, intellectual, and human environment of this noteworthy rectorate in our conversation.

SCHRAMM: Allow me to state the aim of our question more precisely. Throughout his life, Heidegger considered himself a philosopher, not a politician, yet still, for a certain stretch of the path, he considered himself a political guide. We would like to know where such a man saw his political place—before 1933, at the beginning of National Socialist rule, when he took over an important responsibility, and in the following years until 1945, as long as he was still able to work publicly as a professor at the University of Freiburg.

MARTIN: When did you first meet Martin Heidegger, and what was your first impression?

MÜLLER: I began my studies in Berlin. There I primarily "pursued" history and had teachers in that field who deeply impressed me and whom I have remained grateful to throughout my life. They were Friedrich Meinecke and Hans Rothfels.[4] Then I went to Munich, where I returned after a year in Paris. I included philosophy in my studies, because I thought that as a historian I needed a philosophical basis. When I moved to Freiburg to finish my studies, I knew nothing of Heidegger except for his huge reputation. A magical aura emanated from *Being and Time.* Although I had not read the work yet, I said to myself: I want to sit in this man's seminar sometime. Heidegger began his work in Freiburg with an introductory seminar on "Kant's laying of the foundations for a metaphysics of morals." I still remember very well how I tried to find the room on the first floor of the university in which Heidegger was giving his introductory lecture, since the philosophy seminar room with its twenty to twenty-five places did not have enough space. A small man behind me asked me: "What are you looking for?" I said: "I'm looking for Heidegger's lecture room." Then he responded: "I'm looking for it, too. I am Heidegger." Finally we found what we needed on a map and went up together. A number of Heidegger's respected philosophy students sat there. But in the first class he did not want to ask questions of those students he already knew. Instead he asked me many questions and said to me at the end of class: "You must come to my seminar on Aristotle as well." I said: "Professor Heidegger, I am just about to take my state examinations, and two of these philosophy seminars are too much for me." Then he replied: "Oh, that's probably just an excuse. Maybe you don't know enough Greek?" I said: "That's all I know I am capable of: enough Greek." Then he insisted: "You are coming to my advanced seminar." This advanced seminar was a big thing. Not only students, also colleagues were there: Oskar Becker,[5] a philosopher of mathematics who later was a professor at the University of Bonn; Julius Ebbinghaus,[6] who later worked at the University of Marburg; Gustav Siewerth;[7] Simon Moser,[8] later professor at the University of Karlsruhe; Bröcker[9] and his future wife Käthe Oltmanns;[10] finally Eugen Fink.[11] It really was a fantastic seminar where a lot was demanded of the students. And so it happened that I, as quickly as could possibly be imagined, had a closer relationship to Heidegger. None of his students thought about politics at the time. Not a single political word was uttered in these seminars.

MARTIN: When was that?

MÜLLER: In the winter of 1928/1929. It was the last semester that Husserl gave a lecture with a corresponding seminar. It was on the "Phenomenology of Empathy." By chance, Heidegger's relationship to Husserl was mentioned the first time Heidegger and I met. I said: "And incidentally I understand nothing about phenomenology either, and you have announced a 'Phenomenological Seminar on Aristotle.' I don't know what that is supposed to be." "Oh, nonsense!" Heidegger answered. "That's just a gesture for my teacher Husserl. As far as content goes, you don't need to know anything about Husserl. My method of interpretation has nothing at all to do with him." I simultaneously attended Husserl's "Phenomenology of Empathy." And indeed, neither in their methods nor their theories did the two philosophers have anything in common.

SCHRAMM: Heidegger's seminars and lectures, you say, were completely unpolitical. Yet it can be assumed that Heidegger, like all of us, had a world of political conception, either spoken or unspoken. Could you name us the factors that helped to form this world of conception?

MÜLLER: Heidegger cultivated an entirely different style with his students than the other professors. We went on excursions together, hikes and ski trips. The relationship to national culture [*Volkstum*], to nature, and also to the youth movement were, of course, talked about then. The word *national* [*völkisch*] was very close to him. He did not connect it to any political party. His deep respect for the people [*Volk*] was also linked to certain academic prejudices, for example the absolute rejection of sociology and psychology as big-city and decadent ways of thinking. He said: "We must be strong in order to avert such things. Sociology makes an ahistorical system out of history, and psychology does not comprehend that history can only be understood by way of the demands it makes of us and not by way of our own ideas." He inveighed against 'bourgeois' philosophy, because it was a philosophy of values. He liked to say "It is the last decadence of the bourgeoisie. Who can commit themselves to or show enthusiasm for values? We are enthusiastic about certain tasks. Tasks are tasks of creation, and creation is works. A philosophy of works must arise in opposition to the philosophy of values. Only what is concrete commits us, values never commit us."

SCHRAMM: That was hardly a conservative philosophy. Conservative philosophies tend to be philosophies of values. They assume there are values that commit us. Heidegger could have just as well accused Catholic philosophy with what he accused bourgeois philosophy.

MÜLLER: You must consider that a "philosophy of values" plays no part in the works of the great philosophers of *philosophis perennis*, for instance Thomas Aquinas (but also Hegel). They are concerned solely with the good, which must be strived for and willed. In contrast to Max Scheler,[12] for example, Thomas Aquinas does not know the concept of emotion. According to Heidegger, the idea that one could comprehend something as a value through emotion was, from the start, an error. However one may reconstruct the history of his views, his position was hard to categorize into the philosophy of the time. When he received his qualification to teach at the university level, his thinking was close to that of Rickert.[13] Rickert had been the mentor of his postdoctoral thesis. The Catholic philosopher Artur Schneider[14] had been the director of Heidegger's dissertation. It was important for the shaping of Heidegger's character that he came from an half-peasant, petit bourgeois background. When he came to the university, he entered a very strange environment, and this would always be a conflict for him. Two forces pulled within him: On the one hand Freiburg, very famous in the field of philosophy at the time, and on the other small, unprepossessing, Upper Swabian Messkirch. These two homes joined in him to form an unbroken whole. As a radical philosopher, he was shocked by the institutionalized philosophy of the Catholic church. He had to break away from this yoke of the church but could never really leave its tradition. When the institutional church wanted to dictate the manner of the religious to him, it caused an inner conflict that he was never quite able to overcome. He was against this certain ecclesiastical form. But on the other hand he said: "It is a Western tradition, a combination of Greek and Jewish lines, that we will never be able to abandon. Even if this tradition is at an end, we must still take it with us into a new time." It could be said that he suffered under the church. It was a shackle from which he could never quite free himself, or a fishhook that he could never tear out. A love-hate relationship ...

SCHRAMM: Did he ever have a clear, positive, and yet critical relationship to an institution? Is not a basically unclear attitude toward institutions a part of his philosophy, as it is a part of his political conduct?

MÜLLER: I think he saw the necessity for institutions very clearly. This came out in many conversations. For Heidegger everything always revolved around the figure [*Gestalt*]. Thus the Führer figure or the figure of Stefan George[15] or the figure of the worker, and also the form and figure, or shape, of the community. Ernst Jünger[16] had a big influence on him. He did not think abstract values and norms but definite figures one could follow and comprehend were committing. The figure, or shape, that a nation [*Volk*] must assume is the work. And this shape must be, on the one hand, characteristic of the nation, but, on the other, the contradiction objectivity-subjectivity dissolves in it. It is our shape yet still objective shape.

SCHRAMM: Do I understand correctly? Heidegger thought a fundamental significance of modernity, the complicated organization in institutions, vanished, as it were, in two directions: in the fixation on leading figures, leader personalities, behind which the base of their following pales, and in the mythicizing into "figures" of something so of this world like institutions and what they achieve?

MÜLLER: *Mythicizing* is very appropriate. For Heidegger, Hölderlin, who played a very important role for him, was naturally a mythicized Hölderlin figure. As Heidegger saw him, he already anticipated all of today's religious problems. As Heidegger understood him, Hölderlin thought Christianity was great but at its end. And Christ has the task to unite all religions and in so doing overcome confessionality. Now to the problem of institutions: You see, Heidegger was one of the first to be aware of the problem of technological modernity. In this way he was always different from all so-called bourgeois philosophers. He realized that technologizing was a central problem. That is why Ernst Jünger, with his peculiar unity of romanticism and technicism, fascinated him. This kind of thinking is what Heidegger thought was new. He said something like this: "Everything else is left-over, nothing but conservatives of the past." He did not want to identify himself with the bourgeois age. He was no longer a real peasant or petit bourgeois from Messkirch, but he also never became "urbane." Romanticism held him to "Blood and Soil," and technicism pulled him toward the "new society"! Heidegger thought this justified a very different relationship to things, the technical relationship. Certainly, this relationship finally led him on an inevitable wrong track. Heidegger speaks of the "construct" [*Gestell*][17] that cannot be rejected but must be carried through to the end. Then—and this is the missionary–romantic aspect of it—comes the new world. Incidentally, the conviction that a new human being would be born links him not only to Ernst Jünger but also to Ernst Bloch[18] and Marx. In his "Letter on Humanism"[19] Heidegger later showed that Marx was philosophically worth more than the bourgeois philosophers of value after all, because Marx concretely discussed the history of work. What divides Heidegger and Marx is that for Heidegger a great disappointment lies at the end of the "history of works," whereas Marx thinks that the utopia of the new earth will open up. Basically, Heidegger thinks that in Marxism human beings walk the path of alienation to its end. They do not abolish alienation, however, by becoming fully technical human beings. The unity of nature and human beings—the naturalization of human beings, the humanization of nature—basically leads to *both* not being themselves any more.

MARTIN: What you have explained about Heidegger's fundamental philosophical positions reveals a strong continuity. He himself claimed that his inaugural lecture "What Is Metaphysics?"[20] anticipated the content of his rectorial address in many points. According to this, the concept of a reunification of science was only argued further in the address of 1933. Would you agree with this?

MÜLLER: Here you touch on a key question disputed in research on Heidegger: whether his path toward the "turning" was contained in his thinking from the start or whether there was a "break." Was *Being and Time* perhaps still thought anthropologically after all? He himself claimed: "I have never thought anthropologically. I have always thought from Being and the world toward human beings. I approached human beings from the world's destiny, from history and its mission. I did not start from a 'self-realization' of human beings." When he claimed such unity in his thinking, he admittedly added that he had not been capable of finishing it or achieving it then. That is why the second part of *Being and Time*, even the third section of the first part, was never published. He lacked the language to continue it.

Only gradually and in small individual interpretations—not in a self-contained work—could he carry out what he had in mind. According to Heidegger *Being and Time* was always conceived as a break with all of previous philosophy. He paralleled National Socialism with his own intentions in thinking inasmuch as it was a fundamental break with previous politics. That was, of course, utopian. The people he thought capable of this break wanted something very different than he did with his break with previous thinking.

MARTIN: When did he see that he had chosen the wrong companions for his path?

MÜLLER: Regarding the Party, he had already recognized it in 1934. But he kept the belief that something could still be done with the so-called *Führer*, even if his following was useless, much longer than he later admitted to himself. He did not back the Party but one person and the direction, the "movement." That is obscured in a disappointing manner in *Facts and Thoughts*,[21] which was published by his son Hermann. In it, Heidegger did not want to acknowledge the radicalness of his intentions in retrospect. The *Spiegel* interview[22] was the biggest disappointment for me. He should have used the opportunity to admit that at the time he did not want to preserve old values or the old university, but that he had wanted to stand the university "on its head." That is exactly what he had continually said to his students since 1922: "The Humboldtian university belongs to the bourgeois age. It is superbly conceived but no longer possible in that way today."

MARTIN: Then that would mean there was a continuity in Heidegger's thinking on university politics that can be determined from 1922 until beyond 1933?

MÜLLER: I suspect that it continues until 1938. After that he pushed university politics away from him. It cannot be established whether he kept his ideas of university politics until the end. He had burned his fingers so badly that he did not disclose his opinions any more.

SCHRAMM: But he had already burned his fingers in 1934 ...

MÜLLER: Yes, but he still harbored certain hopes then.

MARTIN: Could you tell us something about your own experiences with the "political Heidegger"?

MÜLLER: I experienced wonderful things with Heidegger but also disappointments. At the instigation of Gerhard Ritter,[23] whom I was very close to and whom I greatly admire, I was appointed the head of the newly founded student representation of the faculty of philosophy in the spring of 1933. Heidegger objected that I was politically unsuitable for it and then dismissed me in November 1933, when he was rector.

SCHRAMM: What impression did you have of the goals Heidegger hoped to realize during his rectorate? How do they compare with the plans the National Socialists had in mind? Where did they agree and where did they diverge?

MÜLLER: An agreement could be seen in Heidegger's strong aversion against the fraternities at the time. He thought the students in fraternities, with their traditions, mostly wanted to hold on to an outdated class society. These fraternities were, Heidegger was convinced, not compatible with a radically new future, which was a world of work and could not tolerate a class stratification. As rector, he tried to restructure the fraternities. He even scheduled evenings for them, he visited the duelling corps, other fraternities, and Catholic fraternities as well . . .

SCHRAMM: Once he even talked about the value of the duel.[24]

MÜLLER: Yes, although he was inwardly strongly opposed to fraternities. The duel was an exception. His idea of personal commitment reveals itself here, a certain romantic respect for bravery. But as I said, he thought German fraternity life no longer fit into the technical world.

MARTIN: And here he agreed with National Socialism?

MÜLLER: Indeed. But he also agreed in the idea of "threefold service," which he developed in his rectorial address.

MARTIN: Labor Service, Military Service, Knowledge Service . . .

MÜLLER: Yes. He did not at all think that Knowledge Service was an abstract achievement. It was to have been concretely placed into the service of the community, thus linked to Labor Service and Military Service. Heidegger had an entirely new type of human being in mind: the concretely-knowing-acting human being. Certainly he was no apostle of equality. Not everyone should do the same things, but they should all work together on a common work. They should be united by cooperation (precisely not by "corporation" [student societies]), not by the belief in a value. The work must have leadership if it is to come about. Therefore the leap to a leader [*Führer*] ideology. Aristotle already says with reference to Homer: "οὐκ ἀγαθὸν πολυκοιγανίη εἰς κοίρανς ἐστὶ ἐς βασιλεύς;" that is, that the rule of many does not work. Instead *one* person should make the decisions and take responsibility. This is what one could call Heidegger's "antidemocratic" view. He probably never abandoned it.

SCHRAMM: When we read something like that today, it could easily seem like pure National Socialism to us. But did not the actual National Socialists in 1933 think that it sounded like a strange sort of that academic arrogance they wanted to combat? Knowledge service is moved to the first place. The rectorial address is about the "Self-assertion" of the university. National Socialism had something different in mind. The university should put its powers to work on goals that were determined from outside. Heidegger had, let us say, a more noble picture of the universities. He once compared them to other schools and attached great importance to the fact that at the university one could dedicate oneself to a certain subject one had voluntarily chosen. That probably seemed like academic presumption to "normal" National Socialism.

MÜLLER: I think so, too. Here, again, Heidegger must be understood against the background of his biography. Until his death, he thought the university was something enormously great. For someone who came from small Messkirch to study, to receive a doctorate and the qualification to teach at the university level must have seemed like high goals. Then the position as associate and later full professor at the University of Marburg and, soon after, the position at the University of Freiburg that Riehl,[25] Windelband,[26] Rickert,[27] and Husserl had had before him. It's a wonder he didn't write in his book in the cabin in Todtnauberg: "It has been reached!" He always kept his very high estimation of the university.

SCHRAMM: It would seem, then, that the university was the institution with which he identified most clearly?

MÜLLER: Yes, and which he wanted to mold in an incredibly one-sided fashion according to his own conception. I would not call it personal ambition or an urge for power. Rather, in a certain way, he thought of it as a fulfillment of his life's purpose. That is why he did not need to be pushed into the rectorate or, as he later wanted to think, to accept the burden in order to prevent worse things from happening. No, basically he thought everyone was not radical enough. He wanted to form the model university, the new university, here in Freiburg. He did not want to slow things down, he wanted to urge them on. And then came the big disappointment.

MARTIN: Then Heidegger wrote himself two roles as leader: as philosopher and as rector?

MÜLLER: Yes, and he wanted to be a model example of leadership in both these roles. I never noticed a political ambition in him on any other level. This wanting-to-be-a-leader, in a manner that always remained completely unclear, was a disappointment for me.

SCHRAMM: There is now evidence that beyond the ambition to become the "führer" of the University of Freiburg, he had the still greater ambition to become the leader of the German universities. With this ambition, he was striving for a position that the National Socialists had not intended to have as part of their organizational scheme, let alone a position that was intended for him.

MÜLLER: It is actually amazing that although the National Socialists introduced the appointment of deans and rectors, they still kept, to a large extent, the structure of the university. The oldest Party member of the Freiburg faculty, Professor A.[28] . . .

SCHRAMM: A classicist . . .

MÜLLER: This man, probably wrongly granted the qualification to teach at the university level by the great Wilamowitz-Möllendorf,[29] did not even receive a full professorship during the Third Reich, although he, as the oldest Party member at the University of Freiburg, headed the National Socialist Faculty Alliance and was a feared figure throughout the Third Reich. He could prevent talents from climbing up. But he could achieve hardly anything for himself and the likes of him. The famous "Race Günther,"[30] who was given the honor of a professorship at the University of Freiburg, probably was helped by the protection of his teacher Eugen Fischer.[31] Fischer was an imposing figure, later the director of the Kaiser Wilhelm Institute for Anthropology in Berlin-Dahlem. On the other hand, a man like our colleague Tellenbach,[32] who never had anything to do with the Party, could receive a professorship at the University of Münster and then one at the University of Freiburg under the Nazis. It might be considered a certain counter concession that a historian like Klewitz,[33] a very decent man but politically more accommodating toward National Socialism, was then also employed at our university. But basically, National Socialism could carry out very few changes in personnel policy at the universities.

SCHRAMM: We are also interested in the way Heidegger behaved toward individuals. How did he get along with his Jewish colleagues? And how did he treat people who had convictions that did not suit him?

MARTIN: The enforcement of the Law for the Restoration of Professional Civil Service,[34] the forced retirement of Jewish colleagues, occurred during his rectorate.

SCHRAMM: Here in Baden, action was taken earlier than elsewhere in the Reich.

MARTIN: How did a rector, who later rejected National Socialist racism in his writings because it did not fit into his conception of the world, humanly and personally cope with this? He thought highly of certain elites, but not of an elite achieved through racial selection. Did Heidegger personally place himself in front of colleagues who were supposed to be dismissed, or did he keep himself out of it?

MÜLLER: Here again, a contradiction characteristic of him manifested itself. He was probably never personally spiteful to a Jew. But he never again visited his teacher Husserl, who remained living in Freiburg on Lorettostrasse at the time. Though he also never took action against him either. His statement that he did not voluntarily drop the beautiful dedication to Husserl in the new edition of *Being and Time* published during the war is believable. The publisher had to demand it or the edition would not have appeared. A certain contact between the philosophy department and Husserl was preserved. But both professors, my much admired teacher Honecker[35] as well as Heidegger, did not exactly exhibit what one could call "civil courage." They no longer visited Husserl personally, but sent assistants, like myself, to him. In this manner, Husserl was continually informed about which dissertations were being written and what was happening in the current semester. He was not to consider himself fully isolated. These regular errands to Husserl for both Honecker and Heidegger were—as I said—usually my affair. I always had a very wonderful conversation with Husserl. I asked some questions, and then Husserl talked freely. He was a strongly monological type and, as he had entirely concentrated on his philosophical problems, he did not actually experience the time that had begun in 1933 as "hard," unlike his wife. He was allowed to philosophize however he wanted, and he received the full amount of his salary as professor emeritus. He was spared from persecution. So he had everything that was important to him; and it didn't matter to him that he was no longer allowed to lecture at the university. The Deutsche Notgemeinschaft still paid for his assistant.[36] Heidegger never said a word against Husserl on any occasion. But he never visited him after 1933, and he was missing from Husserl's funeral, like most colleagues of his faculty, because he was ill.

SCHRAMM: He was sorry about that later, as he admitted in the *Spiegel* interview.

MÜLLER: Incidentally, not only Heidegger—as I said—was missing. Gerhard Ritter was, as I remember, the only full professor from the faculty of philosophy to attend. The other full professors in the funeral procession were all from other faculties: for example Euken[37] and Großmann-Doerth.[38]

MARTIN: How did Heidegger behave toward other Jewish professors, like Hevesy,[39] Thannhauser[40] . . .

MÜLLER: He certainly respected these men. But after Thannhauser became a full professor, he called attention, in conversations, to the fact that originally there were only two Jewish doctors working in internal medicine and that finally there were only two non-Jews in this department. It did bother him somewhat.

MARTIN: That was before 1933?

MÜLLER: Yes, before 1933. Thannhauser left relatively soon after Hitler came to power. Heidegger told me he had sent a letter to England for his Jewish assistant Brock[41] so that he would be well received there. Brock has never, I think, denied this. But ever since the moment when Heidegger became rector, no Jewish student who had started a dissertation with him got a doctorate from him.

SCHRAMM: That applies to Helene Weiss,[42] for example . . .

MÜLLER: Yes. Yet he had the deepest respect for her. She was, incidentally,—unlike Alfred Seidenmann,[43] who worked with Heidegger on Bergson—not dependent on a financial guarantee! Heidegger still wanted his Jewish students to receive a doctorate after 1933, but not with him as an advisor. So he used a trick (naturally not a very splendid one) and turned to Honecker. He declared himself willing to accept Heidegger's Jewish doctoral candidates and to advise them until they received their doctorate.

MARTIN: Was Heidegger interested in the fate of Jews from his circle beyond making it possible for them to receive a doctorate?

MÜLLER: Well, his relationship to Wilhelm Szilasi[44] should be mentioned in this context: a close friendship yet a difficult relationship. Until 1933, Szilasi came to Freiburg every summer semester, gave private philosophical seminars, and worked in a way that was close to Heidegger's own ideas. Szilasi told me that Heidegger then said to him in 1933: "We will have to break off our contacts because of the present situation." There were never any angry words. But Heidegger simply let the relationship fall apart, and later it was very difficult and unclear on both sides.

SCHRAMM: What about non-Jews whose political or other views made them vulnerable at the time? Heidegger's denigration of his colleague Staudinger[45] when Heidegger was rector has recently created a sensation.

MÜLLER: The two originally had a good relationship to each other as neighbors. After the Second World War, I often met Staudinger in Ritter's reading group. Staudinger was an incredibly kind person. His first wife was, however, politically probably extremely leftist and was supposed to have been a committed pacifist. Staudinger himself did not have a political nature and probably accepted the political direction she chose. Heidegger should certainly have differentiated here. Aside from him, no one at the university, where the background was well known, took Staudinger's occasional political remarks seriously, let alone took offense.

MARTIN: How do you explain that Heidegger, who was not a militarist, denigrated a colleague to the authorities in Karlsruhe with the argument that he was a pacifist?

MÜLLER: I don't know if Heidegger was asked about it and thus came across it; that is, whether the initiative was his or whether it came from outside. There will always be something strange about the "Staudinger case." Staudinger, who had meanwhile married for the second time, had presumably already left the first period of his life far behind. As far as I know, he married into a family from a Baltic background, and that probably encouraged a different political viewpoint in him.

SCHRAMM: What personal experiences did you have with Heidegger's political assessments?

MÜLLER: After 1933 I did not go to his seminars any more, although

I had previously been one of his "favorite pupils" (along with Eugen Fink, for example, and of course Walter Bröcker and Käthe Oltmanns), because some of the characters who had settled there scared me off. Incidentally, they stayed away again later. The atmosphere in the seminar had already changed again in 1935. In 1937, I was denounced because of my activity for the Catholic student youth group. A further inducement may have been the articles on political topics that I had to write for the encyclopedia *Grosser Herder* at the time. No full professor had the courage left to touch such hot potatoes. A younger man had to step in. Finally Professor A., whom we have already mentioned, realized that I had written these articles and therefore decided I was unacceptable.[46] I was summoned to the vice rector of the university, Theodor Maunz,[47] who told me: "You are lost. Because you have been denounced, Heidegger was asked about your political convictions. He wrote a report in which he praises you as a human being, educator, and philosopher, but he has written one sentence in which he says that you have negative opinions about this state. Go to him. Now that your postdoctoral thesis, your trial lecture, and your participation in the teachers' camp have gone so extraordinarily well, everything else will be fine if he crosses out that sentence. But if the sentence remains, it won't be." So I went to Heidegger. He said with some embarrassment: "I can't cross out that sentence. I was only asked about your political convictions. If I refuse to give that information, it will be just as negative for you. That is why I gave the only answer that corresponds to the truth. But I have wrapped it in a cover of justifiable, good things." My reply: "That won't help me. The sentence is there." Then Heidegger said: "As a Catholic, you should know that one must tell the truth. Consequently, I cannot cross out the sentence." Then I replied: "I am not aware that one has to tell the truth always and everywhere. Instead, the person to whom one is speaking must have a right to the truth. There is no undifferentiated obligation to tell the truth." Heidegger: "No, I will stick to what I was asked. I can't take back my whole report now and say I won't write one at all, because people already know that I have given one to the university to be passed on. Nothing can be done. Don't hold it against me." He apparently still wanted to keep up a good relationship to me. My last words were: "The point is not that I might hold it against you, the point is my existence." Shortly thereafter, I did, in fact, receive a letter from Berlin, passed on by Dean Müller-Blattau, that stated that I was unacceptable to the university for "ideological and political reasons."[48]

MARTIN: When was that?

MÜLLER: I received the notification in the middle of January 1939. I took the obvious step and broke off all my contacts to Heidegger. They were only picked up again in 1945, when Heidegger turned to me. Despite everything that had happened, we had a very good relationship for the second time. But my experience of a certain ambiguity in Heidegger's character could no longer be obliterated.

SCHRAMM: How was the atmosphere in Heidegger's lecture courses and seminars after he resigned from the rectorate? During the time when he taught Hölderlin or . . .

MÜLLER: . . . in the great lecture course on Nietzsche.

SCHRAMM: Could one say that these courses were in any way confrontations with National Socialism? And were they understood to be confrontations? Heidegger later claimed that whoever could listen heard that they were.

MÜLLER: I didn't go to the lecture courses any more. But I followed the Nietzsche course using transcripts. It was obvious that the way he understood Nietzsche was the opposite of what Mussolini or Hitler wanted to make out of him. Heidegger thought there were two terminuses of Western metaphysics: Nietzsche and Marx. Although Marx turned the idealist Hegel around from his head to his feet, as Marx put it, it was, Heidegger said, just as much metaphysics, only it was a reversed Platonism. The dualism between mind and sensorial nature remains. But whereas Plato thinks the mind rules sensorial nature, Marx thinks sensorial nature and work take mind, which is only an epiphenomenon, into their service. Nietzsche does not replace Platonism with materialism but with vitalism. With it, he sets metaphysics a magnificent end. Nietzsche recognizes all the weak points of the great, bourgeois age of modernity and the great, bourgeois-idealistic philosophy. But he does not replace it with a completely new thinking but simply by a turnaround. Heidegger always emphasized: "*That* is not the turning I mean, because it is simply a reversal."

MARTIN: What do the lectures on Hölderlin yield for our question?

MÜLLER: Heidegger was not concerned with Hölderlin's conception of the fatherland, which was what especially interested the National Socialists about this poet. Heidegger thought Hölderlin, whom Heidegger knew through Norbert von Hellingrath[49] from the youth movement, was the positive completion of the metaphysical age. Hölderlin was the only one to recognize the outlines of the postmetaphysical age. He, the friend of Hegel and Schelling, had ventured much further than they had. In his poetic language, he had expressed that there could no longer be a system of mind, but only a history of the sending of the new.

SCHRAMM: Who went to Heidegger's seminars or lecture courses, let's say, after 1934/1935 and until the war, which gradually depopulated the university? How did the milieu in Heidegger's classes differ from what was otherwise common at the University of Freiburg?

MÜLLER: In 1934, Heidegger's lectures were not at all unpolitical. I can remember an improvised sentence from his lecture on logic: "Logic is naturally the correct way of thinking for existing-concrete human beings. The figure of the Führer can also be brought into logic." But Heidegger would not have said anything more like that as early as 1934/1935. After that time, as far as I as a nonparticipant can tell, not a single political word was spoken in his courses. And all the full professors at the time had to open their lectures with their arms raised in the "German greeting." Only unimportant, unnoticed people could disregard this order.

SCHRAMM: Did the circle of people Heidegger was close to change during those years?

MÜLLER: It could not be said that there was a big change. For a long time, there had been people in his closest circle who were, put simply, on the right: like the great national and administrative law scholar Ernst Rudolf Huber[50] and—as already mentioned— Ernst Jünger.[51] The figure of the worker that Jünger had designed, as a romantic *and* at the same time technical appearance, impressed Heidegger.

MARTIN: May I interrupt you here? Did Heidegger not admire Ernst Jünger the dashing officer, the recipient of the *pour-le-mèrite* medal, more than he admired Jünger the literary figure? Did this admiration not compensate for the fact that Heidegger had actually been denied his own experience at the front in the First World War? He volunteered in 1914 but was discharged and sent home because of an illness. He served for two and a half years in

Freiburg at the mail censorship office. In 1918, when he was scheduled for service at the front for the second time, this time near Verdun, he ended up at the weather station.[52]

MÜLLER: Yes, this unheroic personal fate probably contributed to the mythical transfiguration of the experience at the front in Heidegger's thinking. Incidentally, if he had really wanted to go to the front with all his might, there would certainly have been ways and means to get there. It seems to me that he was—to use the common slogan—not a "soldierly type." But, because one can seldom use a simple formula to describe Heidegger, it must be added that he had a considerable amount of physical courage. When we were skiing, he laughed at me a number of times because I made turns and curves where he dashingly raced straight down. And he had not skied from childhood on but had probably only learned it with the help of his wife. The same thing was true about hiking. A boy from Messkirch does not hike and does not ski. But Heidegger did both with competence and even with great passion.

MARTIN: Then an answer to the question of Heidegger's courage will give us a conflicting picture?

MÜLLER: Yes, as so often in questions about Heidegger. He did not exactly have very much "civil courage." When discussing topics on which he was not directly an "expert," it was easy to make him uncertain when one contradicted him. That always surprised me. On such occasions, he would not try to argue but would shyly withdraw as soon as decisive opinions were expressed. An uncertainty, which showed in his facial expressions as well, could restrain him even in situations where he would very much have liked to join in but felt his own incompetence. This was evident, for instance, in discussions on art. Thus he did not dare to say anything about the Brandenburg Concertos by Bach, which he listened to with pleasure and which he considered very great works. I am nevertheless slightly doubtful whether he understood very much about music.

SCHRAMM: Did he listen to them on records?

MÜLLER: Yes. He had a wonderful stereo installed when he was old.

MARTIN: Could we return again to Heidegger's relationship to his professorial colleagues?

MÜLLER: In order to illustrate the contradictoriness of those times:

the vice-rector at the time, Josef Sauer,[53] wrote very harsh opinions about his rectorial colleague Heidegger in his journal, which Herr Ott virtually uses as a key for his assessment of Heidegger. Well, Sauer was, as a man of character, one of the most imposing and magnificent figures in the divinity school. But it would be incorrect to make him the "good" antithesis to the "bad" Heidegger during the time of his "error." Sauer was always a monarchist, a German Nationalist. He had never accepted the Weimar Republic. He had served and stuck out the whole year of Heidegger's rectorate as vice-rector. The fact that he continually advised young Catholics "You must join the SA, you must join the SS" helps to illuminate the time. I, too, let myself be impressed by these arguments and joined the SA. "We must be present there or the whole affair will run away from us and against us." Though he was certainly never a National Socialist. A different case—I don't know if it has ever been carefully researched—was Heidegger's relationship to Möllendorff.[54]

SCHRAMM: The doctor?

MÜLLER: Yes. When the National Socialists came to power, he was the legally elected rector, but, as a member of the German Social Democratic Party, he was unacceptable. He had to resign and later accepted a position in Switzerland. As far as I know, Heidegger's personal relationship to Möllendorff was not destroyed as a result of that.

SCHRAMM: Neither was his relationship to Franz Büchner.[55]

MÜLLER: No. His relationship to Erik Wolf[56] never suffered either. Wolf, who was the dean of the law school, was disavowed by his faculty because he appeared to have revealed himself to be an uncritical Heidegger enthusiast. The Party remained absolutely foreign to Wolf, something he had in common with Heidegger. Wolf, originally a follower of [Stefan] George, also let himself be guided by romantic ideas. He, like Heidegger, was fascinated by the magnificence of events. Yes, he moreover had a certain aestheticism. But his Protestantism helped him to make a radical change. He joined the German Confessional Church.[57]

MARTIN: In this conversation, you have continually attempted to approach an overall appreciation for and criticism of Heidegger's personality. Could you go into this more precisely? "Ambiguity" was one of your main concepts.

MÜLLER: Until 1933, I could count myself among his favorite students in Freiburg (I believe this is not too presumptious), along with Fink and others (Bröcker, Oltmanns, Siewerth, for example). Gadamer was not there any more. When I was working toward my qualification to teach at the university, which Heidegger had himself proposed in 1930, I had the impression that he stood by me. But already during my examination proceedings, a certain ambiguity became clear. Although he assessed my examination very positively, he did not appear at any of my trial lectures. In a certain way, I was never disturbed by this ambiguity, however clearly I was always aware of it. Harmonious, self-content human beings, who can easily identify with themselves, are denied the greatest achievements. Heidegger dealt with a deep ambiguity in himself for most of his life, an ambiguity toward his religion, too. This can be checked in Guido Schneeberger's documentation,[58] which also contains Heidegger's virtually spiteful remarks about the Catholic church. Bernhard Welte[59] told me about a scene from the year 1945. Heidegger was sitting in archbishop [Conrad Gröber's] anteroom to ask him for help. The archbishop's sister came in and said: "Oh, Martin is here again! He hasn't been here for twelve years!" Heidegger answered with embarrassment: "Marie, I have had to atone for it. I am finished." Of course he was in no way finished. Instead he still achieved a number of great things. According to that story, Heidegger must have avoided Bishop Gröber for twelve years.

MARTIN: Although Gröber had, to an extent, discovered and supported him.[60]

MÜLLER: Yes, and especially the last.

MARTIN: Heidegger actually owed his entire career to Gröber.

MÜLLER: I wouldn't go that far. But he always admired Gröber as a father figure. He could never have been spiteful against him personally. This relationship had some aspects in common with Heidegger's relationship to Husserl. Courage and uncertainty often conflicted in him. He always had a hard time with himself. No one could have thought so deeply about certain human phenomena who did not have these problems in himself. The Messkircher and the professor, for instance, then the independent thinker and the religiously rooted—such contrasts describe some of the "ambiguities" of his nature. His mother was almost a bit too pious, and he was never quite able to break away from her. A picture of his mother was always on his desk. Another example: On the hikes that I went on with him, we sometimes visited churches and chapels. To my great amazement, he took holy water and genuflected. I once pointed the inconsistency of this out to him. "But you have distanced yourself from the church. You don't believe in transsubstantiation. Why a genuflection? You don't think Christ is in the altar." Heidegger replied: "Certainly not. Transsubstantiation—that is a misuse of Aristotelian physics by scholastics. But I am not a run-of-the-mill pantheist. One must think historically. And in a place where so many have prayed, the godly is close in a very particular way. However you may interpret the figure, I believe that the godly was also once unusually close in the figure of Christ. Today it is probably no longer so. But such a church, where people have worshiped for centuries, is a place where one must have reverence." He rejected the church's dogma, the "yoke of the church." But at the same time, he saw that the proximity of godliness had prevailed over the church throughout the centuries, and that it is now disappearing from it. That is why he had this strange "Adventism."

At some point there will be a new religion, for human beings will never be without religion; after all, they are *homo religiosus*. Heidegger saw a certain contradiction in the legacy that has come down to us. The legacy must not be thrown away; it must be built upon. But from it one must go on to new shores. Here he adopted Hegel's famous triple "lifting" [*Aufhebung*]. To lift up means *tollere*—it is no longer valid [as in to lift a ban]. It can mean *conservare*—to save [as in to lift something out to save it]. And finally it can mean *elevare*—to lift up. And when it has been lifted up, then it is standing someplace very different than before. These problems deeply or, to use a label, "existentially" moved him. He did not manage to solve any of the problems that he had torn open with such magnificence. Well, to philosophize means to remain questioning. Anyone who can deal with these problems actually has no need for philosophy any more. Therefore his last hypothesis, which I always contradicted: Either one thinks *or* one believes, because with belief comes the answer. Thinking is only thinking in the Heideggerian sense when it persists in its answerlessness. I think that a certain (though not in the usual meaning of the word) nihilism lies in this. It leads to the answerless thinker evading answers and responsibility in the political as well. That is not what Heidegger intended; yet still, after all, it is what he did.

Heidegger's Resoluteness And Resolve

HANS JONAS

JONAS: Heidegger was, without a doubt, the most important philosophical thinker Germany had at the time. One could perhaps
say, the most important philosophical thinker of this century. At
the time, there were two names in philosophy if what one wanted
to learn was not simply conventional or traditional university
philosophy. One was the already aged Husserl in Freiburg, the
founder of phenomenology, which was still closely tied to the
philosophical tradition but already was, in some respects, a new
beginning. At that time in Germany it was the most highly regarded philosophy next to neo-Kantianism. And the neo-
Kantianists, who were especially based in Marburg, Hermann
Cohen, who was already dead at the time, Paul Natorp, and
Nicolai Hartmann,[1] were worthy but not original philosophers.
The phenomenologists had originality. In Freiburg there was a
young lecturer and assistant of Husserl named Martin Heidegger. The rules of the university, or rather, the rules Husserl had
introduced, made it so that young philosophy students were not
allowed to begin by entering Husserl's seminars. First, they
were sent to an introductory seminar, which was given by his

Source: *Interview by Prof. Dr. Andreas Isenschmid with Hans Jonas for Swiss radio,
broadcast on 9 October 1987. First publication. The title was provided by the editors.*

197

young assistant Martin Heidegger. I therefore simultaneously had the double impact of these two powerful and very individual teacher personalities, thinker figures: Edmund Husserl and Martin Heidegger. Of the two Heidegger was the much more exciting.

ISENSCHMID: And why?

JONAS: My answer may sound very surprising at first. However, I am speaking entirely autobiographically. First, because he was much more difficult to understand. This was strangely attractive for a young and ardent philosophy student who was still in the apprenticeship stage: a strange attraction, a totally compelling assumption that there must be something hidden behind it that was worth being understood, that something was going on there, that work was being done on something new.

ISENSCHMID: Someone once said: I didn't understand a word, but I knew that it was philosophy.

JONAS: Exactly. That was precisely it. I don't understand it, but that must be it. Here one is coming close to the center of philosophical thinking. It's still a mystery, but something is going on here in which (how should I say it) the last concerns of thinking in general, of philosophy, are dealt with. And also, by then Husserl's thinking had become settled to the effect that his lectures were a constant repetition of what he had already said, what was in his books, which were well worth studying. But it could not be said that you received new outlooks from Husserl when you sat in his seminar or in his lectures. Rather you entered a school, so to speak. And somehow (although it could be said that Heidegger later also taught a school of thinking) that was not what I wanted. It goes without saying that my students now learn a set teaching from me, too, but I did not want simply to become a member of a school that was, in a certain way, convinced of itself and its final truth.

ISENSCHMID: Heidegger brought up the last concerns of philosophy, an old topic but in a completely new language and, I believe, with a completely new point of view. What were the secrets of this Heideggerian manner of speaking about the last concerns of philosophy?

JONAS: Well, that could perhaps be concisely explained by contrasting two words that actually became *termini technici.* Husserl spoke of the analysis of consciousness. Heidegger spoke of the ways of *Dasein.* Consciousness here, *Dasein* there: it was more than a terminological difference.

Husserl thought pure consciousness built the world up in itself, essentially in so-called noetic acts; that is, acts of cognition, of knowledge. This begins with the sensory perception of how objectivity is built up in the consciousness and then rises up to the intellectually abstract forms in which the world is organized in the consciousness. This pure consciousness stood opposite the world, in a certain sense completely abstract and independent of it. The world was its product, a product of consciousness. A very strange thing to say. As if the body, the interconnection with the world did not exist. As if here the pure self builds its world of objects itself. That was still the legacy of German idealism, the legacy of Kant and the entire philosophy of consciousness, which Fichte and Hegel and so on continued after Kant. But in contrast with Hegelian philosophy, it was no longer speculative—as Husserl said again and again—but descriptive. Phenomenology is descriptive; it describes phenomena. But which phenomena? The phenomena of consciousness.

Heidegger spoke of *Dasein*, and not of *Dasein* that pictures the world through acts of knowledge, but of *Dasein* whose way of Being is care and which is concerned with something. And he defines *Dasein* as that Being which is concerned in its being with this Being. Husserl does not make such statements. Husserl thought this pure self was essentially an intellectual self. The intelligible and intellectual self of the pure consciousness that (as I said) had the world as its object, and object [*Gegenstand*] means *standing opposite* [*gegenüberstehend*]. Heidegger's *Dasein* was experienced in an entirely different way: as interwoven with care into the world. It is concerned with something that means It is. Yes, it is actually essentially on the way. To say it perhaps very unphilosophically (Heidegger did not use this expression) it is a "tormented self" and not a self that sovereignly sets itself opposite the world.

ISENSCHMID: And how did your picture of Heidegger, your picture of his thinking as well, shift with what you heard about Heidegger during and after the war? Did a shadow fall onto Heidegger and his thinking? What happened then?

JONAS: What happened happened long before the war; namely in 1933. Heidegger came out of his hiding place then. Until then, he had never expressed any political affinities or even sympathies; yes, a certain "Blood-and-Soil" point of view was always there: He emphasized his Black Forest-ness a great deal; I mean his skiing and the ski cabin up in Todtnauberg. That was not only because he loved to ski and because he liked to be up in the mountains; it also had something to do with his ideological affirmation: one had to be close to nature, and so on. And certain remarks, also ones he sometimes made about the French, showed a sort of (how should I say it?) primitive nationalism. That was the way Heidegger was, and, at the time, I did not connect it to his philosophy or his philosophy to it; rather, those were his personal idiosyncrasies. He pursued a certain cult, for example, in the way he dressed. He had thought up a kind of traditional costume that accentuated the landscape: knee breeches with long socks, a vest, I think it was an Alemannic one, a costume, which he also wore during lectures, that was half thought up by him and half copied from the Black Forest peasants. You didn't think about it too much, because, after all, you weren't there to deal with Martin Heidegger's idiosyncrasies but with his thinking and his teaching.

And he was a magnificent teacher. He was not only a tremendously original teacher but also a fascinating teacher. And I have never again seen such careful notes being taken as during his lectures. I took the transcripts of his lectures with me when I emigrated and still had them, after all my migrations, in exile, until I finally put them at the disposal of the Heidegger Archive in the sixties. We not only very religiously and very precisely took notes on Heidegger's lectures and supplemented them among each other from personal transcripts, we also studied them before Heidegger published his books.

ISENSCHMID: But what is the connection between those two components, the magnificent thinker and teacher Heidegger and the chauvinist, who came out of his hiding place in 1933? Or were these components always connected subterraneously?

JONAS: Yes, one must say the latter. But it took a long time for me to realize it. In 1933, when he gave that infamous rectorial address, justifiably called treacherous in a philosophical sense and actually deeply shameful for philosophy, I was simply appalled and spoke with friends about it and said: "That from Heidegger, the most important thinker of our time." Whereupon I heard the reply: "Why are you so surprised? It was hidden in there. Some-

how it could already be inferred from his way of thinking." That
was when I realized, for the first time, certain traits in Heidegger's thinking and I hit myself on the forehead and said: "Yes, I
missed something there before."

ISENSCHMID: In which traits was it hidden?

JONAS: You ask very difficult questions. In this context, I can only
answer with simplifications. Such a simplification is provided by
the concept of resoluteness. Heidegger published *Being and
Time* in 1927; that is, after I had studied with him for a number of
years. Here, for the first time, he presented to the philosophical
public what he had to say about the authenticity and the inauthenticity of existence in his analysis of *Dasein*. It said that the
Being of *Dasein* can take place in different modes, in different
ways of Being, of which one is the predominant one of ordinariness. *Dasein* is caught up or entangled in "One" [Man],[2] that is,
the not actually personal, the leveled-off, anonymous Being of
society, in which it can't really be said, I mean this and that, I
think this and that, I want that, but instead one says, one thinks,
one acts or behaves in such a way. That means that *Dasein* is not
lived by the authentic self but by this anonymous world of society. Authentic existence, in contrast to *Dasein* lived by the
leveled-off Being-in-the-world of "One," is gained by a kind of
self-contemplation. This self-contemplation is particularly stimulated by the so-called preliminary run toward death.

For Heidegger—perhaps because of experiences during the
First World War, I don't really know—the relationship to one's
own death, the relationship to one's own finality (not necessarily
through this alone, but certainly in part) was one of the impetuses that throws *Dasein* back on its self and lets it free itself from
the rule of the "One": toward its authenticity. The characteristic
of this authenticity is resoluteness: you must resolve something
for yourself. Resoluteness as such, not *for what* or *against what*
one resolves oneself, but *that* one resolves oneself becomes the
authentic signature of *authentic* Dasein. Opportunities to resolve
oneself are, however, offered by historicity. Heidegger had developed his own doctrine fully independent of political reality. It
was a doctrine of a process of deterioration occurring in history,
in the history of thinking. In this process, the origins had been
lost, had become a routine of thinking, as it were. The intensity with which he studied the Greeks and disclosed them to
us—particularly Aristotle, but also the pre-Socratics, Plato,

Augustine—this return to what he called the origins of thinking was connected to his very negative evaluation of where Western philosophy had finally arrived after following these original impetuses. He had shown the descent, the derivation of philosophical thinking, as it was represented by, for instance, the neo-Kantianism of German lectern philosophy, by German university philosophy.

There was a memorable meeting in the late twenties in Davos, the famous conversation between Heidegger and Ernst Cassirer. On the one side, there was the older Cassirer, a very distinguished man, tremendously schooled in the tradition of Western philosophy, a man who had been very determined by Kant but who had thought further independently, the actual *homo humanus* in the traditional sense. And opposite him was this (one could almost say) "barbarian" Heidegger, in contrast to whom everything that really mattered became shadowy. One could say it was a kind of pictorial catastrophe: the most respected German university philosopher, Cassirer, who stood opposite this new urger and questioner in the person of Heidegger. I was later told that Cassirer was deeply disgusted and had naturally felt that the hearts, the feelings of the listeners were completely with Heidegger. That was an experience that was painful enough, but in addition, he found this "black-haired demon" he had to deal with deeply disturbing in an antipathetic sense. Here Cassirer had very correct insights.

In any case, in January 1933, when the moment had arrived, history offered the opportunity for resoluteness. One should throw oneself into this new destiny. One should finally take the leap away from the whole compromising, weak, civilized, subdued negotiations of the intellect at the German universities (particularly in philosophy but also in general), and leap into the events of a new beginning. Suddenly the tremendous questionability of Heidegger's entire approach indeed became clear to me. If he accused idealistic philosophy of a certain idealism—forms of thinking were studied, the categories in which the world is organized, and all studied from a certain distance—he himself could be accused of something much more serious: the absolute formalism of his philosophy of decision, in which the decision in itself is the greatest virtue. Purely hypothetically, it could be said that it would have been possible to decide against it. And then it would indeed have been a very formidable decision, a decision to swim against the tide. But in Hitler and in

National Socialism and in the new departure, in the will to begin a new Reich, even a thousand-year Reich, he saw something he welcomed. Somehow, for a time, he identified this with his own endeavors to find a beginning, to return from this track, this downhill track of a philosophizing that distanced itself ever further from the origins, toward something that would allow a new start. He identified the decisiveness as such (of the Führer and the Party) with the principle of decisiveness and resoluteness as such. When I realized, appalled, that this was not only Heidegger's personal error but also somehow set up in his thinking, the questionability of existentialism as such became apparent to me: namely, the nihilistic element that lies in it. That went together with what I had recognized as an essential feature of the gnostic agitation at the beginning of the Christian age, which also contained a strongly nihilistic element.

APPRECIATIONS

and yet had an extraordinary influence. In Heidegger's case, however, there was nothing tangible on which this fame could be based. There was nothing written, except for notes taken on his lectures, which were passed around among students. These lectures dealt with texts that were generally familiar; they contained no doctrine that could be reproduced or transmitted. There was hardly anything more than a name, but the name traveled throughout Germany like the rumor of the secret king. This was something totally different than a "circle" centered around, and directed by, a "master" (like, for instance, the circle around Stefan George), which, although familiar to the public, separates itself from it by the aura of a mystery that supposedly only the members of the circle know about. Here there was neither a mystery nor a membership. Those who had heard the rumor knew each other, since they were all students; some became friends, and later cliques were formed here and there. But there never was a circle, and there was nothing esoteric about his following.

Who heard the rumor, and what did it say? At the German universities at the time, after the First World War, there was no rebellion but there was a widespread discontent with the academic industry of teaching and learning in all the faculties that were more than mere professional schools. This discontent was shared by all the students for whom studying meant more than the preparation for a job. Philosophy was not something one studied to earn money; rather, it was the study of resolute starvelings who, for precisely that reason, were hard to please. These students were not in the least interested in wisdom of the world or of life. For anyone who was searching for the solution to all riddles there was a rich selection of ideologies and ideological parties available; it wasn't necessary to study philosophy to choose among them. However, these students also did not know what they did want. The universities generally offered them either the schools of philosophy—the neo-Kantians, the neo-Hegelians, the neo-Platonists, etc.—or the old philosophical discipline, in which philosophy was neatly divided into separate fields (epistemology, aesthetics, ethics, logic, and so on) and, rather than be communicated, was done in by endless boredom. Even before Heidegger entered the scene, there were a few rebels against this comfortable and, in its way, quite solid academic industry. Chronologically speaking, there was Husserl and his call "To the things themselves"; that is, "away from theories, away from books," and toward establishing philosophy as a rigorous science that could take its place among the other academic disciplines. This call was, of course, still completely naïve and completely unrebellious, but it was something to which first Scheler and somewhat later Heidegger could refer. And then there was Karl Jaspers in Heidelberg, who was consciously rebellious and came from a tradition other than the philosophical. He, as is known, had long been friends with Heidegger precisely because the rebellious element in Heidegger's plans attracted him as something primordially philosophical in the midst of all the academic talk *about* philosophy.

What these few had in common was (to put it in Heidegger's words) that they could differentiate "between an object of scholarship and a matter of thought,"[1] and that they were fairly indifferent to the object of scholarship. At that time, the rumor reached those who knew, more or less explicitly, about the break in tradition and the "dark times" that had begun. Because of this, they thought erudition in matters of philosophy to be idle play and were only willing to submit to academic discipline because they were concerned with the "matter thought," or, as Heidegger would say today, with the "matter of thinking."[2]

The rumor enticed them first to Freiburg to the lecturer [*Privatdozent*] and later to Marburg. According to the rumor, there was someone who actually attained the things Husserl had proclaimed, someone who knew they were not simply an academic matter but concerns of thinking human beings—not just yesterday and today, but from time immemorial—and who, precisely because he saw that the thread of tradition had broken, was in the process of rediscovering the past. The technically decisive point was that, for instance, Plato was not talked *about* nor his theory of Ideas described; instead a single dialogue was pursued throughout an entire semester and was questioned step by step. In the end, a series of very relevant and contemporary problems took the place of a thousand-year-old doctrine. Today this sounds very familiar to us, because so many use this method nowadays; but no one did it that way before Heidegger. The rumor said quite simply: Thinking has come alive again; the cultural treasures of the past, believed to be dead, are made to speak, and it turns out that they produce things altogether different than it had been presumed that they said. There is a teacher; one can perhaps learn thinking.

The secret king reigned in the realm of thinking, a realm that is entirely of this world, but is so concealed in it that one is never quite sure whether it exists at all; but it is a realm that has more inhabitants than is commonly believed. How else could one ex-

plain the unprecedented, often subterranean, influence of Heideggerian thinking and thoughtful reading, which went so far beyond
his circle of students and what is generally understood to be philosophy?

For it is not Heidegger's philosophy, whose existence we can
justifiably question (as Jean Beaufret has said), but Heidegger's
thinking that has helped so decisively in determining the spiritual
physiognomy of this century. This thinking has a probing quality
that is unique to it. If one wished to capture it and put into language, one could say its probing quality lies in the transitive use of
the verb *to think*. Heidegger never thinks "about" something; he
thinks something. In this entirely uncontemplative activity, he
probes the depths, but not to discover, let alone bring to light, an
ultimate, secure foundation in a dimension of depth that could be
said to have been previously undiscovered. Rather he remains in
the depths in order to lay down paths and set up "path marks" (a
collection of his texts from 1929–1962 is called "path marks," *Wegmarken*). This thinking may set itself tasks. It may deal with "problems." It is, of course, always concerned with, or, more exactly,
excited by, something specific; but it cannot be said that it has a
goal. It is unceasingly active, and even the laying down of paths
serves more to open up a new dimension than to head toward a
goal that has been previously sighted. These paths may be called
"wood paths" (after the title, *Holzwege*, of a collection of his essays
from 1935–1946). Because these "wood paths" do not lead to a
point outside the woods and they "suddenly end in places un-
walked," they are incomparably more suitable to the person who
loves the woods and feels at home in them than the carefully laid
out "problem streets" on which the investigations of professional
philosophers and scholars rush back and forth. The metaphor of
"wood paths" has hit something very essential. Not, as might seem
at first, because someone has strayed onto a wrong track, but
because someone, like the woodcutter whose business is the
woods, goes on paths he has cleared himself; and clearing the path
is no less a part of his work than cutting wood.

Heidegger has laid down a vast network of such paths of thinking
in this dimension of depth, which was first explored by his probing
thinking. The single immediate result, understandably noticed and
even imitated, is that he caused the edifice of traditional metaphysics to collapse. This edifice, in which, for a long time, no one
had felt quite comfortable anyway, collapsed the way a structure
whose foundations are no longer secure enough will collapse

when underground tunnels are burrowed. This is a historical matter, perhaps even of the first order; but it need not trouble those of
us who do not belong to the guilds, including the historical. The
fact that Kant could, from a certain perspective, justifiably be called
"the all-crushing one" has little to do with who Kant was, in contrast to what his historical role was. As for Heidegger's share in the
collapse of metaphysics, which was imminent anyway, what we
owe him, and only him, is that the collapse happened in a manner
worthy of what had preceded it; that metaphysics was *thought*
through to the end and not simply overrun, as it were, by what
came after it. "The end of philosophy," as Heidegger calls it in *Zur
Sache des Denkens*, but it is an end that is an honor to philosophy
and holds it in honor, prepared for by someone who was deeply
bound to it. Throughout his life, Heidegger based his seminars and
lectures on the texts of the philosophers. Only in old age did he
venture to give a seminar on one of his own texts. *Zur Sache des
Denkens* contains the "protocol of a seminar on the lecture 'Time
and Being,' " which forms the first part of the book.

I have said that people followed the rumor in order to learn thinking. What they then experienced was that thinking as pure
activity—and that means thinking driven neither by thirst for
knowledge nor the urge for cognition—can become a passion
which does not so much rule all other capabilities and gifts as it does
order them and prevail through them. We have grown so accustomed to the old oppositions of reason versus passion, of spirit
versus life, that the thought of a *passionate* thinking, in which thinking is unified with aliveness, is somewhat disconcerting to us.
Heidegger himself once expressed this unification (according to a
well-documented anecdote) in a single statement when, instead of
the usual biographical introduction, he said at the beginning of a
lecture on Aristotle: "Aristotle was born, worked, and died." That
such a thing exists is, indeed, as we were later able to realize, the
condition of the possibility of there being philosophy at all. But it is
more than questionable whether we would have discovered this,
especially during this century, without the existence of Heidegger's
thinking. This thinking, which rises out of the simple fact of being-
born-in-the-world and now "thinks reflectively on the meaning that
reigns in all that is,"[3] can no more have a final goal—cognition or
knowledge—than life itself can. The end of life is death, but human
beings do not live for death's sake, but because they are living
beings; and they do not think for the sake of any arbitrary result, but
because they are "thinking, that is, musing beings."[4]

A consequence of this is that thinking acts in a peculiarly destructive or critical way toward its own results. Certainly since the philosophical schools of antiquity, philosophers have exhibited a fatal inclination toward system building, and we often have difficulty today to dismantle the structures they have built and then to discover what was actually thought. But this inclination does not stem from thinking itself, but from very different needs, which are themselves quite legitimate. If one wanted to measure thinking in its immediate, passionate liveliness by its results, then one would fare as with Penelope's veil: what was spun during the day would relentlessly undo itself during the night, so that the next day it could be started again. Each of Heidegger's writings, despite occasional references to previous publications, reads as though he was starting from the beginning and only incorporating, as needed, language already coined by him—a terminological language, in which the concepts are only "path marks" by which a new way of thought orients itself. Heidegger refers to this peculiarity of thinking when he emphasizes "the extent to which the *critical* question, which is the matter of thinking, necessarily and constantly is a part of thinking"; when he, with reference to Nietzsche, speaks of "the ruthlessness of thinking, beginning ever anew"; when he says that thinking "has the character of a reversal." And he practices this reversal when he subjects *Being and Time* to an "immanent criticism," or establishes that a certain interpretation of Platonic truth is "no longer viable," or speaks generally of the thinker's "backward glance" at his own work, "which always becomes a *retractatio,*" not as cancellation but as a new start to thinking what has already been thought.[5]

Each thinker, if he grows old enough, must strive to unravel the actual results of his thinking, and he does this simply by thinking them through again. (He will say with Jaspers, "And now, just when you really wanted to start, you must die.") The thinking "I" is ageless; it is both the curse and the blessing of the thinker, as long as they only genuinely exist in thinking, that they became old without aging. And the passion of thinking is like other passions; what are commonly known as the qualities of the person, whose totality, structured by the will, amounts to something like the character, cannot hold their own against the onslaught of passion that seizes and, in a sense, takes possession of the person. The thinking "I" that is "standing within" the raging storm, as Heidegger says, and for which time literally stands still, is not just ageless, it is also, although always specifically other, without qualities. The thinking "I" is everything but the self of consciousness.

Moreover, thinking is, as Hegel once remarked on philosophy in a letter to Zillmann in 1802, "something solitary." This is not only because I am alone in the "soundless dialogue with myself," as Plato called it (*Sophist* 263e), but because something "unutterable" always reverberates in this dialogue, something which cannot fully be brought to sound through language, cannot be made to speak, and therefore is not only not communicable to others but also not to the thinker himself. It is presumably this "unutterable," which Plato describes in his Seventh Letter, that makes thinking such a solitary occupation and yet forms the very different nurturing grounds from which thinking arises and constantly renews itself. It is easy to imagine that (though this is probably not at all the case with Heidegger) the passion of thinking might seize the most sociable of human beings and, as a consequence of the solitude thinking requires, destroy him.

The first and, as far as I know, the only one to speak of thinking as a *pathos*, something to be endured with suffering, was Plato, who, in the *Theaetetus* (155d), calls wonder the beginning of philosophy; by this he naturally does not at all mean the surprise we have when we encounter something strange. For the wonder that is the beginning of thinking—as surprise may be the beginning of the sciences—applies to the everyday, to the self-evident, to things we are thoroughly acquainted and familiar with. This is also the reason why it cannot be pacified by any knowledge whatsoever. Heidegger once spoke, completely in Plato's sense, of the "ability to wonder at the simple," but, in contrast to Plato, he adds "and to accept this wonder as one's abode."[6] This addition seems to me decisive for a reflection on who Martin Heidegger is. For perhaps many people know (so we hope) thinking and the solitude that is connected to it; but, undoubtedly, their abode is not there. When wonder about the simple overcomes them and they, giving in to the wonder, engage in thinking, then they know that they are torn away from their habitual place in the continuum of transactions and occupations in which human affairs take place and that they will return there again after a short while. The abode of which Heidegger speaks lies therefore, metaphorically speaking, apart from the habitations of human beings; and however stormy it may become in this place, these storms are a degree more metaphorical than the storms we mean when we speak of the storms of the age.

Compared with other places in the world, the places of human affairs, the abode of the thinker is a "place of stillness."[7]

Originally it is wonder itself that produces and spreads stillness, and it is because of this stillness that being shielded against all sounds, including the sound of one's own voice, becomes an indispensable condition for the development of thinking from wonder. Enclosed in this stillness there is already a peculiar transformation which affects everything that gets caught in the vicinity of this thinking. In its essential seclusion from the world, thinking only has to do with things and matters that are absent and withdrawn from direct perception. If you stand face to face with another person, you perceive him in his bodily presence, but you do not *think* of him. If you do, a wall has already been erected between you and the person you have encountered. You are secretly withdrawing yourself from the direct encounter. In order for it to be possible to get close to matters or to human beings through thinking and directly perceive them, they must lie in the distance. Thinking, says Heidegger, is "coming-into-nearness to what is distant."[8]

This point can easily be demonstrated by a familiar experience. We go on journeys in order to view things in faraway places; in the course of this it often happens that it is only when we look back in recollection, when we are no longer under the power of our immediate impression, that the things we have seen come very near. It is as if they only disclose their meaning when they are no longer present. This inversion of relationships—that thinking distances what is near, or withdraws itself from what is near, and draws what is distant into nearness—is decisive if we want to find an answer to the question of where the abode of thinking is. Recollection, which becomes remembrance in thinking, plays such an important role as a mental faculty in the history of thinking about thinking, because it guarantees us that nearness and distance, as they are perceptible to the senses, are actually capable of such an inversion.

Heidegger only occasionally, by suggestion, and then mostly negatively, talked about the abode he inherited, the abode of thinking—for instance, when he said that thinking's questioning "is not part of the usual order of everyday life," does not "gratify urgent or prevailing needs"; indeed, "questioning itself lies outside order."[9] But this relationship of nearness-distance and its inversion in thinking pervades Heidegger's entire work like a keynote to which everything else is attuned. Presence and absence, concealing and revealing, nearness and distance—their interlinkage and the connections that prevail among them have next to nothing to do with the truism that there would be no presence unless absence was experienced, no nearness without distance, no revealing without concealing. Seen from the perspective of thinking's abode, the "withdrawal of Being" or "forgetfulness of Being" does indeed prevail in the surrounding of this abode, in the "ordinary order of everyday life" and human affairs; that is, the withdrawal of that with which thinking—which, by nature, keeps to the absent—is concerned. The annulment of this "withdrawal" is always paid for by a withdrawal from the world of human affairs; this is even true, and is, indeed, especially true, when thinking, in its own isolated stillness, reflects on just these affairs. That is why Aristotle, with the great example of Plato still vividly in view, urgently advised philosophers not to play at being kings in the world of politics.

"The ability to wonder at the simple" is, at least occasionally, presumably inherent in all humans; the thinkers known to us from the past and present should then be distinguished by having developed the ability to think, or having developed a thinking that is suitable to them, from this wonder. However, the ability to "accept wondering as one's abode" is a different matter. This is extraordinarily rare, and we only find it documented with a degree of certainty in Plato. More than once and most drastically in the *Theaetetus* (173d to 176), he described the dangers of such an abode. It is also here that he tells, apparently for the first time, the story of Thales and the Thracian peasant girl who witnessed how the "wise man," his gaze upward to watch the stars, fell into a well. She laughed that someone who wanted to know the sky should be so ignorant of what lies at his feet. Thales, if we can believe Aristotle, was immediately very offended—especially since his fellow citizens used to make fun of his poverty—and wanted to prove by a large speculation in oil presses that it is easy for a "wise man" to get rich if he only really sets his mind to it (*Politics*, 1259a 6ff.). And since books, as everyone knows, are not written by peasant girls, the laughing Thracian child was later subjected to Hegel's statement that she just did not have a sense for higher things.

In the *Republic* Plato, as we know, wanted not only to put an end to poetry but also to forbid laughter, at least to the class of guardians; he feared the laughter of his fellow citizens more than the hostility of those opinions opposed to the thinker's claim to absolute truth. Perhaps he knew that the thinker's abode, seen from the outside, could easily seem like the Aristophanic Cloud-cuckooland. At least he knew that thinking, if the thinker wants to market his thoughts, is incapable of fending off the laughter of the others.

This might be one of the reasons why he, at an advanced age, left for Sicily three times in order to help set the tyrant of Syracuse straight by giving him lessons in mathematics, which seemed to him an indispensible introduction to philosophy. He did not notice that this venture, seen from the peasant girl's perspective, must seem considerably more comical than Thales' mishap. To an extent he was right in not noticing; for as far as I know, no one laughed, and I know of no description of this episode that even smiles. Evidently, human beings have not yet discovered what laughter is good for—perhaps because their thinkers, who have always been ill disposed toward laughing, have left them in the lurch in this respect, although some of them have racked their brains about the immediate causes of laughter.

Now we all know that Heidegger, too, once gave in to the temptation to change his "abode" and to involve himself in the world of human affairs. And as far as the world is concerned, he was served much worse than Plato, because the tyrant and his victims were not on the other side of the ocean, but in his own country.[10] As far as he himself is concerned, I believe the matter is different. He was young enough to learn from the shock of the collision, which drove him back to his inherited abode after ten short hectic months thirty-five years ago, and to settle what he had experienced in his thinking. What emerged from this was the discovery of the will as will to will and thus as the will to power. In the modern age, much has been written about the will, but despite Kant, despite Nietzsche, not much has been thought about its essence. In any case, no one before Heidegger saw the extent to which this essence is opposed to thinking and affects it destructively. To thinking belongs composure and serenity [*Gelassenheit*]. And seen from the perspective of the will, the thinker must say, only apparently in paradox, "I will non-willing"; because only "by going through this," only by "weaning ourselves from willing," can "we let ourselves get involved in the sought-for essence of thinking that is not a willing."[11]

We who wish to honor the thinkers, although our abode may lie in the midst of the world, can hardly help thinking it striking and perhaps infuriating that Plato and Heidegger, when they got mixed up in human affairs, turned to tyrants and Führers. This should be imputed not only to the circumstances of the time and still less to a preformed character, but rather to what the French call a *déformation professionelle*. For the inclination toward the tyrannical could be demonstrated theoretically in many of the great thinkers (Kant is the great exception). And if this inclination is not demonstrable in what they did, then merely because only very few even of them were prepared to go "beyond the ability to wonder at the simple" and "accept this wondering as their abode."

It finally does not matter where the storms of their centuries carried these few. For the storm that blows through Heidegger's thinking—like the one that still sweeps toward us from Plato's works after thousands of years—does not originate from the century he happened to live in. It comes from the primeval, and what it leaves behind is something perfect that, like all that is perfect, returns home to the primeval.

In France

JEAN BEAUFRET

WHEN HEIDEGGER WAS IN Paris in 1955, one cause of his astonishment was the sheer fact of his being there. Before stepping through the gate at Gare de l'Est, he paused for a while and said thoughtfully: "Why, I am in Paris!"

Frau Heidegger asked him: "And what's your impression of it?"

"I am astonished—at myself."

A further cause of astonishment was the statue of Charlemagne by Notre Dame. "Oh yes," I told him, "those are our roots, too. There's even a Lycée Charlemagne close by, in the Marais area. St. Charlemagne was celebrated for a long time in all the French schools. And wasn't Napoleon, on this very spot, the last emperor of the West, as the Germans still know? Today, however, the West has sailed to America."

He called Paris "A playing city! Even the policeman on the street plays with his stick."

The meeting with René Char, under a chestnut tree in Ménilmontant, was the best get-together during Heidegger's stay. We had a cheerful dinner that summer night, doing full justice to Frau Heidegger's cooking. The conversation unexpectedly shifted to Melville and *Billy Budd* which, as it turned out, both men greatly admired. Char, who is so quick to huddle in a corner when things do not look promising, felt completely at ease and spoke while Heidegger listened. I can still hear Char saying: "A poem has no memory. I am asked to go forward."

And, as we were seeing our guest home after midnight, Heidegger whispered to me in German: "What Char said is accurate."

219

Then he went on in French: "That is the difference between thought and poetry. Poetry moves forward, while thought is essentially memory, even if poetry remains its viaticum."

The visit to Braque's studio in Varengeville was no less intense and equally simple. Braque offhandedly served us his best white wine. We had started talking about Impressionism, and I said to Braque, somewhat heedlessly: "When you moved away from Impressionism—" Whereupon Braque sharply broke in: "It's not I who moved away from Impressionism. They're the ones who departed." Then, turning to his guests, he said amiably, while showing them the paintings he was working on: "Do stroll about, and look at everything." Braque's weakened state of health forced him to remain in an easy chair. It was only as we were leaving that he stood up, accompanying his visitor to the center of the lawn that stretched out in front of the studio. It was there that Beda Allemann snapped the highly revealing photograph that is reproduced on page 100 of Biemel's small book *Heidegger* (Reinbek bei Hamburg: Rowohlt, 1973). The snapshot tells us wordlessly: "Everything speaks renunciation into the same. Renunciation does not take. Renunciation gives. It gives the inexhaustible strength of simplicity."

Returning from Normandy, Heidegger asked me if we would be passing through the countryside of Gérard de Nerval. A short time earlier, when a small selection of the latter's work was published in France, Heidegger and I had read a few of Nerval's sonnets together and also the passage in *Sylvie* in which the hero and the girl, who are paying a morning visit to Sylvie's aunt in Othys, go up to the bedroom, from which they emerge, holding hands and dressed up as a married couple of the previous century. At their entrance,

> the aunt cried out as she turned around: "Oh, my children!"
> And she began weeping, then smiled through her tears.

Heidegger had said to me in French: "I never realized there was anything like this in French literature."

"Nerval's countryside is very near," I told him as we approached Paris. I then steered the car across the delicate landscapes of Valois, which are watered by the Thève, and we drove all the way to Ermenonville, where Rousseau spent his final days; there, one can still find

> the wise man's grave,
>   the splendid sage, who, surrounded by
>   murmuring poplars, slumbers on the isle.

Heidegger gazed silently at this secret domain, "half dreamt," says the poet, and where "the heart of France beat for over a thousand years." His communion was a profound understanding of what I, without explanations, let him divine—something that revealed itself to us in the peacefulness of the waning summer, as evoked by another utterance of Nerval's: "Ponds shone here and there through the red leaves, which stood out against the gloomy verdure of the pines."

Provence! In 1956 we met in Lyon, which Heidegger wanted to see and where the Rhône was still a river. After spending the night in a peaceful refuge, an old house isolated in a park (Heidegger called it a *Märchen*, a fairy tale), we went to Ponsas, near Tain l'Hermitage. This was the entranceway to Provence. The more intense light, the rocky outcroppings, the rugged landscape forth, Grignan, Vaison, the lunch on an outdoor terrace in Malaucène, the climb up the Ventoux, the crossing of the Lubéron, and, at last, Aix, where Cézanne's road lay ready for us, waiting to be discovered. Today it's an easy matter. But in those times you had to look hard for the very faint trail in order to follow it all the way to the stone balcony, which offers a sudden view of Mount Sainte Victoire. Two years later, when Heidegger was speaking on "Hegel and the Greeks" at the University of Aix, he told the audience crowding the vast amphitheater about the walk that he so greatly cherished: "Here, I found Cézanne's road, to which, from start to finish, my own road of thinking corresponds in its fashion."

However, Provence was also, indeed above all—after the travels in Greece—the period of the Thor seminars. The invitation was extended by René Char, who wanted personally to reveal the Provence of Avignon to Heidegger: The Thor conversations took place in utter privacy. "When I thought about it," said Char, "I felt it would be best if we kept to ourselves."

How right he was! Going all alone, we visited several members of Char's family as well as Eugen Fink and his wife, who, while traveling through France by way of Thor, joined us for lunch at the Chasselas. In the late afternoons, we would often visit Madame Mathieu at her home, in the midst of a domain of fruit trees; Madame Mathieu was the epitome of the countryside, its discreet generosity. One of our favorite hiking routes led up to her cabin in Rebanqué; the vista beyond its terrace is dominated by a Delphic massif. Nowhere was Greece any closer to us. From the terrace, the view extended across the olive trees on the terraced slopes descending toward the plain of Vaucluse. We knew that the Rhône was flowing in the distance, still invisible. Under the eyes of the gods, who were also present, we remained there—as Madame Mathieu put it, "all the way to the stars." One day, we were watching her as she strolled along in her antiquated costume, crossing the fields, walking like someone who knows the road even when it seems to fade out. "Hera!" Heidegger said to me. It was across the proximity that distance was suddenly manifested, giving sense to Goethe's utterance before the original statute of man: "The purpose and striving of the Greeks is to make human beings divine, not make divinity human. This is theomorphism and not anthropomorphism."

Heidegger cherished those images of France just as he remains present in the memories of his hosts. He would often ask me to give him the name of the restaurant where we had lunched when returning from Normandy, the restaurant nestling in the park through which the Epte flows; or the name of the château where we had spent the night one year later just before reaching Provence. And whenever I see Henry Mathieu, we conjure up the time we visited his mother in her home and also at Rebanqué—as captured in a photograph that shows her under her arbor, offering Heidegger a bunch of local grapes.

René Char is at the center of those meetings: as the Other in a dialogue in which poetry and thought correspond most intimately, albeit on mountains with separate peaks; and as the Friend that he was from the very start. One night, as we were leaving a restaurant in Gordes, to which Char had invited us, Heidegger said somewhat wistfully: "One never spends an evening like this in Germany." To which Char instantly replied: "Nor do we spend such evenings in France when you are not here."

Words in Memory of Martin Heidegger from the Academy of the Arts in Berlin

WALTER JENS

M ARTIN HEIDEGGER, a human being and his contradictions: a scholar who knew the history of philosophy from Thales to Husserl, from Duns Scotus to Rickert like no other and who still, although not quite contemptuous, thought "science" was the profession of the laborers and not of the masters. Following in Nietzsche's footsteps, he thought science was *only* science, not philosophy, not to speak of thinking and poetry.

Heidegger: a man who lectured on the most subtle problems of scholastic philosophy in such a way that his listeners could believe that the leader of a medieval disputation was standing before them, and who at the same time declared philosophical positivism to be "incompatible with the matter of thinking."

Heidegger: an artist of thinking who had two languages in which to make himself understood, the Greek of the pre-Socratics and the Latin of scholasticism. He invented a third, highly artificial language for himself: a German that bordered on image and concept. In between poetry and theology, he tried to name a Being with the

Source: Erinnerung an Martin Heidegger. *ed. Günther Neske (Pfullingen: Neske, 1977), pp. 149–153.*

help of this language. This Being could no longer be grasped with a set formula, but instead could only be circumscribed, hinted at, and thus evoked in constantly new attempts. As a "clearing," as "unconcealedness," as the "coming toward," as the "only matter."

Martin Heidegger: a philosopher who never denied his provincial background in his attire, his gestures, and his language; he denied neither his dialect nor that relationship to his home that Ernst Bloch describes with the code "Gothic chamber." Yet he is (the history of the effect of his philosophy proves it) the most far-reaching German philosopher of the twentieth century: not *despite* but *because of* his individuality in adapting to the most varied aspects.

A man, once again, and his contradictions: strict adherence to defined terms lies, almost directly, next to what is vague and associative, more whispered than formulated. If axiom follows axiom in a Cartesian manner in one place, elsewhere a systematic explanation of developed theories is avoided from the start. Contradictions everywhere! Scholastic quibbling about words—games with glass pearls by the theologian from Messkirch!—and a form of etymologizing that frequently loses itself in arbitrariness. The sharpest operations of thought and insecure incantations supplement each other in this work. But as contradictory, strange, and confusing as this gigantic work may seem (there appear to be worlds between the postdoctoral thesis on *Duns Scotus' Doctrine of Categories and Theory of Meaning* and the rectorial address at the University of Freiburg, between the precise description of the existing *Dasein* in *Being and Time* and the evocation of the lightening Being in his later work) and as diverse as are the attempts to find a language for something no longer nameable, something that has fallen into oblivion during the history of Western metaphysics: Being in its unconcealedness. . . . it must still be emphasized that Heidegger's work, despite all its contradictions, is self-contained and unified.

Between *Being and Time* and the later work, the main accent may have shifted from the question of the subject to the question of the object, from the existence of human *Dasein* to the destiny of Being that makes existence possible at all. The discrepancy between what is, the world, and human beings and the absolute Being may have enlarged to become, as Karl Löwith has shown, pure opposition in his later work: Being "is" not, it lets itself. . . . All of this does nothing to change the fact that, when seen from a distance, Heidegger's philosophy appears at once uniform and consistent if one realizes that he, however different his *answers* are, has always asked the same question: What characterizes the relationship between what is, which we transcend, and Being, without which we would not be, between the ontological that belongs to the realm of what is actual and derived and the ontic, which belongs to the realm of what is real and thus true?

A consistent path—not dissimilar to the path of his great opposite Ernst Bloch. From theology via the interpretation of the world back to theology. Johann Peter Hebel and the lift into the universe. Radicality of thinking; the authentic language; the attempt to find, here thus and there thus, a *tertium comparationis* between poetry and thinking. The reverence for art and the disdain for positivistic play with the matter at hand. Indeed, there are grounds for comparison—and also contrast. To dream of the "warm stream" of fascism the way Heidegger did, with the necessary amendments, in his Freiburg rectorial address, would have certainly been the last thing that would have occurred to an Ernst Bloch, despite all of his errors. But still the parallels between their lives, worthy of being described by a Plutarch, reach farther than might seem at first glance. How quickly, on this side and that side political misjudgments were revised, naturally and without sentimentality. When Heidegger refused the appointment in Berlin in the fall of 1933, the die was cast. Anyone who does not want to admit this denounces a man who had the courage (a courage that others, almost as famous as he, did not have) to keep the following statement in *Being and Time* throughout the entire rule of fascism:

> The following investigation would not have been possible if the ground had not been prepared by Edmund Husserl, with whose *Logische Untersuchungen* phenomenology first emerged. . . . If the following has taken any steps forward in disclosing the "things themselves," the author must first of all thank E. Husserl, who by providing his own incisive personal guidance and by freely turning over his unpublished investigations, familiarized the author with the most diverse areas of phenemonological research during his student years in Freiburg."[1]

Hommage to Husserl, a bow to the ostracized man, repeated from edition to edition. This gesture, attesting his courage and character, acquits Heidegger, whose supposed political convictions are much maligned. It attests the unwavering nature of a man who did not make things easy for himself, neither as a philosopher nor as an academic teacher. I will never forget the magic, that mixture of sobriety and bold speculation, that became apparent as soon as he began to meditate on propositions by Heraclitus in Lecture Hall 1 at the University of Freiburg. He never casually improvised for a moment; everything down to the microphilological was always superbly prepared ... just as he was prepared for each point in seminars as well. Whoever wanted to protest had to do so in writing and was taken as seriously as someone of equal rank.

He demanded a lot, but he never for a moment flaunted his superiority. "Half like a king and half like a father," Grillparzer described Goethe, and that is the way Heidegger seemed to us young students in Freiburg at the time. I cannot imagine that there is anyone, not one person, who can say that his life has not been more serious, his thinking has not been more vital, his questions have not been more logically consistent after having worked with this man, this Alemannic Socrates (for that is the way he seemed to us in the seminars: not lecturing but questioning and probing). We learned from Martin Heidegger what it means to be approached by a matter and to set out on the path, accepting the risk that thinking, under the influence of the matter, might change on the way. "As it says in *Identity and Difference*, "It is therefore advisable to pay more attention to the path and less to the content."

Throughout his life, Martin Heidegger demonstrated how someone might think and speak in zones where no one had been before him. We thank him for that. Whatever we think of him, we are all his students—the students of a man who wanted to have these words inscribed on his gravestone: "He was born, worked, and died." But it should be added: Because he worked, the world was different after his death than before his birth.

Postscript
GÜNTHER NESKE

NOW THAT Hermann Niemeyer and Vittorio Klostermann have died, I am the last of the publishers who, together with Martin Heidegger, supervised the publication of his works over a period of decades. After the Chilean Victor Farías appeared on the scene, Martin Heidegger has once again become the focus of fierce discussion, and it was not surprising that I was asked by many different people to comment on this topic. I do it in my own way and have collected a number of documents that will be preserved for a biography to be written later. In what follows I mention several events that might be helpful in better understanding our topic and its context.

During a long walk one night through the completely empty streets of Frankfurt, Ernst Bloch and I talked about the publication of his collected works, something Ernst Bloch wanted to entrust to me. "Are you not at all afraid to entrust me with your work, when Heidegger was entangled in National Socialism by his assumption of the rectorate in 1933?"

"Not in the least," Bloch answered. "Heidegger was taken in by Hitler and I was taken in by Stalin."

Back again in Leipzig, Bloch asked for Minister of Culture Becher's[1] consent to publish his works in my publishing house. Becher declared himself not responsible to make such a decision. Bloch thereupon asked the Chairman of the Council of the State Ulbricht[2] for his permission. Ulbricht refused on the grounds that Neske was an "existentialist" publisher and was thus out of the question.

Ernst Bloch knew about the serious consequences of an episode that happened to me in June 1933 in Bethel near Bielefeld on the occasion of a so-called open evening in the apartment of the Old Testament scholar Wilhelm Vischer, my teacher at divinity school. My fellow student Reichl, one of the twelve invited students of theology, asked me what I thought of Hitler. Angry about this impertinent question, I answered: "Hitler is the devil's affair. The whole thing will end in the destruction of Germany." The following day I was questioned by the "honorary" NSDAP county leader, then the head doctor of the large hospital in Bielefeld, Dr. Löhr, and I admitted I had made the statement. Friedrich von Bodelschwingh asked me to leave the divinity school. I went to Tübingen and tried to work there without attracting attention, which I succeeded in doing for a while. Then Gau student leader Schumann found out about me, I received warnings from Stuttgart, and there was finally nothing left for me to do but to leave Germany.

I first went to Basel to study with Karl Barth, then became a tutor in a private home in Lugano, and later went to Rome to study ecclesiastical history at the Gregoriana.

Incidentally, it was symptomatic of the political situation at the beginning of 1933 that many important public figures, scientists, university teachers, writers, artists, and musicians saw Hitler's takeover of government as the rescuing change Germany needed. Large sections of the population thought of him as the savior of the nation. These circumstances have largely been forgotten. They all made it easy for Hitler. I could name many famous names from the time in addition to Heidegger, although some soon realized they had made a fundamental error.

The passage in the *Spiegel* interview in which Heidegger points out the essay by Spranger should also be understood in that context. The essay appeared with the title "March 1933" in the highly respected journal *Erziehung*, and it is worth looking at today, because it makes the heterogeneous circumstances of that destiny-determining time clear. Spranger soon recognized his error, temporarily gave up his professorship, distanced himself from the regime, and was arrested in 1944 because he belonged to the resistance.

Many years later, after the Second World War, I met Martin Buber in the apartment of the unforgettable editor Erna Krauss in Tübingen. I wanted to ask him to write a contribution to the *festschrift* for Martin Heidegger's seventieth birthday. Buber looked at me with concentration and asked which topic I would suggest for his contribution. "Perhaps you would be willing to write on the Hebrew verb הָיָה in our language *to be*?" I think the word יהוה, the word *God*, which comes from this root, is the most frightening word in the world: I was who I was, I am who I am, I will be who I will be. The dissolving of time in one word. And this word could not be spoken. Instead one reads אדני, *Lord*.

Martin Buber looked at me with friendliness and said: "You will get what you want."

In a letter from Jerusalem on 16 April 1959, Martin Buber wrote to me that he could not fulfill my request after all because his wife was very ill. All his time would be spent in caring for his wife. He asked me to understand this.

And another thing: Hitler had ordered that a new final edition of Nietzsche should be prepared. A committee of scholars, among them Martin Heidegger and Walter F. Otto, were commissioned to do the work. The meetings of the committee took place in the Nietzsche Archive in Weimar. One day, Dr. Goebbels conveyed on behalf of Hitler that all the passages in Nietzsche's work in which Nietzsche expresses contempt for antisemitism had to be eliminated. As I know, Heidegger was then afraid that there would be a renewed (political) intrusion into the work and decided to end his collaboration at that time.

In March 1988, I turned to the general director of the German library in Leipzig with the inquiry whether papers documenting these events still existed in Weimar. I received from the Goethe and Schiller Archive in Weimar, which also holds the files of the former Nietzsche Archive, a letter written on 10 May 1988. It said: "According to our knowledge of the material we have here, a resignation from the academic committee can only be documented for Heidegger. It took place at the end of 1942 without real reasons being given."

Heidegger—Bloch—Spranger: Are we capable of doing justice to the dialogue between power and spirit? Or are we only victims of the spirit of the times?

Pfullingen, 14 September 1988   Günther Neske

APPENDICES

Comments by Martin Heidegger's son and executor

On the Edition of the Interview Published on 31 May 1976 in Der Spiegel.

DR. HERMANN HEIDEGGER

On 31 May 1976 *Der Spiegel* reported in a memo, not quite accurately, on the history of the interview, which appeared in the same edition. The history actually was as follows: In a first public response, Martin Heidegger wrote a letter to *Der Spiegel*[1] in reaction to untruthful statements about him written in the *Spiegel* essay "Heidegger—Midnight of a world's night." At the end of February 1966 Erhart Kästner, who had contacts with editors of *Der Spiegel*, suggested to them that they interview Martin Heidegger. On hearing Kästner's suggestion, Martin Heidegger himself manifested an unambigous resistance: "But I will under no circumstances agree to a *Spiegel* interview that is in any way organized."[2] On 23 March 1966 Rudolf Augstein, prompted by Kästner, wrote a two-page, empathetic letter to Heidegger and offered to interview him. Only after Heidegger received encouragement from Kästner and other friends and, above all, Augstein's letter, did he agree to such a conversation.

The *Spiegel* interview took place in Martin Heidegger's house in Freiburg-Zähringen on the Rötebuck on 23 September 1966. Martin Heidegger, Rudolf Augstein, Georg Wolff, Heinrich Wiegand Petzet, the stenographer Steinbrecher, a technician, and the photographer Digne Meller Marcovicz were the participants.

It had been previously agreed that the transcript of the tape recording would be linguistically and factually revised and supplemented by Martin Heidegger as well as by the *Spiegel* editors. Some of the wording of the conversation, which had remained unchanged in Martin Heidegger's first revision, was only edited and improved by the *Spiegel* in their second revision and was left and accepted by Martin Heidegger in the "second *Spiegel* version."

After Heidegger had revised and refined his own verbal responses, *Der Spiegel* reformulated some of the questions Rudolf Augstein had posed during the interview, some were moved to different places, and some new questions were squeezed in. Heidegger first read these changes in the "second *Spiegel* version." But *Der Spiegel* also edited Heidegger's revised text without making it clear to Martin Heidegger which spots had been edited when they sent him the "second *Spiegel* version." It is unclear, and cannot be clarified any more, whether Martin Heidegger noticed the spots in his text that had been changed by the *Spiegel* in the "second *Spiegel* version." In the "second *Spiegel* version," Heidegger's answers are therefore sometimes given to questions that were originally formulated differently. Some of the linguistic reformulations of Heidegger's text made by *Der Spiegel* in the "second *Spiegel* version" were undoubtedly editorial improvements and were accepted by Martin Heidegger through his "agreed" at the end of the whole manuscript, and these I have kept in the version presented here. Heidegger's corrections of the text that were left out by *Der Spiegel* in the "second *Spiegel* version" were added again. A comparison between the first revision by Georg Wolff and the first revision by Martin Heidegger shows that often new formulations were searched for and statements were crossed out at the same points, and that Heidegger accepted but also rejected Wolff's suggestions.

Quite a few times, therefore, statements and questions made by *Der Spiegel* were reformulated, sometimes even posed differently, after Heidegger's revision. Heidegger's answers, however, remained the way they had been given to the originally posed *Spiegel* questions, so that, even in the version signed by Heidegger, his answers are given several times to questions that were no longer published. He apparently concentrated on his own text during his last check and did not even consider that, despite the fact that *Der Spiegel* had concluded its major editing, questions might have been changed and new ones squeezed in.

Martin Heidegger apparently received the "second *Spiegel* version," in which, as previously mentioned, not all of his supplements were included, for final editing without the transcript of the tape recording in the version he had corrected. Heidegger had not written down his supplements and improvements on the copy of the transcript remaining with him. After he made a few supplementary corrections, Martin Heidegger's signed the "second *Spiegel* version" with his final "agreed" on 28 March 1967.

A careful comparison with the *printed version* published in 1976 revealed that *Der Spiegel* had later, without Heidegger's knowledge, added the subtitles, squeezed in questions, changed the *Spiegel* text linguistically, and left out more sentences. On the other hand, the *Spiegel* editors also crossed out, changed, and in minor ways improved Martin Heidegger's sentences linguistically twice, without Heidegger's knowledge.

The text that is presented here is the text that Martin Heidegger accepted for printing with his signature. The changes and supplements made later by the *Spiegel* editors were changed back again or crossed out. All Heidegger's texts that had been crossed out by *Der Spiegel* after Heidegger's final editing and without his knowledge were added again. The texts Martin Heidegger had added in handwriting in his first revision but had been silently left out of the second version by *Der Spiegel* were added again in the appropriate places. The subtitles, which were inserted later by the *Spiegel* editors and which Martin Heidegger did not know about, were taken away.

Mistakes Martin Heidegger had overlooked during his final editing were corrected. In his statement about Husserl's lecture in Berlin, Heidegger, on the basis of a report in the *Voss'sche Zeitung* that described a "sort of sports palace atmosphere," had been mistaken about the place of the event and the first name of the reporter Mühsam.[3] These two sentences were corrected by me to correspond to the facts.

Martin Heidegger was never informed of the final editing done later by the *Spiegel*, so that he never found out which changes were still made, which subtitles were given to the interview, and which pictures were incorporated into the text with which captions.

Linguistic changes that were made later by *Der Spiegel* and do not influence the content were kept. All the changes in content—supplements, deletions, other sentences—made after Heidegger's final editing were brought back to the state they were in when Martin Heidegger signed his name.

Letter to
Martin Heidegger
23 August 1933
KARL JASPERS

Dear Heidegger,   Heidelberg, 23 August 1933

Thank you for your rectorial address. I was glad to become acquainted with the authentic version after having read about it in the newspaper. The fact that you start out from the ancient Greeks moved me again as a new and, at the same time, self-evident truth. You agree with Nietzsche in that. The difference is that one can hope that you will be able to philosophically interpretively realize what you say. Your address has a believable substance. I am not speaking of style and density, which make this address, of all the documents of a present academic will, the only one up to now that will endure. My trust in your philosophy, which has grown in

Editorial Note. In the rest of the letter, which will only be completely printed in the publication of the correspondence between Jaspers and Heidegger that is at present being prepared by Hans Saner and Walter Biemel, Jaspers writes about the reform of medical studies and the new university constitution. It needed, he wrote, a correction or addition if a "hive of intrigue" dependent on coincidence was to be avoided. The letter closes with an invitation to Heidegger for October and a note added in handwriting asking whether Heidegger's rafting trip with his son had been successful.

strength since the spring and our conversations then, is not disturbed by the characteristics of this address that are in keeping with the times, by something in it that seems a little forced to me, or by sentences that appear to me to have a hollow sound. All in all, I am just glad that someone can speak that way, that someone can touch genuine limits and origins.

Letter to Gerd Tellenbach

5 June 1949

KARL JASPERS

To the Rector of the University of Freiburg
Herr Professor Dr. Tellenbach
Magnificence,[1]   Basel, 5 June 1949

Through his achievements, Professor Martin Heidegger is recognized throughout the entire world as one of the most important contemporary philosophers. There is no one in Germany who can surpass him. His philosophizing, almost concealed, in touch with the deepest questions, and only indirectly discernible in his writings, makes him a perhaps unique figure today, in a world that is lacking in philosophy.

It is a duty that arises from the affirmation of intellectual status and intellectual ability for Europe and for Germany to ensure that a man like Heidegger can continue his work in peace and can print it.

This is only guaranteed if Heidegger is granted the status of professor emeritus. With it, he gains the right, not the obligation, to give lectures. He would then also have influence again as a teacher. I think this is acceptable and even desirable. In my report in 1945, I

Source: *Letter 5 June 1949 to Gerd Tellenbach, then rector of the University of Freiburg. First publication; with the kind permission of Jaspers' executor, Hans Saner.*

expressed the principle that one would have to temporarily depart from the idea of the university in which everyone of intellectual status, even if they are foreign to the university's liberality, should be able to have influence. The education of the youth, its critical thinking weakened by National Socialism, demanded that one did not expose them right away to all the possibilities of uncritical thinking. Following the development in Germany up to now, I can no longer keep this principle. As I suggested in my report, the possibility of Heidegger's reinstatement should be examined after a few years. The time seems ripe to me. The German university can, in my opinion, no longer leave Heidegger on the outside.

I therefore very warmly support the proposal to grant Heidegger the rights of an emeritus professor.

Yours very respectfully,
Karl Jaspers

On the Origin of the Work of Art[1]

HANS BARTH

On a lecture given by Martin Heidegger
Neue Zürcher Zeitung, *20 January 1936*

MUCH WATER HAS FLOWED down the Rhine since Heidegger divulged new results of his philosophical endeavors to a broader public. The rectorial address on "The Self-Assertion of the German University" given in 1933 cannot, to the best of my knowledge, be judged as an essential expression of his spirit. For that it is too poor. Many must therefore have awaited with suspense the lecture, organized by the student body, that he delivered at the University of Zürich on 17 January. We probably have to consider it a great honor that Heidegger would speak here, in a democratic state; for a time at least, he was thought to be one of the philosophical spokesmen for the new Germany. But still, many remember that Heidegger dedicated *Being and Time* in "admiration and friendship" to the Jew Edmund Husserl and that he eternally connected his interpretation of Kant with the memory of the half-Jewish Max Scheler. The one in 1927, the other in 1929. As a rule, human beings are not heroes—not even the philosophers, although there are exceptions. Therefore it can hardly be demanded that someone swim against the tide. Only a certain obligation to one's own past will heighten the standing of philosophy, which is not only knowing but was once also wisdom.

Anyone who heard Heidegger's lecture (and numerous, attentive, and influential listeners were gathered there) will hardly expect that I reproduce its content in Heidegger's own language. This language may be greatly admired by poets; often it is violent, often playful, feigning depths where a sober description of the findings would be more desirable. It is obvious that inaccuracies may occur in any rendition. In this case, it is not only the translator who is to blame. I cannot presume to reproduce even a considerable fraction of this complex and associative lecture.

Works of art are strewn throughout the world. They are products of an artist. But being-produced is not yet work-being. For the work should rest within itself. Once created, it has a life independent of its creator; indeed the work seems indifferent to its artist. Artworks are not because artists have produced them, but because artworks are possible, they may be produced. The scientific, conservational, and marketing occupation with artworks is the art industry, which only comprehends and judges the artwork as object-being. Philosophy, however, asks about the essence of the artwork. In this question, a circular movement characteristic of all philosophy immediately reveals itself. This circular movement is virtually the criterion to ascertain whether we are dealing with a philosophical question. That about which we are asking must already be answered in some way. What we are looking for we must already have. Every determination of the features of artworks presupposes that we have always already singled out artworks from the abundance of what there is. The question on the artwork is the question on the ground that makes the artwork possible.

Artworks are displayed, "set up." Every setting up is a consecration, in which what is holy in the artwork is revealed, and a praising. What does an artwork set up in its work-being? It reveals a world, a world is set up, a world that is not the sum of all countable things that we deal with in everyday life but means "the joint that prevails over our *Dasein* and to which everything that has been ordered upon us submits" and that we must decide upon. The artwork produces, "sets forth," of itself. What does it set forth? The work sets the earth up and forth. What is concealed is revealed in it. Concealedness appears at one with openness. What is revealed is the truth. The artwork is a way in which truth "happens," like the act of the creator of the state and the act of the philosopher are other ways of the revealing of truth. As a setting-into-work of truth, the artwork is an origin and thus a beginning. The beginning is unmediated. The end and thus the ascent or descent are already concealed in the beginning. The work of art is never timely. Rather it is always ahead of the time and is thus the measure of time. The basic relation to the artwork is a knowing, knowing about the truth.

At the end, Heidegger refers to a wonderful, sharp conclusion from Hegel's *Aesthetics*, in which the thought is expressed that an aesthetics only emerges at the end of an epoch's great art. The question whether such an end is applicable to the West remains unanswered, even though Hölderlin spoke the incomparably beautiful words:

"Schwer verlässt was nahe dem Urprung wohnet, den Ort."
"Reluctantly that which dwells near its origin departs."[2]

Heidegger Once Again

[*Neue Zürcher Zeitung,* 23 January 1936]

EMIL STAIGER

T HE COMMENTS ON Martin Heidegger's lecture (see No. 105) have aroused the wrath of a scholar of German. In the following, we give this Heidegger enthusiast a chance to speak. We only regret that Dr. Emil Staiger did not give an argumentative justification of Heidegger but was content to spiritedly praise the philosopher. Herr Staiger accuses the reporter of a lack of objectivity, because he had started his account with a "political 'wanted' poster." That was done, however, intentionally; it will not do to divide the philosophical and the human, thinking and being, by abysses. Herr Staiger agrees with me that a reproduction of such a lecture cannot be dealt with "journalistically" at all. But whether placing Heidegger directly next to Hegel, Kant, Aristotle, and Heraclitus, as Herr Staiger quite seriously does, is not an extremely "journalistic" evaluation, is a question I would like to hand over to the interested reader and expert to decide. Light of heart, I will leave the literary historian the responsibility for this virtually colossal estimation of Heidegger.

A criticism like the one Heidegger's lecture received from bth. [Hans Barth] cannot remain uncontradicted. Its lack of objectivity is blatantly obvious. bth. starts his account with a political "wanted" poster, which assures him the applause of his audience.

245

He then finds fault with Heidegger's language and finally compiles several sentences he had jotted down during the lecture. Meanwhile bth. presumes that he cannot "reproduce even a considerable fraction of the lecture." And indeed, such a task is completely impossible to deal with journalistically. One wonders if it would not have been better to remain silent or to just point out the external circumstances of the lecture and to thank the student body that made it possible and organized it.

It is thoroughly muddled to place Heidegger's political views in the foreground the way bth. does, as muddled as if one wanted to open an assessment of the *Critique of Pure Reason* with a comment on Kant's views on the French Revolution. Admittedly, if one does not see the essential problem of Heidegger's philosophy at all, the problem "Being and time" in which the "and" is questioned, then one would have to count him among the greats of the day and measure and judge him from the perspective of the day. But Heidegger does not stand next to Oswald Spengler or Tillich, to name only two philosophers from opposite camps; Heidegger stands next to Hegel, next to Kant, Aristotle, and Heraclitus. And once that is recognized, one will still always regret that Heidegger ever got himself involved in the day—the way it is always tragic when the spheres are confused—but one will not lose one's admiration for him, as little as one loses reverence for the *Phenomenology of Spirit* in picturing the Prussian reactionary.

It should not be said that the situation of science is so endangered that it may no longer separate the practical and the theoretical. Certainly we, only poor bondsmen laboring in its vineyards, would be better off not to lose touch with the day and its problems. We would do better to keep ourselves away from the abstract solitariness of the scholar's chamber, which can easily relax weaker spirits. But if someone, like Heidegger, is such a "friend of what is essential, simple, and constant," "in which 'friendship' alone, the turning toward what is can take place, and from which turning the question on the concept of Being—the basic question of philosophy—emerges" (*Kant and the Problem of Metaphysics*), then to take offense at the historical contingency of a thinking is truly to stare at the shadow on the first step and not to see the white temple that rises above it into the timeless. Let us be thankful that we can live as contemporaries of a thinker who will probably appear more essential to later generations than much that excites us today.

The reprimand bth. thought was necessary directed itself against

Heidegger's language. "This language may be greatly admired by poets; often it is violent, often playful, feigning depths where a sober description of the findings would be more desirable." We admire this language without being poets, admire it precisely as a scientific language and because it is *not* everything that bth. claims it is. Violent? We call it primordial, the way otherwise in German philosophy only Hegel's language is primordial, the way otherwise no one, including all the poets, speaks primordially in the German tongue today. Playful? We call it masterful, a regal handling, whose development we have the great fortune to be able to follow in a sequence from Heidegger's early writings to this lecture in Zurich. And in such primordial masterfulness, this language is sober the way everything genuine, the philosophically genuine as well as the poetically genuine, is sober. It is the language of a disclosed [*entschlossen*] *Dasein*, a *Dasein* that sees the things themselves and nothing else. Only someone who, admittedly like most of those who talk about Heidegger, sees wisdom's final solution in the chapters that are on "anxiety," on "one," and on "conscience" and is unaware of the question on time (and it is only in approaching this question that these subjects are touched upon at all) can claim that this language feigns depths. Anyone who bears the last pages of *Being and Time* and the piece *The Essence of Reasons* in mind has to realize that every expression that Heidegger used is the only one out of the wealth of the German language that holds the necessary dialectic tension (I will refer here only to "disputing the strife" [*Bestreiten des Streites*], which means both "denying" and "carrying out" the strife), and that everything had its place, the way everything has its place in a Bach fugue, as if it had been there for an eternity.

But who realizes that today? Heidegger says in *Being and Time*: "Distantiality, averageness, and leveling down, as ways of being for the 'they,' constitute what we know as 'publicness' [*die Öffentlichkeit*]. Publicness proximally controls every way in which the world and *Dasein* get interpreted, and it is always right—not because there is some distinctive and primary relationship-of-Being in which it is related to 'things,' or because it avails itself of some transparency on the part of *Dasein* which it has explicitly appropriated, but because it is insensitive to every difference of level and genuineness . . ."[1]

Emil Staiger

Letter to Günther Neske

18 August 1988

EBERHARD JÜNGEL

Dear Herr Neske,

Your question why I dedicated my study entitled "Metaphoric Truth," which appeared in a special issue—done together with Paul Ricouer—of the journal *Evangelische Theologie* in 1974, to Martin Heidegger arrived yesterday and surprised me like a lightning bolt out of the blue. To answer that question would be to retrospectively comment on a past decision that speaks for itself. And, for good reason, Ernst Jünger warns that whoever comments on himself sinks beneath his own level. But there are more important reasons that cause me not to evade your question. I will just have to bravely endure the danger of sinking beneath my own level.

The external cause for the dedication was a visit to Heidegger. It was an intensive encounter, in which concentrated attention and liberating casualness could be experienced as a seamless whole. It ended with a reflection on the connection between thinking and thanks. "And God," I had asked, "should we not also *think* God?" Heidegger answered: "God is what is most worthy of thought, but here language fails." I contradicted him. He accepted my contradiction, knowing that theology cannot honor the mystery entrusted to it by remaining silent. But it was more important to me that he apparently did not want to discredit the thesis of God as what is most worthy of thought by mentioning some philosophical theology or other.

Again and again when I studied Heideggerian texts as a student (and at that time it was not easy to get Heidegger's works in the German Democratic Republic at all) I experienced a concentration that did not tire me but rather made me wide awake, a concentration that I experienced again in my encounter with him. It probably put one into such a state of unusual alertness because this gathering of thoughts taught one to rediscover things one had taken for granted and that were all too familiar in a completely new way. One could learn how to see in the school of his thinking. What had been thought, both one's own thoughts and thoughts of tradition, was "destroyed" in order to expose *what is to be thought*. And still tradition's long-used paths of thinking were taken seriously as paths. Only if one is under way oneself will one be able to understand these paths creatively and appreciate them critically. Tallying results was foreign to this thinking. It remained (understandably enough, as a question on a Being that is not identical with anything that is) without a result and yet was, in its resultlessness, more effective and beneficial for theology than all contemporary philosophy. The twentieth century's pathos of reality was opposed by a thinking that had no fear of the fear of nothing. In concerning myself with it, I experienced a radical alienation from everything that had a claim to reality through the possibilities that emerge from a more primordial nearness to what is. Heidegger set off the primacy of possibility—not achievable through human actions—over the reality of everyday phenomena against the overpowering Aristotelean tradition. The intensity with which this thinker did this let at least some of the primordial, fresh colors of creation light up here and there in the midst of all the murkiness. For me, Heidegger was and is the *thinker of what is possible*. That is why I dedicated that study to him in 1974. In it, I had tried to consider the primacy of the possible in language using what I called metaphorical truth and thus to call attention to the peculiarity of religious speech, which awards what is real with a foreign possibility (*potentia aliena*) to which it is not entitled, but which God has intended for it and which it will thus receive.

1974: That was a time when Heidegger was, as a rule, only struggled with for the purpose of political or quasi-political demonstration at German universities—even at their theological faculties, where previously people had "Heideggered" in an unbearable fashion. As a philosopher of hope, Ernst Bloch, looking deep into the world, was, in his own way, a thinker of or rather a conjurer of the possible. He dominated more than the scene in Tübingen. Eloquently. Heidegger's thinking, however, was presented along the lines of Karl Löwith's critique, but without its objective differentiation and personal dignity. It was seen to necessarily end—and perish—in the National Socialist option, and thus it was dismissed. It is one thing that I, as a student of Karl Barth, the "father of the Confessional Church," and the incorruptible Rudolf Bultmann, consider Heidegger's political (or was it, which would not make matters at all better, an extremely apolitical?) engagement for National Socialism not worth defending. I had hoped that, after 1945, he would make a clearer acknowledgement of his own failure than the statement, which could be read autobiographically: "He who thinks greatly must err greatly."[1] But must one then be blind or even—in all-too-bourgeois obedience to the dictate of "intellectual" fashion—pretend to be blind to the obvious fertility of Heidegger's thinking? Even Jürgen Habermas has called the early products of this thinking "the most important philosophical event since Hegel's *Phenomenology*."

Without ever being seduced into a "mixophilosophicotheologia" (as Abraham Calov called it) by Heidegger's texts, I had experiences with his thinking that encouraged me and made it possible for me to discuss theology really *theologically*; that is, starting from its ground. In doing so, I tried to be serious theologically with the reference that "thinking does not overcome metaphysics by climbing still higher, surmounting it, transcending it somehow or other; thinking overcomes metaphysics by climbing back down into the nearness of the nearest . . . The descent leads to the poverty of the ek-sistence of *homo humanus*."[2]

In the *neue hefte für philosophie*,[3] I tried to show that the fertility of Martin Heidegger's thinking is also proved by the criticism that it provokes against itself. Only a thinking whose *compelling* sovereignity is equally a *liberating* sovereignity can provoke counter-reflections. And that is what I wanted to gratefully attest in my dedication in a time when freedom was often discussed but the liberating strength of thinking was only seldom experienced. Freedom itself is compelling in gratitude.

So much, Herr Neske, as an answer to your lightning bolt from the blue, which, you can see, did not strike me but did bring an old decision back into the light again.

Sincerely yours,
E. Jüngel

A Greeting to the Symposium in Beirut in November 1974

MARTIN HEIDEGGER

LET ME FIRST thank you for this symposium held in honor of my eighty-fifth birthday. My special thanks is owed to all the gentlemen who have taken on important topics for the discussion of my thinking and will thus direct the participants of the symposium toward clarifying and critical conversations.

The age of technological-industrial civilization holds a steadily increasing danger, whose foundations are thought about all too little: The truth that speaks from the fundamental revitalizing effect of poetry, the arts, and of reflective thinking can no longer be experienced. These realms have been falsified to become mere instruments of the civilization industry. The language that rests in them disappears in the fleetingness of the rapid flow of information, which lacks the strength to shape formatively and enduringly.

That is why a thinking is necessary that resolutely persists in discussing the old fundamental questions in a more *questioning* manner, the questions that prevail over the disquiet of mortals' stay in the world continually anew.

This urgent confrontation with metaphysics is not old-fashioned polemics against its teachings about God, the world, and human beings; rather, it first brings the basic ontological features of the technological-scientific world civilization into the view of a reflective thinking.

Above all there is *one* thing that should be recognized in its entire scope. What is characteristic of modern technology, which will, historically calculated, later become apparent, is not a consequence, let alone an application, of modern science; rather, the subject matter of this science has already been determined by the essence of modern technology, which still, for the time being, conceals itself. This, in turn, rests on a unique manner in which Being prevails over what is in the industrial age.

Presumably modern world civilization is executing the transition to the final phase of the ephochal destiny of Being in the sense of a determination of Being as the unconditional orderability [*Bestellbarkeit*] of what is, including being human.

It is therefore necessary first to inquire about the origin of this danger and then to perceive its scope. But this demands that the question of what is characteristic of Being as such be asked. On this path of thinking, contemporary humans could perhaps be brought before a higher possibility of *Dasein.* This is a possibility that they cannot prepare themselves, but that will also not be granted to them by the benevolence of Being without the action of their questioning thinking.

The questioning thinking of Being is in itself an action that abandons what is most characteristic of it, if it, understood as mere theory, delivers itself all too quickly to an unthought practice and the groundless machinations of organization and institution.

Martin Heidegger

Dedications

DEDICATIONS ARE, as a rule, expressions of gratitude and close personal ties. They moreover reveal, especially in philosophical publications, the school or tradition of thinking from which an author comes or to which he feels committed. This is true of Heidegger's dedication in his fundamental book *Being and Time* to his teacher and "fatherly friend" Edmund Husserl; such was Heidegger's usual form of address in his letters to Husserl (see p. 255 in this volume). *Being and Time* was, in addition, originally published in the organ of the phenomenological movement *Jahrbuch für Philosophie und phänomenologische Forschung* (vol. 8; Halle: Niemeyer, 1927) that was edited by Husserl. In this same journal Husserl's *Ideen zu einer reinen Phänomenologie und phänomenologischen Philosophie* (vol. 1, 1913) and Scheler's *Der Formalismus in der Ethik und die materiale Wertethik* (vol. 1, 1913, and vol. 2., 1916) had previously been published. *Being and Time* was also presented as a separate edition in the same year, 1927. The dedication, nothing extraordinary in and of itself, attracted special attention because it disappeared from the book for a short time (more precisely, only in a single edition, the fifth edition printed in the year 1941). The dedication reappeared in the sixth edition in 1949, printed by the publishing house Niemeyer, which had moved in the meantime in exile, so to speak, from Halle to Tübingen.

The omission of the dedication was often quickly interpreted to be an expression of Heidegger's National Socialist convictions, a conscious ideological dissociation from his Jewish teacher. Heidegger himself very clearly dismissed this misrepresentation two times: once in the concluding comments to his collection *Unterwegs zur Sprache*[1] and then in the *Spiegel* interview given in

1966 and published in 1976 (see this volume p. 41). There Heidegger explains that the dedication was omitted at the proposal and wish of his publisher Hermann Niemeyer so that a possible ban of the book might be counteracted.

That Heidegger is not retrospectively glossing things over or even distorting them is apparent from two facts. On the one hand, the dedication was kept in the fourth edition in 1935, one year after Heidegger's controversial rectorate, and, on the other, the fifth edition, like all the previous and later editions, contained the footnote to page 38:

> If the following has taken any steps forward in disclosing the "things themselves," the author must first of all thank E. Husserl, who, by providing his own incisive personal guidance and by freely turning over his unpublished investigations, familiarized the author with the most diverse areas of phenomenological research during his student years in Freiburg.[2]

In this connection, Heidegger's dedication of his book *Kant und das Problem der Metaphysik*[3] to the half-Jewish Max Scheler is also noteworthy.

Rudolf Bultmann's dedication of his collected essays with the title *Glauben und Verstehen* to Heidegger, a dedication Bultmann expressly kept in the second edition,[4] should also be mentioned: "This book remains dedicated to MARTIN HEIDEGGER in grateful memory of our time together in Marburg."

NOTES

Notes on Text

Introduction

1. Martin Heidegger, *Existence and Being*, intro. Werner Brock (Chicago: Regnery, 1949). The collection includes "Hölderlin and the Essence of Poetry," "Remembrance of the Poet," "On the Essence of Truth," "What is Metaphysics?," and a summary of *Being and Time.*

2. Richard Rorty, "Taking Philosophy Seriously," *The New Republic*, 11 April 1988, p. 31.

3. Tom Rockmore and Joseph Margolis in their foreword to Victor Farías, *Heidegger and Nazism*, trans. Paul Burrell, Dominic Di Bernardi, and Gabriel R. Ricci (Philadelphia: Temple University Press, 1989), p. ix.

4. Farías, *Heidegger and Nazism*, p. 84.

5. Alfred de Towarnicki, "Visite à Martin Heidegger," *Les Temps Modernes*, 1945/46.

6. Victor Farías, *Heidegger and Nazism*, p. 167. See also the German edition of the book, *Heidegger und der Nationalsozialismus*, trans. Klaus Laermann (Frankfurt: Fischer, 1989), p. 232, for a fuller discussion.

7. *Heidegger and Nazism*, pp. 192–205.

8. Krieck was a former grammar school teacher whose fortunes rose with those of the Party; in 1933 he was appointed professor and a few months later rector in Frankfurt, only to leave Frankfurt in 1934 for the more prestigious Heidelberg.

9. *Heidegger and Nazism*, pp. 168–169. See also Ott, *Martin Heidegger. Unterwegs zu seiner Biographie* (Frankfurt/New York: Campus, 1988), p. 244, and "Facts and Thoughts," p. 15 below.

10. *Heidegger and Nazism*, p. 205–206.

11. *Ibid.*, pp. 207–209.

12. See especially Ott, pp. 45–119.

13. See Emil Kettering, "Heidegger und die Politik: Stationen einer Diskussion" (Tübingen: Neske, 1988), pp. 129–141, trans. this volume, p. 127.

14. Karl Löwith, "Les implications politiques de la philosophie de l'existence chez Heidegger," *Les Temps Modernes*, vol. II, 1946: pp. 348.

15. Alfons de Waelhens, "La philosophie de Heidegger et le nazisme," *Les Temps Modernes*, vol. IV, 1947/48: pp. 115–127, and Eric Weil, "Le cas Heidegger," *ibid.*, pp. 128–138. See also Löwith, "Réponse a A. de Waelhens, "*ibid.*, pp. 370–373, and de Waelhens, "Réponse a cette réponse," *ibid.*, pp. 374–377.

16. See Jürgen Habermas, "Mit Heidegger gegen Heidegger denken. Zur Veröffentlichung von Vorlesungen aus dem Jahre 1935," *Philosophisch-politische Profile* (Frankfurt: Suhrkamp, 1971), pp. 67–75. Also "Heidegger—Werk und Weltanschauung," his introduction to the German edition of Farías, *Heidegger und der Nationalsozialismus*, pp. 30–32.

17. *Einführung in die Metaphysik* (Tübingen: Niemeyer, 1953), p. 152.

18. "Facts and Thoughts," below, p. 15.

19. Christian E. Lewalter, *Die Zeit*, 13 August 1953.

20. Heidegger's letter, published in *Die Zeit* 24 October 1953, is now reprinted in the editor's postscript to *Einführung in die Metaphysik, Gesamtausgabe* (abbreviated as *GA*), vol. 40 (Tübingen: Klostermann, 1983), pp. 232–233. See also Jürgen Habermas, "Martin Heidegger. Zur Veröffentlichung von Vorlesungen aus dem Jahre 1935," *Philosophisch-politische Profile* (Frankfurt: Suhrkamp, 1971), pp. 67–75. It now appears that the parenthetical remark was indeed added later. The postscript to this volume of the *GA* informs us that the relevant page is missing in the manuscript and Rainer Marten, who helped read proofs when Heidegger prepared the manuscript for publication in 1953, does not recall the parenthetical remark. See Habermas, "Heidegger—Werk und Weltanschauung," Farías, *Heidegger und der Nationalsozialismus*, p. 399, fn. 71.

21. See the *Spiegel* interview, p. 41 below. In a letter to S. Zemach of 18 March 1968 Heidegger claims, however, that the context of the 1935 lecture, which shows his opposition to National Socialism, should have ruled out the kind of reading offered by Habermas. *GA*, vol. 40, p. 233.

22. Georg Lucács, *Die Zerstörung der Vernunft*, now available in *Werke*, vol. 9 (Neuwied: Luchterhand, 1962).

23. Paul Hühnerfeld, *In Sachen Heidegger* (Hamburg: Hoffmann und Campe, 1959).

24. Theodor W. Adorno, *Jargon der Eigentlichkeit* (Frankfurt: Suhrkamp, 1964).

25. Guido Schneeberger, *Nachlese zu Martin Heidegger* (Bern: Guido Schneeberger, 1962). A selection of the materials Schneeberger had assembled was published in English misleadingly as Martin Heidegger, *German Existentialism*, trans. and intro. Dagobert D. Runes (New York: Philosophical Library, 1965).

26. Ott has called attention to Jean Beaufret's correspondence with the revisionist historian Robert Faurisson in 1978 which the latter published in *Annales d'Histoire Révisionniste* (no. 3, 1987). In a later issue of the same journal (no. 4, 1988), Faurisson was to claim Beaufret and Heidegger as his revisionist precursors. Although Ott calls the latter claim totally unjustified, he adds that the letters cast "a bad light on the environment in which the Heidegger reception in France flourished." See Ott, *Heidegger*, p. 15.

27. "Nur noch ein Gott kann uns retten," *Der Spiegel*, 23 November 1976, pp. 193–210. The conversation itself took place on 23 September 1966. See also "Spiegel Gespräch mit Martin Heidegger," *Antwort. Martin Heidegger im Gespräch*, ed. Günther Neske and Emil Kettering (Pfullingen: Neske, 1988), pp. 81–111; trans. pp. 00 below, which gives essentially the text of the interview authorized by Heidegger. Cf. "Feststellungen des Nachlaßverwalters Dr. Hermann Heidegger zur Edition des 'Spiegel'-Gesprächs vom 31. Mai 1976," *ibid.*, pp. 112–114; tr. p. 41 below, and Heinrich W. Petzet, "Nachdenkliches zum Spiegel-Gespräch," *ibid.*, pp. 115–126; tr. pp. 67–75 below.

28. Martin Heidegger, *Die Selbstbehauptung der deutschen Universität: Rede, gehalten bei der feierlichen Übernahme des Rektorats der Universität Freiburg i. Br. am 27.5. 1933. Das Rektorat 1933/34; Tatsachen und Gedanken* (Frankfurt: Klostermann, 1983); tr. p. 81 below.

29. Victor Farías, *Heidegger et le nazisme*, tr. from the Spanish and German by Myriam Benarroch and Jean Baptiste Grasset (Lagrasse: Verdier, 1987). The revised and much longer German edition appeared a year later as *Heidegger und der Nationalsozialismus* (Frankfurt: Fischer, 1989). It was translated from the Spanish and French by Klaus Laermann. The English edition, *Heidegger and Nazism* (Philadelphia: Temple University Press, 1989), edited by Joseph Margolis and Tom Rockmore, was translated from the French and the German.

30. Farías, pp. 19–121 and 209–211. See also Ott, pp. 183–184, 201–213.

31. See Richard Wisser, ed., *Martin Heidegger im Gespräch* (Freiburg und München: Karl Alber, 1970), p. 68; tr. p. 120 below.

32. *Antwort*, p. 9; tr. p. 33 below.

33. *Ibid.*, p. 15; tr. p. 38.

34. *Ibid.*, p. 15; tr. p. 38.

35. See p. 158 below.

36. See pp. 197–203 below.

37. See p. 238 below.

38. See p. 207 below; see also Gadamer, p. 141 below.

39. See Elizabeth Young-Bruehl, *Hannah Arendt. For Love of the World* (New Haven and London: Yale University Press, 1982).

40. See pp. 217 below. On Hannah Arendt's changing estimate of Heidegger since 1945 see Otto Pöggeler, " 'Praktische Philosophie' als Antwort an Heidegger, in Bernd Martin, ed., *Martin Heidegger und das 'Dritte Reich.' Ein Compendium* (Darmstadt: Wissenschaftliche Buchgesellschaft, 1989), pp. 68–72.

41. Below, p. 35.

42. See the *Spiegel* interview, p. 41 below and "Facts and Thoughts," p. 15 below.

43. See Spiegel interview, p. 41 below, Rectoral Address, p. 5 below.

44. *Spiegel* interview, p. 41 below.

45. "Facts and Thoughts," p. 15 below. In fact Heidegger was in office for a year.

46. Victor Farías, *Heidegger and Nazism*, p. 4.

47. *Ibid.*, p. 4.

48. *Ibid.*, p. 5.

49. Martin Heidegger, *Über Abraham a Santa Clara* (Messkirch: Stadt Messkirch, n. d.), p. 15.

50. Farías, *Heidegger and Nazism*, pp. 288–297.

51. In the original French edition, Farías places the concentration camp in the Frankfurt suburb (p. 293). The German edition corrects this mistake, to which Ott had called attention in his review, without comment (p. 378). The English edition, although in part based on the German, somewhat inexplicably repeats the original error (p. 289).

52. See especially Hugo Ott, "Martin Heidegger als Rektor der Universität Freiburg i. Br. 19 1933/34." *Zeitschrift für die Geschichte des Oberrheins*, 132 (1984): pp. 343–358; "Martin Heidegger und die Universität Freiburg nach 1945. Ein Beispiel für die Auseinandersetzung mit der politischen Vergangenheit," *Historisches Jahrbuch*, 105 (1985): pp. 95–138.

53. Roger-Pol Droit, "Heidegger était-il nazi?" *Le Monde*, 14 October 1987.

54. Christian Jambet, "Préface," Victor Farías, *Heidegger et le nazisme*, p. 13.

55. Jacques Derrida. "Heidegger's Silence," p. 145 below.

56. The relationship between the French and German versions is somewhat unclear. Some passages in the French edition were deleted in the German, which adds many others and an entirely new chapter on Heidegger's contributions to the magazine *Der Akademiker* in the years 1910–1912. While the French edition is said to be "translated

from the German and the Spanish," the German is said to be "translated from the Spanish and French." What happened to the original German text? Given the very considerable differences between the two editions, one wishes that the German edition had included a clarifying preface. The English edition offers a translation of the French with the addition of some of the material added in the German, especially a chapter on "Heidegger's contribution to the *Akademiker*."

57. Jürgen Habermas, "Heidegger—Werk und Weltanschauung," Farías, *Heidegger und der Nationalsozialismus*, p. 12.

58. *Ibid.*, p. 13.

59. *Ibid.*, p. 14.

60. *Ibid.*, p. 34–35.

61. François Fédier, *Heidegger: anatomie d'un scandale* (Paris: Éditions Rober Laffont, 1988), pp. 30–31.

62. Hans-Georg Gadamer, "Superficiality and Ignorance," see p. 141 below.

63. See Jacques Derrida, "Heidegger's Silence," p. 145 below.

64. Hugo Ott, "Wege und Abwege. Zu Victor Farías' kritischer Heidegger-Studie," *Neue Züricher Zeitung*, 27 November 1987; tr. below p. 133.

65. Correction by Günther Neske. "Hans Barth. Notizen zur Person: geb. 1904, Studium der Jurisprudenz, 1929–1943 Feuilleton-Redakteur bei der Neuen Züricher Zeitung, von 1946–65 Inhaber des Lehrstuhls für Philosophie an der Universität Zürich, gest. 1965.

"Hauptwerke: Fluten und Dämme—Der philosophische Gedanke in der Politik (1943), Wahrheit und Ideologie (1945), Die Idee der Ordnung (1958), Masse und Mythos (1959)."

66. Herbert Marcuse, 28 August 1947, reprinted in *Pflasterstrand* 279/280 (1988).

67. Unpublished typescript of "Die Gefahr," p. 25.

68. "Die Gefahr," p. 26.

69. "Die Gefahr," p. 26.

70. Cited by Wolfgang Schirmacher from a typescript of the second of the Bremen lectures, "Das Gestell," which was later revised, enlarged, and published as "Die Frage nach der Technik" ("The Question of Technology"). All but the statement about agriculture were deleted from the published version. See *Technik und Gelasenheit* (Freiburg: Alber, 1983), p. 25. An ecological postmodernist of sorts, Schirmacher cites the passage, not to criticize Heidegger but to underscore the need to take a step beyond modernism.

71. Philippe Lacoue-Labarthe discovered this "scandalously insufficient" quote in Schirmacher's book. Maurice Blanchot found it in Labarthe's *La fiction du politique* (Breteuil: Collection du Trois, 1988). See "Penser l'Apocalypse," *Le Nouvel Observateur* (22 Jan 1988), p. 44. Also

Lévinas, "Comme un consente," *Le Nouvel Observateur* (22 Jan 1988), p. 46, and Sheehan, "Heidegger and the Nazis," *New York Review of Books* (16 June 1988), pp. 41–42.

72. Jürgen Habermas, "Heidegger—Werk und Weltenschaung," Farías, *Heidegger und der Nationalsozialismus*, p. 32.

73. See Otto Pöggeler, "Todtnauberg," *Spur des Wortes. Zur Lyrik Paul Celans* (Freiburg/München: Alber, 1986), pp. 259–271.

74. Derrida, below, p. 145.

75. Gadamer, below, p. 141.

76. "Facts and Thoughts," p. 15 below.

77. Hannah Arendt, below p. 211 (German 237).

78. Farías, *Heidegger and Nazism*, p. xvi.

79. René Wellek, "Literary History and Literary Criticism," *History as a Tool in Critical Interpretation*, ed. Thomas F. Rugh and Erin R. Silva (Provo, Utah: Brigham Young University Press, 1978), p. 43.

80. *Sein und Zeit*, 7th ed. (Tübingen: Niemeyer, 1953), p. 310. Tr. John Macquarrie and Edward Robinson, *Being and Time* (New York: Harper & Row, 1962).

81. *Sein und Zeit, GA* 2, p. 179.

82. *Ibid.*, 2, p. 216.

83. See p. 20 below.

84. Below, p. 13.

85. See p. 12 below.

86. See p. 21 below.

87. *Being and Time*, par. 62.

88. Below, p. 238.

89. Hans Barth, "Vom Ursprung des Kunstwerks," *Antwort*, p. 266; tr. below p. 242.

90. Emil Staiger, "Noch einmal Heidegger," *Antwort*, p. 270; tr. p. 247.

91. See p. 62 below.

92. Martin Heidegger, *Hölderlins Hymnen "Germanien" und "Der Rhein," GA*, vol. 39 (Frankfurt: Klostermann, 1980), p. 1.

93. *Ibid.*, p. 6.

94. *Spiegel* interview, p. 45. Freiburger Studentenzeitung, 3 November 1933.

95. *Ibid.*, p. 16.

Preface to The Rectoral Address

1. Translator's note. *Judenplakat*. In the spring of 1933 Joseph Goebbels' newly established Reichsministerium für Volksaufklärung und Propaganda directed the NS-Deutsche Studentenbund, the National Socialist

student organization, to engage in a campaign "against the un-German spirit." Starting on 12 April (Heidegger was elected rector of the University of Freiburg on 21 April), twelve theses were to be posted in every university. At the same time, students were to "cleanse" not only their own libraries but also those of their friends, and even public libraries that did not primarily have a research function, of *zersetzendes Schrifttum*, literature that was thought to pose a threat to the integrity and purity of the German spirit. On 10 May these books were publicly burned.

2. Translator's note. Georg von Hevesy (1885–1966) was a professor of chemistry at the University of Freiburg from 1926 to 1934. He emigrated to Denmark in 1934, where he worked at the University of Copenhagen, and fled to Sweden in 1943, the year he won the Nobel Prize for Chemistry. He returned to Freiburg after the war.

3. Translator's note. Siegfried Thannhauser (1885–1962), professor of internal medicine at the University of Freiburg, was forced to retire from the university in 1934 and emigrated to the USA, where he assumed a visiting professorship at Tufts.

4. Translator's note. The bilingual edition is entitled "*L'Auto-affirmation de l'université allemande*," trans. by Gerard Granel and appeared in the *Editions Trans-Europ-Repress*, 1982. This translation had been preceded by an earlier version, also by Granel, published under the same title in *Phi*, supplement to *Annales de l'Université de Toulouse Le Mirail*, 1976. A translation by François Fédier of both the retrospective remarks of 1945 and the rectorial address appeared in *Le Débat*, No. 27 (November 1983) under the titles "*Le rectorat 1933–34*" and "*L'Université allemande envers et contre tout elle-même.*"

5. Translator's note. "Nur noch ein Gott kann uns retten," *Der Spiegel*, 31 May 1976, Nr. 23, pp. 193–219. An English translation is in this volume.

The Self-Assertion of the German University

1. Translator's note. Here Heidegger uses *hohe Schule*. Like the more common word *Hochschule*, *hohe Schule* means "institution of higher education." However, the word has a special aura, especially in the way Heidegger uses it. I have thus chosen to translate it later in the text as " 'high' school."

2. Translator's note. Throughout Heidegger's rectorial address, I have translated *Dasein* as "existence." I have interpreted Heidegger's use of *Dasein* here to mean just that and have decided not to use the untranslatable technical term *Dasein*.

3. Translator's note. Proclaimed on 1 May 1933, the *neue Studentenrecht* sought to organize students according to the *Führerprinzip* in an effort to integrate the universities into the National Socialist state.

4. Translator's note. Carl von Clausewitz (1780–1831), for many years

head of the Prussian War College, was the author of the influential
Vom Krieg (*On War*).

The Rectorate 1933/34: Facts and Thoughts

1. Translator's note. Wilhelm von Möllendorff (1887–1944), a distinguished anatomist, was elected rector for the academic year
1933/1934. Hugo Ott, the Freiburg historian, writes in his recently
published biography of Heidegger that Möllendorff was not forced out
of office by Minister Wacker but resigned voluntarily because of his
unwillingness, as a "strong believer in democracy and the republic,"
to carry through with Nazi politics in the university. See Hugo Ott,
Martin Heidegger. Unterwegs zu seiner Biographie (Frankfurt/New
York: Campus Verlag, 1988), p. 139.

2. Translator's note. Joseph Sauer (1872–1949), a church historian
known especially for his work in Christian archeology and the history
of Christian art, served as rector of the University of Freiburg for the
academic year 1932/1933 and was vice-rector during Heidegger's rectorate.

3. Translator's note. *Was ist Metaphysik?* (Bonn: Cohen, 1929); "What Is
Metaphysics?" trans. by David Farrell Krell, *Basic Writings*, ed. David
Farrell Krell (New York: Harper & Row, 1977), p. 96. The translation is
my own.

4. Translator's note. *Vom Wesen der Wahrheit* (Frankfurt: Klostermann,
1943); "On the Essence of Truth," trans. by J. Glenn Gray in *Basic
Writings*.

5. Translator's note. Now available in *Wegmarken*, vol. 9 of the *Gesamtausgabe* (Frankfurt: Klostermann, 1976); "Plato's Doctrine of Truth,"
trans. by John Barlow, *Philosophy in the Twentieth Century*, eds. William Barrett and Henry D. Aiken (New York: Harper & Row, 1962).

6. Translator's note. *Politische Wissenschaft*. Political means "politicized"
here. As Heidegger explains in the *Spiegel* interview (see p. 45 in this
volume), *political science* was understood to mean that "science as
such, its meaning and its value, is appraised for its practical use for the
nation [*Volk*]." This led to attempts to create a "German mathematics,"
a "German physics," and so on.

7. Translator's note. The paths of Ernst Jünger (b. 1895), essayist and
writer, and Martin Heidegger continued to meet. See *Zur Seinsfrage*,
now available in *Wegmarken* and translated as *The Question of Being*
by William Kluback and Jean T. Wilde (Boston: Twayne, 1958). This
was written as a response to Ernst Jünger's *Über die Linie* (Frankfurt:
Klostermann, 1958). Both essays were originally written to honor the
other on his sixtieth birthday.

8. Translator's note. Werner Brock (1901–1974) was Heidegger's assis-

tant from 1931 to 1933. In 1934 he went to Cambridge on a research fellowship. He returned to teach at the University of Freiburg in 1946.

9. Translator's note. In *Holzwege*, now vol. 5 of the *Gesamtausgabe* (Frankfurt: Klostermann, 1977); "The Word of Nietzsche: 'God is dead,'" trans. by William Lovitt, *The Question Concerning Technology and other Essays* (New York: Harper & Row, 1977).

10. Translator's note. Heidegger's translation of the Heraclitus fragment offers a key to his use of the word *Auseinandersetzung*, a word that is difficult to translate. *Auseinandersetzung* means confrontation, but by hyphenating the word (*Aus-einander-setzung*), Heidegger calls attention to its roots. Confrontation then comes to mean a "setting apart," in which those who are thus set apart reveal themselves. This interpretation of what confrontation means should be kept in mind.

11. Translator's note. This translation fails to preserve the play on the words *Selbst-be-hauptung* (self-assertion) and *Selbst-ent-hauptung* (self-decapitation).

12. Translator's note. Gaustudentenführer Gustav Adolf Scheel made a name for himself as the National Socialist student leader at the University of Heidelberg. He soon advanced to more important positions, became the student leader of the Gau of Baden and finally of all the students in the Reich.

13. Translator's note. Long a committed National Socialist, Ernst Krieck (1882–1947) was made a full professor at the University of Frankfurt in 1933 and at the University of Heidelberg in 1934. A leading National Socialist theorist on education, Krieck protested in his journal *Volk im Werden* against the non-German character of Heidegger's thinking.

14. Translator's note. Ministerialrat Eugen Fehrle, classicist and folklorist, was a professor at the University of Heidelberg after 1934.

15. Translator's note. See note 2 to Hermann Heidegger's "Preface."

16. Translator's note. Erik Wolf (1902–1977), an authority on legal history, was a professor at the University of Freiburg after 1930. For more information on Heidegger's relationship to Wolf, see the interview with Max Müller in this volume (p. 193) and Alexander Hollerbach, "Im Schatten des Jahres 1933: Erik Wolf und Martin Heidegger," *Freiburger Universitätsblätter* nr. 92: *Martin Heidegger, Ein Philosoph und die Politik* (Freiburg: Rombach, 1986), pp. 33–47.

17. Translator's note. *Technology* does not quite capture the meaning of *Technik*, which also means "technique." *Wissenschaft* tranformed into *reine Technik* suggests that science no longer questions its method and is dominated by it.

18. Translator's note. This lecture was given on 9 June 1938 and published under the title "Die Zeit des Weltbildes" in *Holzwege*, now vol. 5 of the

Gesamtausgabe. Translated as "The Age of World View" by Marjorie Grene in *Boundary 2*, 4 (1976), also as "The Age of the World Picture" by William Lovitt in *The Question Concerning Technology.*

19. Translator's note. ". . . *im dichtenden Denken und Singen des Deutschen.*" See *Hölderlins Hymnen "Germanien" und "Der Rhein,"* a lecture course given in the winter semester 1934/1935, now available in the *Gesamtausgabe,* vol. 39 (Frankfurt: Klostermann, 1980).

20. Translator's note. 30 June 1934 was the day Ernst Röhm, the head of the SA, and many others were murdered on the pretext that a putsch had been planned against the Nazi regime.

21. Translator's note. Alfred Bäumler was perhaps the most prominent philosopher to identify with National Socialism. Best known for his works on Nietzsche and Kant, Bäumler had become a professor of pedagogy and philosophy at the Technical University of Dresden in 1929, professor of political pedagogy in Berlin in 1933, where he also became the head of the "Office of Science" under the auspices of Alfred Rosenberg, whom Hitler had put in charge of the ideological training of the Party.

22. Translator's note. Hans Georg Gadamer was Heidegger's student at the University of Marburg—see his book *Philosophische Lehrjahre* (Frankfurt: Klostermann, 1977)—as was Gerhard Krüger. Walter Bröcker became Heidegger's assistant after Werner Brock emigrated. As of December 1934, National Socialist "teachers' camps" had to be successfully attended by anyone wanting to receive qualification to teach at the university level.

23. Translator's note. "Der Ursprung des Kunstwerkes," *Holzwege*; "The Origin of the Work of Art," trans. by Albert Hofstadter, *Poetry, Language, Thought* (New York: Harper & Row, 1971), pp. 17–81, reprinted in *Basic Writings*, pp. 149–187.

24. Translator's note. "Wie wenn am Feiertage . . . ," *Erläuterungen zu Hölderlins Dichtung, Gesamtausgabe,* vol. 4 (Frankfurt: Klostermann, 1981).

25. Translator's note. "Heimkunft/An die Verwandten," *Erläuterungen zu Hölderlins Dichtung*; translated as "Remembrance of the Poet" by Douglas Scott in *Existence and Being*, ed. Werner Brock (Chicago: Regnery, 1967).

26. Translator's note. See Johannes Lotz, *Martin Heidegger und Thomas von Aquin: Mensch, Zeit und Sein* (Pfullingen: Neske, 1975), and Karl Rahner, *Geist und Welt: zur Metaphysik der endlichen Erkenntnis bei Thomas von Aquin* (Innsbruck: Rauch, 1939).

27. Translator's note. Hans and Sophie Scholl were members of the White Rose resistance group that led student opposition to the Nazis at the University of Munich early in 1943. The group had connections to other universities in Germany, where other resistance groups had

formed. Hans and Sophie Scholl were executed, as were other students and their friend and adviser, the philosopher Kurt Huber.

28. Translator's note. Nicolai Hartmann (1882–1950) insisted on the primacy of ontology. In this connection, he attacked Heidegger's fundamental ontology for its subjectivism.

29. Translator's note. See *Systematische Philosophie*, ed. Nicolai Hartmann (Stuttgart/Berlin: Kohlhammer, 1942) with contributions by Arnold Gehlen, Erich Rothacker, Nicolai Hartmann, O. F. Bollnow (who wrote the essay on existential philosophy), Hermann Wein, and Heinz Heimsoeth.

Spiegel Interview with Martin Heidegger

1. Translator's note. Heidegger is referring to his cabin in Todtnauberg.

2. Translator's note. Wilhelm von Möllendorff was to have served as rector of the University of Freiburg for the academic year 1933/34, but, according to historian Hugo Ott, voluntarily resigned soon after he assumed office in April 1933. See note 1 to Martin Heidegger's "The Rectorate 1933/34." Both Heidegger and Möllendorff lived on Rötebuckweg in Freiburg-Zähringen.

3. Translator's note. See note 1 to Hermann Heidegger's "Preface."

4. Translator's note. See "What Is Metaphysics?" trans. by David Farrell Krell, *Basic Writings*, ed. by David Farrell Krell (New York: Harper & Row, 1977), p. 96. This translation is, however, my own.

5. Translator's note. Martin Heidegger, *Die Selbstbehauptung der deutschen Universität* (1933; Frankfurt: Klostermann, 1983), p. 15; an English translation, "The Self-Assertion of the German University," is in this volume.

6. Translator's note. *Die Selbstbehauptung der deutschen Universität*, p. 19; "The Self-Assertion of the German University," p. 13 in this volume.

7. Translator's note. Friedrich Naumann (1860–1919) was a minister and a political and social theorist who called for social reform as well as for German economic and political imperialism. After his own party failed, he joined the Freisinnige Vereinigung in 1903, which merged with the Progressive People's Party in 1910. He was elected to the Reichstag in 1907, and in 1919 he was one of the founders of the German Democratic Party.

8. *Der Spiegel's* note. The essay appeared in the magazine *Die Erziehung*, edited by A. Fischer, W. Flitner, Th. Litt, H. Nohl, and Ed. Spranger. "März 1933," *Die Erziehung*.

9. Translator's note. This is a quote from an article Heidegger published in the *Freiburger Studentenzeitung* on 3 November 1933. Reprinted in Guido Schneeberger, *Nachlese zu Heidegger* (Bern: 1962): 135–136. An

English translation by William S. Lewis, may be found under the title
"German Students," *New German Critique* 45 (Fall 1988): 101–102.
This translation is, however, mine.

10. Editor's note. The book Heidegger shows his interviewers is *Vernunft
und Existenz.* Heidegger also presents Jaspers' book *Descartes und die
Philosophie*, which has a dedication from Jaspers to Heidegger written
in 1937.

11. *Der Spiegel*'s note. Hermann Niemeyer, Heidegger's publisher at the
time.

12. Translator's note. Martin Heidegger, *Unterwegs zur Sprache*
(Pfullingen: Neske, 1959), p. 269; *On the Way to Language*, trans. by
Peter Hertz (New York: Harper & Row, 1971), pp. 199–200. This trans-
lation is my own, except for the passage from *Being and Time*, trans. by
John Macquarrie and Edward Robinson (New York: Harper & Row,
1962), p. 489.

13. Translator's note. See note 3 to Hermann Heidegger's "Preface."

14. Translator's note. See note 2 to Hermann Heidegger's "Preface."

15. Translator's note. Albert Leo Schlageter (1894–1923), a former student at the University of Freiburg, was shot by the French occupation
army in the Ruhr on 26 May 1923. For one of Heidegger's speeches on
Schlageter, see Schneeberger, *Nachlese zu Heidegger*: 47–49. An English translation can be found in "Martin Heidegger and Politics: A
Dossier," *New German Critic*, 45 (Fall 1988): 96–97.

16. Editor's note. The cited headline has not yet been able to be verified.

17. Translator's note. See note 16 to Martin Heidegger's "The Rectorate
1933/34."

18. Translator's note. See note 22 to Martin Heidegger's "The Rectorate
1933/34."

19. Editor's note. Here the *Spiegel* edited a reformulated statement by Dr.
H. W. Petzet into the Heidegger text. Heidegger accepted it in the final
version, probably because it was factually accurate.

20. *Der Spiegel*'s note. Professor Dr. Gerhard Ritter (author of *Carl Goer-
deler und die deutsche Widerstandsbewegung*), at the time full professor of modern history at the University of Freiburg, was imprisoned
on 1 November 1944 in connection with the attempted assassination of
Hitler on 20 July 1944. He was freed on 25 April 1945 by the Allied
troops. The historian became professor emeritus in 1956 and died in
1967.

21. Translator's note. The *Volkssturm*, an army for home defense, was
organized toward the end of the Second World War and consisted of
men and boys unable to serve in the regular military.

22. Translator's note. See Martin Heidegger, *Einführung in die Metaphysik*, 2nd. ed. (Tübingen: Max Niemeyer, 1958), p. 152. English

translation: *An Introduction to Metaphysics*, trans. Ralph Mannheim (Garden City, N.Y.: Doubleday, 1961), p. 166. The translation is my own.

23. Translator's note. See note 2 to Richard Wisser's "Martin Heidegger in conversation."

24. Editor's note. Martin Heidegger, *Nietzsche*, vol. II (Pfullingen: Neske, 1961), p. 335.

25. Translator's note. Martin Heidegger, "Die Frage nach der Technik," *Vorträge und Aufsätze* (Pfullingen: Neske, 1954), p. 44; English translation: "The Question Concerning Technology," *The Question Concerning Technology and other Essays*, trans. by William Lovitt (New York: Harper & Row, 1977), p. 35. This translation is my own.

26. Translator's note. Martin Heidegger, *Was Heisst Denken?* 2nd ed. (Tübingen: Niemeyer, 1961). An English translation by Fred Wieck and J. Glenn Gray has been published with the title *What Is Called Thinking?* (New York: Harper & Row, 1968). A selection from it is published in *Basic Writings* as "What calls for Thinking," pp. 345–367.

Afterthoughts on the Spiegel Interview

1. Translator's note. See Paul Hühnerfeld, *In Sachen Heidegger. Versuch über ein deutsches Genie* (Hamburg: Hoffmann und Campe, 1959).

2. See "Das Rektorat 1933/34—Tatsachen und Gedanken," *Die Selbstbehauptung der deutschen Universität / Das Rektorat 1933/34* (Frankfurt: Klostermann, 1983), pp. 21–43. Translator's note: An English translation is in this volume.

3. Translator's note. See Karl Löwith, *Denker in dürftiger Zeit* (Frankfurt: S. Fischer, 1953). See also note 1 to Richard Wisser's "Introduction."

4. Translator's note. See note 2 of Richard Wisser's "Martin Heidegger in Conversation."

5. See "Das Rektorat 1933/34," p. 29ff. Translator's note. See "The Rectorate 1933/34," p. 15 in this volume.

6. See "Das Rektorat 1933/34," p. 21 ff. Translator's note. See p. 15 in this volume.

Introduction

1. Translator's note. In 1953, Karl Löwith first published a book he called *Heidegger: Thinker in Destitute Times [Heidegger—Denker in dürftiger Zeit*, now available in Karl Löwith, *Sämtliche Schriften*, vol. 8 (Stuttgart: Metzler, 1984), pp. 32–71]. This title refers to a line from Friedrich Hölderlin's poem "Bread and Wine": "... *und wozu Dichter in dürftiger Zeit*" ("and why poets in a destitute time"). For Heidegger's reaction to this description, see Heinrich Petzet's article in this volume, p. 67.

2. Martin Heidegger, *Aus der Erfahrung des Denkens* (Pfullingen: Neske, 1954), p. 17; "The Thinker as Poet," *Poetry, Language, Thought,* trans. Albert Hofstadter (New York: Harper & Row, 1971), p. 9.

3. Translator's note. Here Wisser refers to Heidegger's line in "The Thinker as Poet": "We may venture the step back out of philosophy into the thinking of Being as soon as we have grown familiar with the provenance of thinking" (p. 10).

4. Translator's note. The word *Holzweg* idiomatically means a wrong track, a path that leads nowhere. Heidegger, however, understands a wood path to be a winding, seldom-walked path that leads to a clearing. This is illustrated by a story told by Carl Friedrich von Weizsäcker about a walk he took with Heidegger near his cabin in Todtnauberg. Heidegger led him down a path through the woods that suddenly ended at a spot where water bubbled out through moss. When von Weizsäcker said "The path has ended," Heidegger answered: "That is the wood path. It leads to the source." Carl Friedrich von Weizsäcker, "Begegnungen in vier Jahrzehnten," *Erinnerung an Martin Heidegger,* ed. Günther Neske (Pfullingen: Neske, 1977), p. 242.

5. Martin Heidegger, *Holzwege* (Frankfurt: Klostermann, 1950), p. 3. Translator's note. For the words *woodcutters* and *foresters*, Heidegger does not use the German *Holzhacker* and *Förster* but the uncommon *Holzmacher* and *Waldhüter.* A literal translation of the words would be "makers of wood" and "guardians of the woods," phrases that redefine the functions of those who "know what it means to be on a wood path."

6. Martin Heidegger, *Identität und Differenz* (Pfullingen: Neske, 1957), p. 8; *Identity and Difference,* trans. by Joan Stambaugh (New York: Harper & Row, 1969).

Martin Heidegger in Conversation

1. Translator's note. See "What Is Metaphysics?" trans. by David Farrell Krell, *Basic Writings,* ed. by David Farrell Krell (New York: Harper & Row, 1977), p. 96. This translation, is, however, my own.

2. Translator's note. Instead of the more usual translations of *Gestell* as "enframing," "framework," or simply "frame," I have decided to use "construct." *Construct* captures more of the ordinariness of the German word *Gestell* (which can be used in such ways as *Brillengestell* ["glasses frame"] or *Büchergestell* ["bookrack"]) than *enframing* does. The prefix *con* also holds some of the same meaning as the German prefix *Ge-:* both can mean "a gathering together." Finally, the verb *to structure,* although it does not contain the variety of meanings that the German *stellen* has, does correspond to the German verb in meaning "putting into place."

3. Translator's note. See "The Question Concerning Technology," *The Question Concerning Technology and Other Essays,* trans. by William

Lovitt (New York: Harper & Row, 1977), p. 24. I have changed Lovitt's translation of *Bestand* as "standing reserve" to "available material."

Afterthoughts and Gratitude

1. Translator's note. ZDF is the abbreviation for *Zweites Deutsches Fernsehen*, Second German Television. Another television network mentioned in this article is the *Arbeitsgemeinschaft der öffentlich-rechtlichen Rundfunkanstalten der Bundesrepublik Deutschland*, Association of the state-owned broadcasting corporations of the Federal Republic of Germany, or ARD for short.

2. *Süddeutsche Zeitung* [Munich], 29 September 1969, Nr. 231.

3. *Evangelische Pressedienst, Kirche und Fernsehen* [Frankfurt-am-Main] 27 September 1969, Nr. 37.

4. *Der Spiegel*, 22 September 1969, Nr. 39, p. 216.

5. *L'Express*, 20 October 1969, Nr. 954.

6. *Die Welt*, 21 October 1969, Nr. 245, p. 19.

7. "Hausmitteilungen," *Der Spiegel*, 3 November 1969, Nr. 45, p. 5.

8. Both letters may be found in *Der Spiegel*, 19 January 1970, Nr. 4, p. 14.

9. "Nur noch ein Gott kann uns retten," *Der Spiegel*, 31 May 1976, Nr. 223, pp. 193–219; an English translation is in this volume.

10. *Der Spiegel*, 31 May 1976, Nr. 23, pp. 3, 5.

11. The three seminars Heidegger held in Provence were published in 1977 together with the seminar held in Zähringen and thus (they are transcripts) were made accessible to the general public. Martin Heidegger, *Vier Seminare. Le Thor 1966, 1968, 1969, Zähringen 1973* (Frankfurt: Klostermann, 1977).

12. Martin Heidegger, *Was ist das—die Philosophie?* (Pfullingen: Neske, 1956); English translation: *What Is Philosophy?* A bilingual edition, trans. by William Kluback and Jean T. Wilde (New Haven: College & University Press, 1958).

13. The reference to Prof. von Rintelen, my teacher, is informative inasmuch as his book *Philosophie der Endlichkeit als Spiegel der Gegenwart* (Fritz Joachim von Rintelen, *Philosophie der Endlichkeit als Spiegel der Gegenwart*, Meisenheim/Glan: Hain, 1951) is alluded to. The book contains a critical confrontation, supported by methodological sympathy but inspired by and grounded in a realistically oriented philosophy of values, with the "existialist philosophical movement," especially with Martin Heidegger. Heidegger had already rejected thinking in terms of values in 1927 in *Being and Time* because "values are determinate characteristics which a thing possesses" (*Being and Time*, trans. by John Macquarrie and Edward Robinson, New York: Harper & Row, 1962, p. 132). He said in his "Letter on Humanism" that "[h]ere and now thinking in values is the greatest blasphemy imagin-

able against Being" ("Letter on Humanism," trans. by Frank A. Capuzzi in collaboration with J. Glenn Gray, *Basic Writings*, ed. David Farrell Krell, New York: Harper & Row, 1977, p. 228. Translator's note: I have changed the translation slightly.).

14. Translator's note. *Dipl. Ing.* is the abbreviation for *Diplomingenieur*, an academically trained engineer.

15. *Martin Heidegger zum 80. Geburtstag von seiner Heimatstadt Messkirch* (Frankfurt: Klostermann, 1969), p. 36.

16. Translator's note. English translation: *On Time and Being*, trans. by Joan Stambaugh (New York: Harper & Row, 1972).

17. Karl Jaspers, *Psychology of World Views*; Jaspers, *Philosophical Autobiography*; Jaspers, *Notes on Heidegger*. Translator's note. Since Wisser wrote this piece, the correspondence between Jaspers and Heidegger has been published: Martin Heidegger/Karl Jasper, *Briefwecshel 1920–1963*, ed. by Hans Saner and Walter Biemel (Frankfurt/ Munich: Klosterman/Piper, 1990).

18. Translator's note. See Martin Heidegger, "German Men and Women— November 10, 1933," trans. William S. Lewis, *New German Critique*, 45 (Fall 1988): 103–104.

19. The statements can be found in Richard Wisser, ed., *Martin Heidegger im Gespräch* (Freiburg/München: Alber, 1970), pp. 13–56; *Martin Heidegger in Conversation*, trans. B. Srinivasa Murthy (New Delhi: Heinemann, 1977).

   Translator's note. Wisser's somewhat unusual use of the word *Gratulanten*, "congratulators," to describe the people he interviewed reflects his presentation of the television program as a sort of birthday card, signed by the "congratulators," for Heidegger's eightieth birthday.

20. Translator's note. I have chosen to translate the Heideggerian term *Gestell* as "construct" instead of the usual "enframing" or "frame." See note 2 to the essay "Martin Heidegger in Conversation with Richard Wisser" in this volume, p. 272.

21. Translator's note. See Martin Heidegger, "The Question Concerning Technology" in *The Question Concerning Technology and other Essays*, trans. William Lovitt (New York: Harper & Row, 1977), p. 24. I have changed Lovitt's translation of *Bestand* as "standing reserve" to "available material."

22. It was edited by Hildegard Feick, who has also worked devotedly on the index to Heidegger. Martin Heidegger, *Schellings Abhandlung über das Wesen der menschlichen Freiheit (1809)*, ed. Hildegard Feick (Tübingen: M. Niemeyer, 1971).

23. *Publik* [Frankfurt-am-Main] Nr. 23: p. 26.

24. *Frankfurter Allgemeine Zeitung*, 19 April 1958.

25. Translator's note. Rudolf Bultmann (1884–1976) was a very prominent theologian and New Testament scholar whose interpretations of the New Testament were greatly influenced by Martin Heidegger's thinking. From 1922 to 1928, Bultmann and Heidegger were colleagues at the University of Marburg, where Bultmann taught from 1921 to 1951.

26. Translator's note. See Martin Heidegger, "The Thinker as Poet," *Poetry, Language, Thought*, trans. by Albert Hofstadter (New York: Harper & Row, 1971), p. 6.

27. Translator's note. See Hermann Mörchen, *Adorno und Heidegger: Untersuchung einer philosophischen Kommunikationsverweigerung* (Stuttgart: Klett-Cotta, 1981); Mörchen, *Macht und Herrschaft im Denken von Heidegger und Adorno* (Stuttgart: Klett-Cotta, 1980).

28. *Die Welt der Bücher* [Freiburg im Breisgau], 3, No. 9 (1968): 459 pp. It has, incidentally, been shortened by a third.

29. "The Thinker as Poet," *Poetry, Language, Thought*, p. 9.

30. Hans Kimmel, *Hochland*, 62 (1970): 368ff.

31. *Martin Heidegger im Gespräch*, p. 55; *Martin Heidegger in Conversation*.

32. *Heidegger. Zum 80. Geburtstag von seiner Heimatstadt Messkirch*, p. 57.

33. "Erst Gebild wahrt Gesicht. / Doch Gebild ruht im Gedicht." Heidegger, *Aus der Erfahrung des Denkens*, p. 14; "The Thinker as Poet," *Poetry, Language, Thought*, p. 7.

34. Translator's note. Here Wisser is referring to another line in Heidegger's "The Thinker as Poet," which Albert Hofstadter has translated as: "We may venture the step back out / of philosophy into the thinking of / Being as soon as we have grown familiar with the provenance of thinking." "The Thinker as Poet," p. 10.

Heidegger and Politics: Stages of a Discussion

1. Martin Heidegger, *Einführung in die Metaphysik* (Tübingen: Niemeyer, 1953), p. 152; English translation: *An Introduction to Metaphysics*, trans. by Ralph Mannheim (Garden City, N.Y.: Doubleday, 1961), p. 166.

2. Annemarie Gethmann-Siefert and Otto Pöggeler, eds., *Heidegger und die praktische Philosophie* (Frankfurt: Suhrkamp, 1988), p. 7.

3. Translator's note. Since the German edition of this book was published, Farías' book has been published in both German and English. For comments on changes made to the book, see Karsten Harries' introduction, p. xi. Hugo Ott's book *Martin Heidegger. Unterwegs zu seiner Biographic* has appeared in German (Frankfurt/New York: Campus Verlag, 1988) and is supposed to be published in an English translation.

4. Martin Heidegger, *Gesamtausgabe*, vols. 39-45, 48, 51-55 (Frankfurt: Klostermann, 1980–1988).

Paths and Wrong Paths

1. Translator's note. See *Das Rektorat 1933/34* (Frankfurt: Klostermann, 1983). An English translation is in this volume.

2. Translator's note. See "Nur noch ein Gott kann uns retten," *Der Spiegel*, 31 May 1976, Nr. 223, pp. 193–219. An English translation is in this volume.

3. Translator's note. See Paul Hühnerfeld, *In Sachen Heidegger. Versuch über ein deutsches Genie* (Hamburg: Hoffmann und Campe, 1959).

4. Translator's note. Guido Schneeberger collected various texts on Heidegger's engagement in National Socialism and published them in 1962. See *Nachlese zu Heidegger* (Bern: privately published, 1962).

5. Translator's note. See Martin Heidegger/Erhart Kästner, *Briefwechsel 1953–1974*, ed. by Heinrich W. Petzet (Frankfurt: Insel-Verlag, 1986).

6. Translator's note. Alfred Rosenberg, who had helped form the Nazi Party in the early twenties, was one of its chief ideologists. On Ernst Krieck, see note 13 to Martin Heidegger's "The Rectorate 1933/34."

7. Translator's note. See note 2. to Martin Heidegger's "The Rectorate 1933/34."

8. Translator's note. See Martin Heidegger, "Schlageter, May 26, 1933," trans. by William S. Lewis, *New German Critique* 45 (Fall 1988): 96–97. Albert Leo Schlageter was a former student at the University of Freiburg who was shot by the French occupation army in the Ruhr area for acts of sabotage.

Superficiality and Ignorance

1. Translator's note. See "The End of Philosophy and the Task of Thinking," trans. by Joan Stambaugh, *Basic Writings*, ed. by David Farrell Krell (New York: Harper & Row, 1977), pp. 373–392.

Admiration and Disappointment

1. Translator's note. See Emmanuel Lévinas, *The Theory of Intuition in Husserl's Phenomenology*, trans. by André Orianne (Evanston, Ill.: Northwestern University Press, 1973).

Last Meeting with Heidegger

1. Editor's note. See p. 37 in this volume.

2. Translator's note. Julius Streicher (1885–1946), National Socialist demagogue and politician, was the founder and editor of the antisemitic periodical *Der Stürmer*.

3. In an analogous fashion, Heidegger got together with a Nietzsche "scholar" like R. Oehler in the academic committee of the Nietzsche

Archive—probably also to prevent "even worse things," although he actually thus covered something evil with his own good name. On the general characteristics of the conduct of Germans toward facts and concepts, see Hegel, *Schriften zur Politik und Rechtsphilosophie* (ed. Lasson; Leipzig: Meiner, 1923), p. 6: "In an eternal contradiction between what they demand and what does not happen according to their demand, they appear to be not only obsessed with reprimands but, when they merely speak of their concepts, also untrue and dishonest. This is because they place necessity in their concepts of justice and obligations, but nothing happens according to this necessity. They themselves are so used to it that partly their words always contradict their deeds and partly they try to make something completely different out of events than they really are and twist the explanation of them to fit certain concepts.... It is precisely because of their concepts that Germans appear so dishonest, admitting to nothing the way it is and not presenting it as nothing more or less than actually lies in the strength of the matter."

4. Translator's note. Löwith's allusion to November 1938 must be a reference to Kristallnacht. The "Night of Crystal," 9 November 1938, was the night synagogues were burned, the windows of Jewish businesses were shattered (the broken glass giving Kristallnacht its name), about a hundred Jews were killed, and some 30,000 Jewish men were sent to the concentration camps Dachau, Buchenwald, and Sachsenhausen.

The Power of Thinking

1. Translator's note. Heinrich Brüning (1885–1970), politician from the Catholic Center Party and German chancellor from March 1930 until May 1932.

2. Translator's note. Ernst Röhm (1887–1934), longtime member of the National Socialist Party and chief organizer of the SA, was feared to be gaining too much power with the Party. On the pretext that Röhm and the SA were planning a putsch, Hitler had Röhm and many others, including former chancellor Kurt von Schleicher and Gregor Strasser, another important Party member, murdered during the night of 30 June 1934.

Martin Heidegger: A Philosopher and Politics

1. Edmund Husserl (1859–1938), professor of philosophy at the University of Freiburg from 1916 until he was named professor emeritus in 1928.

2. *Die Selbstbehauptung der deutschen Universität. Das Rektorat 1933/34*, ed. by Hermann Heidegger (1933; Frankfurt: Klostermann, 1983). Translator's note. An English translation in this volume.

3. Hugo Ott, "Martin Heidegger als Rektor der Universität Freiburg im Breisgau 1933/34, I. Die Übernahme des Rektorats der Universität

Freiburg i. Br. durch Martin Heidegger im April 1933; II. Die Zeit des Rektorats von Martin Heidegger (23 April 1933 until 23 April 1934)," *Zeitschrift des Breisgau-Geschichtsvereins* (*Schau-ins-Land*), 102 (1983), pp. 121–136, and 103 (1984), pp. 107–130; "Martin Heidegger als Rektor der Universität Freiburg 1933/34," *Zeitschrift für die Geschichte des Oberrheins*, 132 (1984): 343–357. Translator's note. Since this interview was conducted, Hugo Ott has published his important biography of Heidegger: *Martin Heidegger. Unterwegs zu seiner Biographie* (Frankfurt/New York: Campus Verlag, 1988).

4. Friedrich Meinecke (1862–1954), historian, 1906–1914 professor at the University of Freiburg, 1914–1928 at the University of Berlin. Hans Rothfels (1891–1976), historian, 1926–1934 professor at the University of Königsberg, forced to retire in 1935, research fellowship at Oxford in 1939, emigration to the USA, 1951–1960 professor at the University of Tübingen.

5. Oskar Becker (1889–1964), philosopher, 1922 lecturer, 1928 associate professor at the University of Freiburg, 1931–1955 at the University of Bonn.

6. Julius Ebbinghaus (1885–1981), philosopher, 1921 lecturer, 1927–1930 professor at the University of Freiburg, after 1940 at the University of Marburg.

7. Gustav Siewerth (1903–1963), educator and philosopher, 1937 lecturer at the University of Freiburg, head of a department of the Görres Society for Education after 1958. Doctoral dissertation on "The Metaphysical Character of Cognition according to St. Thomas Aquinas, Shown on the Essence of the Sensorial Act"; Martin Heidegger was his advisor.

8. Simon Moser (b. 15 March 1901), philosopher, received his doctorate at the University of Freiburg in 1929 with a dissertation on "The 'Summulae in Libros Physicorum' of William of Ockham. A Critical Comparison of their Basic Concepts with Aristotle's Philosophy"; Martin Heidegger was his advisor. Assistant professor at the University of Innsbruck, Austria, in 1935, full professorship at the University of Innsbruck in 1948, professor at the University of Karlsruhe after 1952.

9. Walter Bröcker (b. 19 July 1902), philosopher, doctoral dissertation at the University of Marburg on "Kant's Critique of Aesthetic Judgement" in 1928, postdoctoral thesis on "Aristotelian Philosophy as a Question concerning Movement" in 1934 at the University of Freiburg; Heidegger was his advisor. Assistant professor at the University of Freiburg 1937–1940, professorship at the University of Rostock in 1940, after 1948 at the University of Kiel.

10. Käthe Oltmanns, (b. 1906), doctoral dissertation on "The Philosophy of Meister Eckhart" in 1935; her advisor was Heidegger.

11. Eugen Fink (1905–1975), philosopher and educationalist, doctoral dis-

sertation on "Contributions to a Phenomenological Analysis of Physical Phenomena that are dealt with under the Ambiguous Titles 'To think as if,' 'To merely imagine,' 'Fantasies' "; his doctoral advisor was Husserl. 1928–1938 Husserl's assistant, 1938–1940 co-founder of the Husserl Archive in Louvain, Belgium, military service, postdoctoral thesis in 1946 on "The Idea of 'Transcendental Methodology,' " assistant professorship in 1946, 1948–1971 full professor at the University of Freiburg.

12. Max Scheler (1874–1928), philosopher, professor at the universities of Cologne and Frankfurt-am-Main.

13. Heinrich Rickert (1863–1936), philosopher, in 1891 lecturer, then from 1894 to 1916 professor at the University of Freiburg. Topic of Heidegger's postdoctoral thesis finished in 1915: "Duns Scotus' Theories of Categories and Meaning." (Tübingen: Mohr, 1916).

14. Artur Schneider (1876–1945), philosopher, lecturer at the University of Bonn in 1902, professorship at the University of Munich in 1909, at the University of Freiburg in 1911, at the University of Strasbourg in 1913, after 1921 at the University of Cologne.

15. Stefan George (1868–1933), writer, propagated a new Hellenism in *The new Empire* [*Das neue Reich*] (1928), misunderstood to be the prophet of the Third Reich. With the help of the periodical *Blätter für die Kunst*, which he published, he found supporters who were influential in German intellectual life (George circle).

16. Ernst Jünger (b. 29 March 1895), writer, officer in the First World War; early works: *In Stahlgewittern* (1920); *Der Kampf als inneres Erlebnis* (1922); *Der Arbeiter* (1932).

17. Translator's note. See note 2 to Richard Wisser's "Martin Heidegger in conversation."

18. Ernst Bloch (1885–1977), philosopher; 1933–1949 exile in the USA, professor at the University of Leipzig from 1949–1957, after 1961 guest professor at the University of Tübingen.

19. Martin Heidegger, *Platons Lehre von der Wahrheit. Mit einem Brief über den Humanismus* (Bern: A. Francke Verlag, 1947); "Letter on Humanism," trans. by Frank A. Capuzzi in collaboration with J. Glenn Gray, *Basic Writings*, ed. by David Farrell Krell (New York: Harper & Row, 1977), pp. 193–242.

20. Martin Heidegger, *Was ist Metaphysik?* (1929; Frankfurt: Klostermann, 1949); "What Is Metaphysics?" trans. by David Farrell Krell, *Basic Writings*, pp. 95–112.

21. See note 2 above.

22. Interview held on 23 September 1966, posthumously published in *Der Spiegel*, 31 May 1976, pp. 193–219; English translation in this volume.

23. Gerhard Ritter (1888–1967), historian, 1925–1956 professor at the University of Freiburg.

24. Speech held on 3 May 1933 on the occasion of the first joint duel day of the University of Freiburg's fraternities after the suspension of the ban on the duel (see Guido Schneeberger, *Nachlese zu Heidegger* [Bern: 1962], note 51, pp. 27, 29). The official repeal followed on the Reich level only after a law on 26 May 1933 (paragraph 210a of the Criminal Code). See Wolfgang Kreutzberger, *Studenten und Politik 1918–1933. Der Fall Freiburg im Breisgau.* (Göttingen: Vandenhoeck & Ruprecht, 1972), p. 91.

25. Alois Riehl (1844–1924), philosopher, 1882–1895 professor at the University of Freiburg.

26. Wilhelm Windelband (1848–1915), philosopher, 1877–1882 professor at the University of Freiburg.

27. See above, note 12.

28. Wolfgang Aly (1881–1962), classicist, 1908 lecturer, 1914 associate professor at the University of Freiburg, 1928 language assistant for classics, 1936 lecturer for Greek and Latin philology. Numerous applications by the faculty for an associate professorship for Aly were rejected by the governmental ministry in Karlsruhe; Dismissal in 1945.

29. Ulrich von Wilamowitz-Möllendorf (1848–1931), classicist, professor at the University of Berlin after 1897.

30. Hans F. K. Günther (1891–1968), researcher on race, professor at the University of Jena in 1930, 1935 at the University of Berlin, 1940–1945 professor at the University of Freiburg, suspended and not reemployed. Major work: *Ethnogeny of the German People* [*Die Rassenkunde des deutschen Volkes*] (1922), 14th edition in 1930.

31. Eugen Fischer (1874–1967), anatomist and anthropologist, professor at the University of Würzburg in 1912, at the University of Freiburg after 1914, 1927–1942 director of the Kaiser Wilhelm Institute for Anthropology in Berlin.

32. Gerd Tellenbach (b. 17 September 1903), medieval scholar, professor at the University of Münster in 1942, 1944–1962 at the University of Freiburg, has published an autobiography: *Aus erinnerter Zeitgeschichte* (Freiburg im Breisgau: Wagner, 1981).

33. Hans-Walter Klewitz (1907–1943), medieval scholar, professor of medieval history at the University of Freiburg 1940–1943.

34. 11 April 1933, in Baden on 6 April 1933 by edict of the Reich commissioner (and Gau leader) Wagner.

35. Martin Honecker (1888–1941), philosopher and psychologist, professor at the University of Freiburg from 1924–1941.

36. Eugen Fink, see note 11 above.

37. Walter Eucken (1891–1950), economist, professor at the University of Freiburg after 1927.

38. Hans Grossmann-Doerth (1894–1944), jurist, professor at the University of Freiburg after 1930.

39. Georg von Hevesy (1885–1966), chemist, professor at the University of Freiburg from 1926–1934, emigrated to Scandinavia, Nobel Prize for Chemistry in 1943.

40. Siegfried Thannhauser (1885–1962), doctor, professor at the University of Freiburg after 1931, forced retirement in 1934, emigrated to the USA (Boston). Thannhauser had good contacts with former German chancellor Heinrich Brüning during his exile in America.

41. Werner Brock (1901–1974), philosopher, received his qualification to teach at the university level in 1930 in Göttingen with a postdoctoral thesis on "Nietzsche's Conception of Culture," requalification in 1931 in Freiburg at Heidegger's request, assistant professorship, revocation of the qualification to teach by resolution of Reich commissioner Wagner on 1 October 1933, exile in Cambridge, England, after 1946 associate professor with a salaried teaching position at the University of Freiburg. A budgetary professorship Brock was to have received as an act of reparations was not given him for a number of reasons, in part because of his poor health.

42. Helene Weiss (b. 1898); on Heidegger's suggestion she received her doctorate in Basel, Switzerland, with a dissertation on "Coincidence in Aristotle's Philosophy" in 1935.

43. Alfred Seidenmann (b. 1895), doctoral dissertation on "Bergson's Position on Kant" at the University of Freiburg in 1935.

44. Wilhelm Szilasi (1889–1966), philosopher, spent some years in Freiburg before 1933 as a private scholar, replacement for Heidegger's position as an honorary professor from 1947–1956, after 1956 given a chair in philosophy at the University of Freiburg.

45. Hermann Staudinger (1881–1965), chemist, professor at the University of Freiburg after 1926, Nobel Prize in 1953.

46. Complete quotation of Professor Aly's evaluation of Müller's thesis:
    Max Müller's postdoctoral thesis:
    Because the author has been described to me as an honorable person, the work, whose subject is the overcoming of the natural sciences' conceptions of truth following the premises of Thomism, seems to have been unsuccessfully conceived. For the premises of Thomism are not the premises of our science. However, anyone who still accepts these premises today may find the work a test of a very perceptive and intellectually noteworthy power. Since an assessment of the work would deal with ideological bases, I must refuse to judge it.

The article on "state" in Herder's *Encyclopedia*, which was written by M., according to my information, proves that the author's fundamental conception of the state is politically unacceptable. I therefore think it impossible to entrust a professorship in the philosophical faculty to him. What other, for instance theological, faculties would think about it goes beyond my knowledge. *Aly.*
(Source: Archive of the philosophical faculties, Freiburg im Breisgau, "Habilitation Max Müller.")

47. Theodor Maunz (b. 1 November 1901), professor of national law at the University of Freiburg 1935–1952, 1952 at the University of Munich, 1957–1964 Bavarian Minister of Culture, resigned because of a pro-National Socialist attitude.

48. Joseph Müller-Blattau (1895–1976), musicologist, professor at the University of Freiburg 1937–1952. Letter from the Reich Ministry of Science, Education, and National Education [KP Müller, 85 h] on 23 November 1938, in which it says: "For political and ideological reasons, I could not comply with Dr. phil. habil. Max Müller's application for the issuing of a professorship." (Archive of the philosophical faculties in Freiburg im Breisgau, "Habilation Max Müller.")

49. Norbert von Hellingrath (1888–1916; killed near Verdun), literary historian, began the first historical-critical edition of Hölderlin's collected works.

50. Ernst Rudolf Huber (b. 8 June 1903), national law scholar, professor at the University of Kiel after 1933, after 1937 at the University of Leipzig, after 1941 at the University of Strassbourg, lecturer after 1944 at the University of Heidelberg, honorary professor at the University of Freiburg in 1956, professor at the University of Wilhelmshaven in 1957, in 1962 at the University of Göttingen, named emeritus professor in 1968.

51. See Martin Heidegger's piece in honor of Ernst Jünger's 60th birthday in *Freundschaftliche Begegnungen. Festschrift für Ernst Jünger zum 60. Geburtstag* (Frankfurt: Klostermann, 1955), pp. 9–45. Reprinted under the title *Zur Seinsfrage* (Frankfurt: Klostermann, 1956). (English translation by William Kluback and Jean T. Wilde entitled *The Question of Being.* (Boston: Twayne, 1958)—Translator's note. See also Ernst Jünger's *Über die Linie* (Frankfurt: Klostermann, 1958).

52. The notes, which Heidegger had apparently supplied himself, on Heidegger's military service come from the *Das Deutsche Führerlexikon 1934/35.* Quoted by Guido Schneeberger *Nachlese zu Heidegger. Dokumente zu seinem Leben und Denken* (Bern: 1962), p. 237. Heidegger seems to have had an ambivalent relationship to his time in the military during the First World War. In 1927/1928, he was asked by the university curator at the University of Marburg a total of five times to

fill out a form on his military service so that his work as lecturer at the University of Freiburg would be acknowledged as applicable for pension in Prussia. Heidegger never answered. (Staatsarchiv Marburg, Best. Nr. 310, acc. 1978/15, No. 2729)

53. Joseph Sauer (1872–1949), ecclesiastical historian, lecturer in 1902, after 1905 professor at the University of Freiburg, rector 1932/1933.

54. Wilhelm von Möllendorff (1887–1944), histologist, associate professor from 1919–1922 and after 1927 full professor at the University of Freiburg, elected rector for the academic year 1933/1934, resigned on 21 April 1933.

55. Franz Büchner (b. 20 January 1895), pathologist, awarded the qualification to teach at the University of Freiburg in 1927, associate professor at the University of Freiburg after 1931, full professor at the University of Berlin after 1934, then at the University of Freiburg from 1936 until his retirement in 1960. A sensation was caused by a public lecture Büchner gave on 18 November 1941 on the topic "The Hippocratic Oath" (printed in *Das christliche Deutschland 1933 bis 1945. Dokumente und Zeugnisse.* Katholische Reihe). In it, he clearly stated his position against every form of euthanasia, the destruction of life "unworthy of life." Büchner was named an honorary citizen of the city of Freiburg in 1985.

56. Erik Wolf (1902–1977), philosopher of law, professor at the University of Freiburg after 1930.

57. See Alexander Hollerbach, "Im Schatten des Jahres 1933: Erik Wolf und Martin Heidegger," *Freiburger Universitätsblätter*, 25 (June 1986): pp. 33–47.

58. See above, note 52.

59. Bernhard Welte (1906–1983), Catholic theologian, received his doctorate in 1938 and his qualification to teach at the university level in 1946 from the University of Freiburg, professor at the University of Freiburg 1952–1972.

60. Conrad Gröber (1872 in Messkirch–1948), archbishop in Freiburg from 1932 until his death. As the rector of the Konradi House in Constance, he won the student Heidegger over to philosophy. See Hugo Ott, "Conrad Gröber (1872–1948)," *Zeitgeschichte in Lebensbildern*, vol. 6.: *Aus dem deutschen Katholizismus des 19. und 20. Jahrhunderts*, ed. by Jürgen Aretz et al. (Mainz: Matthias Grünewald Verlag, 1984), pp. 64–75. A critical biography of Gröber has yet to be published. On Gröber's conduct to his clergy during the Third Reich, see the unpublished thesis: Ursula Richter, *Das Verhältnis zwischen Bischof und Klerus in der Herausforderung durch den nationalsozialistischen Staat. Das Beispiel Freiburg im Breisgau* (Freiburg: 1985); Bruno Schwalbach, *Erzbischof Conrad Gröber* (Freiburg: 1986).

Heidegger's Resoluteness and Resolve

1. Translator's note. Hermann Cohen (1842–1918) studied at the Jewish Theological Seminary in Breslau and at the universities of Berlin and Halle, where he received his doctorate in 1865. He became a lecturer at the University of Marburg in 1873 and professor in 1876. He was the founder of the Marburg school of neo-Kantian philosophy, which both Paul Natorp (1854–1924) and Nicolai Hartmann (1882–1950) continued to develop.

2. Translator's note. Although John Macquarrie and Edward Robinson chose to translate *das 'Man'* as "the 'they' " in their translation of *Being and Time*, I have chosen "One" here. "The 'they' " sounds to me more like "the others," and not the anonymous "Man."

For Martin Heiddeger's Eightieth Birthday

1. From *Aus der Erfahrung des Denkens*. Translator's note. See "The Thinker as Poet," *Poetry, Language, Thought*, trans. by Albert Hofstadter (New York: Harper & Row, 1971).

2. *Zur Sache des Denkens*, 1969.

3. *Gelassenheit*, 1959, p. 15; Translator's note. *Discourse on Thinking*, trans. by John M. Anderson and E. Hans Freund (New York: Harper & Row, 1966), p. 46. This translation is, however, my own.

4. Ibid.

5. *Zur Sache des Denkens*, pp. 30, 61, 78.

6. *Vorträge und Aufsätze*, 1957, III, p. 55.

7. *Zur Sache des Denkens*, p. 75.

8. *Gelassenheit*, p. 45.

9. *Einführung in die Metaphysik*, 1953, p. 10.

10. There are many aspects to this escapade, which today—now that the embitterment has died down and, above all, the numerous false reports have been somewhat corrected—is usually called an "error." Among them are aspects of the Weimar Republic, which did not at all show itself to its contemporaries in the rosy light it now has for us, against the horrible background of the years that followed it. The contents of this error differed considerably from the "errors" that were then common. Who else but Heidegger came up with the idea that National Socialism was the "encounter between planetarily determined technology and modern human beings"—except perhaps those who read, instead of Hitler's *Mein Kampf*, some of the Italian futurists' writings, which fascism, in contrast to National Socialism, referred to here and there. This error seems insignificant when measured against the much more decisive errors that consisted of ignoring the reality of the Gestapo's cellars and the torture-hells of the concentration camps, which arose right after the burning of the Reichstag, and escaping into

ostensibly more significant regions. Robert Gilbert, the German folk poet and popular song writer, described in four unforgettable lines what actually happened in that spring of 1933:

Keiner braucht mehr anzupochen
Mit der Axt durch jede Tür
Die Nation ist aufgebrochen
Wie ein Pestgeschwür.

No one needs to knock any more
With an axe through every door
The nation is burst open
like a plague boil.

Heidegger realized his "error" very soon, and then risked much more than was usual at the German universities at the time. But one could not say the same thing about many intellectuals and so-called scholars, not only in Germany, who, instead of talking about Hitler, Auschwitz, genocide, and "extermination" as a policy of permanent depopulation, prefer, according to their own inspiration and taste, to refer to Plato, Luther, Hegel, Nietzsche, or to Heidegger, Jünger, or Stefan George in order to dress up the horrible gutter-born phenomenon with humanities and the history of ideas. It could be said that ignoring reality has become a profession by now. It is an escape, not into a spirituality with which the gutter never had anything to do, but into a ghostly realm of concepts and "ideas." This realm has slipped so far away from documented and experienced reality into the merely "abstract," that the great thoughts of the thinkers have lost all solidity in it and, like cloud formations, have blended and flowed into one another.

11. *Gelassenheit*, p. 32f. Translator's note. See English translation *Discourse on Thinking*, pp. 59–60.

Words in Memory of Martin Heidegger

1. Translator's note. *Being and Time*, trans. by John Macquarrie and Edward Robinson (New York: Harper & Row, 1962), p. 62 and corresponding footnote on p. 489.

Postscript

1. Translator's note. Johannes R. Becher (1891–1958), writer and Minister of Culture of the German Democratic Republic 1954–1958.

2. Translator's note. Walter Ulbricht (1893–1973), chairman of the Council of the State of the German Democratic Republic 1960–1971.

3. Translator's note. Because Becher was Minister of Culture until 1958 and Ulbricht didn't become chairman of the Council of the State of the

German Democratic Republic until 1960, Becher could not have asked Ulbricht as chairman for permission. When Becher was Minister of Culture, Ulbricht was General Secretary of the SED (Sozialistische Einheitspartei Deutschlands), which is probably what Neske means.

Appendices

1. Translator's note. "Heidegger—Mitternacht einer Weltnacht," *Spiegel*, 7 February 1966, p. 110–113; Heidegger's letter to the editor is in *Spiegel*, 7 March 1966, p. 12. The *Spiegel* piece is often, including in Heidegger's letter to the editor, referred to as "Mitternacht einer Welt*m*acht," changing the meaning to "Midnight of a world power."

2. Letter from Heidegger to Kästner, 11 March 1966. Published in Martin Heidegger and Erhart Kastner, Briefwechsel: 1953–1974, ed. by Heinrich W. Petzet (Frankfurt: Insel-Velag, 1986).

3. Translator's note. In the original *Spiegel* text, Heidegger says that Husserl spoke in the Berlin Sports Palace and that Erich, not Heinrich, Mühsam reported on the event; *Der Spiegel*, 31 May 1976, pp. 193–219. Erich Mühsam (1878–1934) was a participant in the soviet republic in Munich in 1919, a political essayist and poet, editor of the anarchist periodical *Fanal*, and was murdered in the Oranienburg concentration camp in 1934.

Letter to Gerd Tellenbach

1. Handwritten note by Jaspers on the letterhead: "Written as an agreed upon letter after a conversation with Tellenbach in Basel."

On the Origin of the Work of Art

1. Translator's note. *Der Ursprung des Kunstwerkes* (1950; Stuttgart: Reclam, 1960); English translation by Albert Hofstadter, "The Origin of the Work of Art," *Poetry, Language, Thought* (New York: Harper & Row, 1971).

2. Translator's note. This translation from Hölderlin's poem "The Journey" is by Albert Hofstadter, "On the Origin of the Work of Art," p. 78.

Heidegger Once Again

1. Martin Heidegger, *Sein und Zeit*, p. 127; *Being and Time*, trans. by John Macquarrie and Edward Robinson (New York: Harper & Row, 1962), p. 165.

Letter to Günther Neske

1. *Aus der Erfahrung des Denkens* (Pfullingen: Neske, 1954), p. 17; English translation by Albert Hofstadter, "The Thinker as Poet," *Poetry, Language, Thought* (New York: Harper & Row, 1971), p. 9.

2. *Brief über den Humanismus* (Frankfurt: Klostermann, 1949) p. 352; English translation by Frank A. Capuzzi in collaboration with J. Glenn

Gray, "Letter on Humanism," *Basic Writings*, ed. by David Farrell Krell (New York: Harper & Row, 1977), p. 231.

3. With Michael Trowitzsch, "Provozierendes Denken," *neue hefte für philosophie*, vol. 23: *Wirkungen Heideggers* (Göttingen: Vandenhoeck und Ruprecht, 1984), pp. 59–74.

A Greeting to the Symposium in Beirut

The philosophical symposium in honor of Martin Heidegger's eighty-fifth birthday in November 1974 in Beirut was initiated by his student Professor Charles Malek. Malek was Lebanon's secretary of state and a signatory of the charter of the United Nations.

The conference took place at the Goethe Institute in collaboration with the American University. Professor Otto Pöggeler gave the main address. Participants were Professor Rifka; the historian Zeise, professor at the American University in Beirut as well as Lebanese ambassador to UNESCO in Paris; and Professor Abou Ssuan among others.

Dedications

1. Martin Heidegger, *Unterwegs zur Sprache* (Pfullingen: Neske, 1959), p. 269; *Gesamtausgabe*, vol. 12, p. 259. English translation *On the Way to Language*, trans. by Peter Hertz (New York: Harper & Row, 1971), pp. 199–200.

2. Translation from Martin Heidegger, *Being and Time*, trans. by John Macquarrie and Edward Robinson (New York: Harper & Row, 1962), p. 489.

3. Martin Heidegger, *Kant und das Problem der Metaphysik* (Bonn: Cohen, 1929).

4. Rudolf Bultmann, *Glauben und Verstehen*, 2nd ed. (Tübingen: Mohr, 1954).

NOTES
ON
CONTRIBUTORS

Hannah Arendt

Born in 1906 in Linden near Hannover; 1924–1925 studied with Heidegger at the University of Marburg (with Hans Jonas, Karl Löwith, and Hans-Georg Gadamer, among others), studied with Karl Jaspers at the University of Heidelberg in 1926, received her doctorate in 1928 at the University of Heidelberg with Jaspers as her advisor with a dissertation on Augustine's concept of love, emigrated to Paris in 1933 and to the USA in 1941, professor at Brooklyn College 1953–1956, then 1963–1967 at the University of Chicago, 1967–1975 professor of political science and humanities at the New School for Social Research in New York. She was married to Günther Stern (Anders) from 1929–1937 and married Heinrich Blücher in 1940. She died in New York in 1975.

Publications on Heidegger: "Was ist Existenzphilosophie?" *Sechs Essays* (Heidelberg: Schneider, 1948), pp. 48–80; "Tradition und Neuzeit. Was ist Autorität?" *Fragwürdiger Traditionsbestand im politischen Denken der Gegenwart. Vier Essays* (Frankfurt): Europäische Verlags-Anstalt, 1957), pp. 9–46, esp. p. 30, and pp. 117–168, esp. p. 143; Hannah Arendt and Karl Jaspers, *Briefwechsel 1926–1969,* ed. by Lotte Köhler and Hans Saner (Munich/Zurich: Piper, 1985), esp. letters 7, 8, 42, 93, 109, 139, 148, 187, 206, 214, 224, 293, 297, 377, 391, 395, and Jaspers's corresponding responses.

Major Works: Between Past and Future (Peter Smith, 1983); *Crisis of the Republic* (Harcourt Brace Jovanovich, 1972); *Eichmann in Jerusalem*

Peter Smith, 1983); *Human Condition* (University of Chicago Press, 1970); *Imperialism* (Harcourt Brace Jovanovich, 1968); *On Revolution* (Penguin, 1977); *On Violence* (Harcourt Brace Jovanovich, 1970); *The Origins of Totalitarianism* (Harcourt Brace Jovanovich, 1973).

Notes: Hannah Arendt's relationship to Martin Heidegger after she emigrated changed from an initial position of harsh criticism to one of restrained closeness. Her article written for Heidegger's birthday could be seen as a high point. After Hannah Arendt visited Heidegger in Freiburg in 1950, their correspondence, interrupted in 1933, was picked up again. Unfortunately the correspondence between Hannah Arendt and Heidegger, which would certainly be very informative, has not yet been published. For the personal relationship between Hannah Arendt and Martin Heidegger, see the biography by Elisabeth Young-Bruehl, *Hannah Arendt For Love of the World.* (New Haven and London: Yale University Press, 1982)

Hans Barth

Born 1904; studied jusrisprudence, editor of the feuilleton of the *Neue Zürcher Zeitung* 1929–1943, chair in philosophy at the University of Zurich 1946–1965. Died 1965.

Major Works: Fluten und Dämme—Der philosophische Gedanke in der Politik (Zurich: Fretz & Wermuth, 1943); *Wahrheit und Ideologie* (Zurich: Manease Verlag, 1945); *Die Idee der Ordnung* (Erlenbach-Zurich: Rentsch, 1958); *Masse und Mythos* (Reinbek bei Hamburg: Rowohlt, 1959).

Jean Beaufret

Born 1907 in Auzances; after studying at the École normale, he taught there and after 1944 at the École Normale Supérieur, after 1946 at the Lycée Henri-IV, and after 1955 at the Condorcet; since 1946 friendship with Martin Heidegger, with whom he gave seminars in 1966, 1968, 1969, and 1973 in Le Thor and Zähringen; died in 1982.

Publications on Heidegger: Dialogue avec Heidegger, 3 vols. (Paris: Editions de Minuit, 1973, 1974); *Le chemin de Heidegger* (Paris: Impr. Jugain, 1985); "Qu'est-ce que la métaphysique?" *Heidegger Studies*, vol. 1 (Oak Brook, Illinois: 1985) pp. 101–117.

Jacques Derrida

Born 1930; 1964–1984 professor of philosophy at the École Normale Superieur, 1983–1984 founding director of the Collège International de Philosophie, since 1984 Directeur de recherche at the École des Hautes Etudes en Sciences Sociales.

Publications on Heidegger: Marges de la philosophie (Paris: Editions du

Minuit, 1972); English translation: *Margins of Philosophy*, trans. by Alan Bass (Chicago: University of Chicago Press, 1982); *De l'esprit: Heidegger et la question* (Paris: Galilée, 1987). English translation: *Of Spirit: Heidegger and the Question*, trans. by Geoffrey Bennington and Rachel Bowlby (Chicago: University of Chicago Press). References to Heidegger's work may be found in many of Derrida's other writings.

Major Works: De la Grammatologie (Paris: Editions du Minuit, 1967); English translation: *Of Grammatology*, trans. by Gayarti Chakravorty Spivak (Baltimore: Johns Hopkins University Press, 1976); *La Voix et le phénomène, introduction au problème du signe dans la phénoménologie de Husserl* (Paris: Presses universitaires de France, 1967); English translation: *Speech and phenomena, and other essays on Husserl's theory of signs*, trans. by David B. Allison (Evanston: Northwestern University Press, 1973); *L'écriture et la différence* (Paris: Editions du Seuil, 1967).

Hans-Georg Gadamer

Born 1900 in Marburg; studied German, art history, philosophy, and classics, received his doctorate in 1922 with Paul Natorp as his advisor, received his qualification to teach at the university in 1929 at the University of Marburg with Heidegger as his advisor, after 1939 full professor of philosophy at the University of Leipzig, 1947–1949 at the University of Frankfurt, after 1949 at the University of Heidelberg as Karl Jaspers' successor, lives in Heidelberg.

Publications on Heidegger: Heideggers Wege. Studien zum Spätwerk (Tübingen: Mohr, 1983); *Philosophische Lehrjahre. Eine Rückschau* (Frankfurt: Klostermann, 1977), esp. pp. 210–221; in addition, references to Heidegger's thinking may be found in many of Gadamer's works.

Major Works: Platons dialektische Ethik (1931; Hamburg: Meiner, 1968), *Wahrheit und Methode. Grundzüge einer philosophischen Hermeneutik* (Tübingen: Mohr, 1960; 4th rev. ed. 1975), also in *Gesammelte Werke*, vols. 1 and 2 (Tübingen: Mohr, 1986); *Gesammelte Werke*, 10 vols. (Tübingen: Mohr, 1985 ff.).

Hans L. Gottschalk

Born 1904, the only son of the philosopher Jonas Cohn (change of name 1922); 1938–1948 curator of Mingana Collection of Oriental Manuscripts and Fellow of Selly Oak Colleges in Birmingham, England, 1948–1974 full professor of Arabic and Islamic studies at the University of Vienna.

Karl Jaspers

Born 1883 in Oldenburg; 1916–1921 associate professor of psychiatry at the University of Heidelberg, 1921–1937 professor of philosophy at the same university, 1937–1945 prohibition to teach because he refused to leave his Jewish wife, reinstatement in 1945, 1948–1969 professor of philosophy at the University of Basel. Died in Basel in 1969.

Publications on Heidegger: Philosophische Autobiographie, rev. ed. (Munich: Piper, 1977), pp. 92–111; *Notizen zu Martin Heidegger*, ed. by Hans Saner (Munich: Piper, 1978); *Hannah Arendt/Karl Jaspers: Briefwechsel 1926–1969*, ed. by Lotte Köhler and Hans Saner (Munich/Zurich: Piper, 1985); (see letters 6, 9, 40, 46, 92, 107, 146, 149, 184, 296, 298, 378, 393, and their replies from H. Arendt as well as the commentarial notes.) All these publications were published posthumously. At least indirectly, Jaspers' debate with Rudolf Bultmann, which is essentially also a debate on Heidegger, belongs here, too: *Die Frage der Entmythologisierung* (Munich: Piper, 1954). English translation: *Myth and Christianity; an inquiry into the possibility of religion without myth* (New York: Noonday Press, 1958).

Major Works: Allgemeine Psychopathologie (1913; 4th fully rev. ed Berlin: Springer, 1946), English translation by J. Hoenig and Marian W. Hamilton: *General Psychopathology* (Chicago: University of Chicago Press, 1963); *Psychologie der Weltanschauungen* (1919; 2nd fully rev. ed. Berlin: Springer, 1922), English translation: *Psychology of World Views; Philosophie*, 3 vols. (Heidelberg: 1932); *Von der Wahrheit. Philosophische Logik*, first volume (Munich: 1947), English translation by Jean T. Wilde, William Kluback, and William Kimmel: *Truth and Symbol* (New York: Twayne Publishers, 1959); *Die Großen Philosophen*, 3 vols. (1957; Munich: Piper, 1981), English translation by Ralph Manheim: *The Great Philosophers*, 3 vols. ed. by Hannah Arendt (New York: Harcourt, 1957–1966); *Die Atombombe und die Zukunft des Menschen* (Munich: Piper, 1960), English translation by E. B. Ashton: *The Future of Mankind* (Chicago: University of Chicago Press, 1961); *Der philosophische Glaube angesichts der Offenbarung* (Munich: Piper, 1961), English translation by E. B. Ashton: *Philosophical Faith and Revelation* (New York: Harper & Row, 1967); *Wohin treibt die Bundesrepublik?* (Munich: Piper, 1967), English translation by E. B. Ashton: *The Future of Germany* (Chicago: University of Chicago Press, 1967.

Notes: Throughout his life, Jaspers thought Heidegger was the only contemporary thinker who essentially concerned him. Friendship with Heidegger, 1920–1933, a "fighting comradeship" against the traditional professorial philosophy and for a renewal of the university. Human "failing" on Jaspers' part when Heidegger gave him his detailed review of Jaspers' book *Psychologie der Weltanschauungen* to read, and Jaspers did not respond. Breaking off of communication after 1933. After 1945, various attempts to regain closeness all failed. Throughout his life, Jaspers planned to write a long confrontation with Heidegger's work, which he admitted to not having read completely. He did not finish it. After his death, his *Notes on Martin Heidegger* were found lying on his desk. The chapter on Heidegger, written already in the middle of the fifties, was similarly only allowed to be included in his *Philosophische Autobiographie* after his death. The eagerly awaited edition of the correspondence between Jaspers and Heidegger is presently being prepared by Hans Saner and Walter Biemel. Translator's note. Since the German edition was published, the book has appeared: Martin Heidegger/Karl Jaspers, *Briefwechsel 1920–1963*, ed. by Hans Saner and Walter Biemel (Frankfurt/Munich: Klostermann/Piper, 1990).

Walter Jens

Born 1923 in Hamburg; studied classics and German at the universities of Hamburg and Freiburg, received his doctorate in 1944, 1963 professor and from 1968 to 1988 full professor of general rhetoric at the University of Tübingen.

Major Works: Hofmannsthal und die Griechen (Tübingen: 1955); *Statt einer Literaturgeschichte*, 7th rev. ed. (1957; Pfullingen: Neske, 1978); *Eine deutsche Universität. 500 Jahre Tübinger Gelehetenrepublik* (Munich: Kindler, 1977); *Ort der Handlung ist Deutschland. Reden in crinnerunjafeindlicher Zeit* (Munich: Droemer Knaur, 1984).

Hans Jonas

Born in 1903 in Mönchengladbach; studied philosophy, theology, and art history in Freiburg, Berlin, Heidelberg, and Marburg, received his doctorate in 1928 with Heidegger and Rudolf Bultmann as his advisors, emigrated first to England, then in 1935 to Palestine, 1938–1939 and 1946–1948 lecturer at Hebrew University in Jerusalem and at the British Council School for Higher Studies 1946–1948, professor at McGill University in Montreal in 1949, 1950–1954 professor at Charlton University in Ottawa, 1955–1976 at the New School for Social Research in New York, recipient of the Peace Prize of the German Book Trade in 1987. Lives in the USA.

Publications on Heidegger: "Heidegger und die Theologie," *Heidegger und die Theologie. Beginn und Fortgang der Diskussion*, ed. by Gerhard Noller (1964; Munich: Kaiser, 1967), pp. 316–340; "Wandel und Bestand. Vom Grunde der Verstehbarkeit des Geschichtlichen," *Durchblicke. Martin Heidegger zum 80. Geburtstag*, ed. by Vittorio Klostermann (Frankfurt: Klostermann, 1970), pp. 1–27.

Major Works: Gnosis und spätantiker Geist, 2 vols (Göttingen: Vandenhoeck und Ruprecht, 1934 and 1954); *Organismus und Freiheit. Ansätze zu einer philosophischen Biologie* (Göttingen: Vandenhoeck und Ruprecht, 1973); *Das Prinzip Verantwortung. Versuch einer Ethik für die technologische Zivilisation* (Frankfurt: Insel Verlag, 1981); *Technik, Medizin und*

Ethik. Zur Praxis des Prinzips Verantwortung (Frankfurt: Insel Verlag, 1985).

Notes: Jonas has been very reticent with positions on his teacher Heidegger in his recent publications; in *Das Prinzip Verantwortung*, for example, the name Heidegger is not mentioned.

Eberhard Jüngel

Born in Magdeburg in 1934; studied theology at the universities of Naumburg, Berlin, Zurich, and Basel, received his doctorate in theology in 1961, after 1961 he was an assistant professor of New Testament studies and systematic theology at the Ecclesiastical University in East Berlin, after 1966 full professor af systematic theology at the University of Zürich, after 1969 full professor of systematic theology and the philosophy of religion at the University of Tübingen.

Publications on Heidegger: "Gott entsprechendes Schweigen? Theologie in der Nachbarschaft des Denkens von Martin Heidegger," *Martin Heidegger—Fragen an sein Werk. Ein Symposion* (Stuttgart: Reclam, 1977), pp. 37–45; "Metaphorische Wahrheit. Erwägungen zur theologischen Relevanz der Metapher als Beitrag zur Hermeneutik der narrativen Theologie," *Entsprechungen* (1980), pp. 103–157; with Michael Trowitzsch, "Provozierendes Denken," *neue hefte für philosophie*, vol. 23: *Wirkungen Heideggers* (Göttingen: Vandenhoeck und Ruprecht, 1984), pp. 59–74.

Major Works: Paulus und Jesus (Tübingen: Mohr, 1962); *Zum Ursprung der Analogie bei Parmenides und Heraklit* (Berlin: de Gruyter, 1964); *Gottes Sein ist im Werden* (Tübingen: Mohr, 1965); with Paul Ricoeur, *Metapher. Zur Hermaneutik religiöser Sprache* (Munich: Kaiser, 1974); *Gott als Geheimnis der Welt* (Tübingen: Mohr, 1977); *Entsprechungen. Gott—Wahrheit—Mensch* (München: Kaiser, 1980); *Barth-Studien* (Gütersloh: Gütersloher Verlagshaus, 1982).

Emil Kettering

Born 1957 in Thaleischweiler/Pfalz; studied philosophy, German, and education 1977–1986 at the Johannes Gutenberg University in Mainz, received his doctorate in 1986 with Prof. Dr. Richard Wisser as his advisor, Johannes Gutenberg University prize in 1986, since 1 April 1986 assistant to Prof. Dr. Josef Reiter in the philosophy department of the Johannes Gutenberg University.

Publications on Heidegger: NÄHE. Das Denken Martin Heideggers. (Pfullingen: Neske, 1987); "NÄHE im Denken Martin Heideggers." *Martin Heidegger—Unterwegs im Denken. Symposion im 10. Todesjahr.* (Freiburg/Munich: Alber, 1987), pp. 111–130.

Emmanuel Lévinas

Born 1905 in Kaunas, Lithuania, studied philosophy 1923–1929, at the University of Strasbourg, 1928–1929 at the University of Freiburg with Husserl and Heidegger, naturalized in France in 1930, became professor of philosophy in 1962, appointed professor at the University of Poitiers in 1964, at the University of Paris-Nanterre in 1967, and at the Sorbonne in 1973, recipient of the Karl Jaspers Prize in 1983. Lives in Paris.

Publications on Heidegger: De l'existence à l'existant, 4th ed. (1947; Paris: Vrin, 1986); *En découvrant l'existence avec Husserl et Heidegger*, 3rd ed. (1949; Paris: Vrin, 1974). References to Heidegger may be found in many of Lévinas' works.

Major Works: Totalité et Infini. Essai sur l'extériorité (The Hague: Nijhoff, 1961), English translation: *Totality and infinity: an essay on exteriority*, trans. by Alphonso Lingis (The Hague/Boston: Nijhoff, 1979); *Autrement qu'être ou au-dela de l'essence* (The Hague: Nijhoff, 1974); *De Dieu qui vient á l'idée* (Paris: Vrin, 1982).

Notes: Lévinas is Jewish and took a vow during the Second World War never again to set foot on German soil. He broke with Heidegger because of the latter's initial engagement with National Socialism. According to statements Lévinas later made, he was unable to study Heidegger's later work the way he had his earlier work because of Heidegger's political engagement.

Karl Löwith

Born 1897; studied philosophy in Freiburg with Husserl and Heidegger, whom he followed to Marburg in 1923 after receiving his doctorate. In Marburg he wrote his postdoctoral thesis [*Habilitationschrift*] on "The Individual in the Role of Fellow Human Being" [*Das Individuum in der Rolle des Mitmenschen*] with Heidegger, 1934–1951 to Italy, Japan, and the USA, professor at the New School for Social Research in New York, returned to Germany in 1952, when he received an appointment as professor of philosophy at the University of Heidelberg at Hans-Georg Gadamer's instigation. Taught at the University of Heidelberg until he retired. Died in 1973.

Publications on Heidegger: Das Individuum in der Rolle des Mitmenschen (München: Drei Masken Verlag, 1928); "Les implications politiques de la philosophie de l'existence chez Heidegger," *Les Temps Modernes*, vol. 2, (1946): pp. 343–360 (see "Der europäische Nihilismus" (1940), *Sämtliche Schriften*, pp. 475–540, esp. pp. 514–528); *Heidegger—Denker in dürftiger Zeit* (Frankfurt: S. Fischer, 1953). (3rd rev. ed. Göttingen: Vanderhoeck und Ruprecht, 1965; also collected in *Sämtliche Schriften*, vol. 8 (Stuttgart: Metzler, 1984) along with further essays on Heidegger); *Mein Leben in*

Deutschland vor und nach 1933. Ein Bericht (Stuttgart: Metzler, 1986), esp. pp. 27–45 and 56–59.

Major Works: Nietzsches Philosophie der ewigen Wiederkehr des Gleichen, 3rd rev. ed. (Hamburg: Meinder, 1978); *Von Hegel zu Nietzsche* (Zurich/ New York: Europa Verlag, 1941); *Weltgeschichte und Heilsgeschehen* (Stuttgart: Kohlhammer, 1952); *Sämtliche Schriften,* 9 volumes (Stuttgart: Metzler, 1981 ff.).

Notes: At the time he wrote this, Löwith supposed that this meeting with Heidegger in Rome in 1936 would be the last. After that, Heidegger did not answer Löwith's letters, and after the war there was a break between Löwith and his teacher for a long time. At the reunions of the Altmarburger, for example, Löwith left when Heidegger came and vice versa. In 1969, Löwith participated in a colloquium in Heidelberg in honor of Heidegger's eightieth birthday, gave a lecture, and reconciled himself with him.

For Heidegger's opinion on Löwith's book *Heidegger—Denker in dürftiger Zeit,* see Heinrich W. Petzet, *Auf einen Stern zugehen. Begegnungen mit Martin Heidegger 1929–1976* (Frankfurt: Societäts-Verlag, 1983), p. 68 in this volume.

Max Müller

Born 1906 in Bad Offenburg (Baden); studied philosophy and history at the University of Berlin, University of Munich, and after 1928 with Heidegger at the University of Freiburg, received his doctorate in 1930, *Habilitation* in 1937, after 1946 full professor of philosophy at the University of Freiburg, after 1960 at the University of Munich, named honorary professor of the University of Freiburg in 1971, deputy president of the Martin Heidegger Society. Lives in Freiburg.

Publications on Heidegger: Existenzphilosophie im geistigen Leben der Gegenwart (Heidelberg: Kerle, 1949); 3rd rev. ed. in 1964; 4th rev. ed. with the title *Existenzphilosophie. Von der Metaphysik zur Metahistorik,* ed. by Alois Halder (Freiburg/Munich: Alber, 1986); in addition, references to Heidegger's works may be found in many of Müller's writings.

Major Works: Sein und Geist. Systematische Untersuchungen über Grundprobleme und Aufbau mittelalterliche Ontologie (2nd rev. ed.: Freiburg/ Munich: Alber, 1981; 1st ed. 1940); *Erfahrung und Geschichte. Grundzüge einer Philosophie der Freiheit als transzendentale Erfahrung* (Freiburg/ Munich: Alber, 1971); *Philosophische Anthropologie,* ed. by Wilhelm Vossenkuhl (Freiburg/Munich: Alber, 1974); *Der Kompromiss* (Freiburg/ Munich: Alber, 1981).

Hugo Ott

Born 1931; studied in Freiburg and Munich, 1969 professor at the Pädagogische Hochschule in Freiburg, since 1971 professor of economic and social history at the University of Freiburg, recipient of the Fürstabt Martin Gerbert Prize in 1975, guest professor at the University of Florida, Gainesville, in 1982.

Publications on Heidegger: "Martin Heidegger als Rektor der Universität Freiburg i. B. 1933/34," *Zeitschrift für die Geschichte des Oberrheins*, vol. 132 (1984): pp. 343–358; "Martin Heidegger und die Universität Freiburg nach 1945. Ein Beispiel für die Auseinandersetzung mit der politischen Vergangenheit," *Historisches Jahrbuch*, vol. 105 (1985): pp. 95–128; "Martin Heidegger und der Nationalsozialismus," *Heidegger und die praktische Philosophie*, Annemarie Gethmann-Siefert and Otto Pöggeler, eds. (Frankfurt: Suhrkamp, 1988), pp. 64–77; *Martin Heidegger. Unterwegs zu seiner Biographie* (Frankfurt/New York: Campus Verlag, 1988).

Heinrich Wiegand Petzet

Born 1909 in Bremen; studied history and art history, attended lectures given by Heidegger, received his doctorate in 1938 in Berlin with Walter Elze as his advisor, 1929–1976 acquaintance and friendship with Heidegger. Lives in Freiburg im Breisgau.

Note: On the history of the *Spiegel* interview, see also Martin Heidegger/ Erhart Kästner. *Briefwechsel 1953–1974*. Heinrich W. Petzet, ed. (Frankfurt: 1986), pp. 79–83.

Georg Picht

Born 1913 in Strasbourg; studied classics and philosophy, after 1958 head of the Forschungsstätte der Evangelischen Studiengemeinschaft in Heidelberg, after 1965 professor of the philosophy of religion at the divinity school of the University of Heidelberg. Died in 1982.

Major Works: Wahrheit—Vernunft—Verantwortung. Philosophische Studien (Stuttgart: Klett, 1969); *Hier und Jetzt. Philosophieren nach Auschwitz und Hiroshima*, 2 vols. (Stuttgart: Klett-Cotta, 1980/1981); *Vorlesungen und Schriften*, (Stuttgart: Klett-Cotta, 1985–1987).

Emil Staiger

Born 1908 in Kreuzlingen, Switzerland; professor of literature at the University of Zürich after 1943.

Publications on Heidegger: "Ein Briefwechsel mit Martin Heidegger," *Die Kunst der Interpretation* (Zurich: Atlantis Verlag, 1955), pp. 34–49; also in Martin Heidegger, *Gesamtausgabe* vol. 13 (Frankfurt: Klostermann, 1983), pp. 93–109. In addition, scattered references to Heidegger may be found, especially in Staiger's theoretical writings.

Major Works: Die Zeit als Einbildungskraft des Dichters (Zurich: Atlantis

Verlag, 1959); *Meisterwerke deutscher Sprache* (Zurich: Atlantis Verlag, 1943); *Grundbegriffe der Poetik* (Zurich: Atlantis Verlag, 1946); *Goethe*, 3 vols. (Zurich: Atlantis Verlag, 1952–1959); *Stilwandel. Studien zur Vorgeschichte der Goethezeit* (Zurich: Atlantis Verlag, 1963); *Friedrich Schiller* (Zurich: Atlantis Verlag, 1967).

Richard Wisser

A shorter version of "Afterthoughts and Gratitude" then entitled "The Television Interview" appeared in *Erinnerung an Martin Heidegger*, ed. by Günther Neske (Pfullingen: Neske, 1977), pp. 257–287.

Born in Worms in 1927; studied philosophy, psychology, and comparative culture studies at the universities of Mainz and Córdoba, Argentina; received his doctorate in 1954; the qualification to teach at the university level [Habilitation] in 1966; full professor of philosophy at the University of Mainz after 1971.

Publications on Heidegger: "La voix qui pense et sa pensée. Martin Heidegger," *Les Etudes Philos.* 4 (Paris, 1958), pp. 495–500; "Humanismus und Wissenschaft in der Sicht Martin Heideggers," *Integritas*, ed. by Dieter Stolte and Richard Wisser (Tübingen: Wunderlich, 1966); "Das Fragen als Weg des Denkens. Martin Heideggers Verantwortung von Technik, Wissenschaft und Humanismus im Hinblick auf den Menschen als Da des Seins," *Verantwortung im Wandel der Zeit* (Mainz: v. Hese und Koehler, 1967), pp. 273–323; "Martin Heidegger und der Wandel der Wirklichkeit des Wirklichen," *Aeropag* 5 (1970), pp. 79–90; "Aneignung und Unterscheidung. Existenzphilosophie im Kampf um die Existenz der Philosophie: Karl Jaspers und Martin Heidegger," *Theologie und Philosophie* (1984), pp. 481–498; also in *Karl Jaspers Today. Philosophy at the Threshold of the Future*, ed. by L. Ehrlich and R. Wisser (Washington, D.C: 1988) pp. 341–361; "Hegel und Heidegger, oder die Wende vom Denken des Denkens zum Seinsdenken," *Synthesis Philosophica* 4 (Zagreb, 1987) pp. 301–326; "Martin Heideggers vierfältiges Fragen. Vor-läufiges anhand von 'Was ist Metaphysik?' " *Martin Heidegger—Unterwegs im Denken. Symposion im 10. Todesjahr*, ed. by Richard Wisser (Freiburg/Munich: Alber, 1987), pp. 15–50.

A Selective Bibliography on Heidegger and Politics

Amended for the English edition by Karsten Harries. Entries are Listed in Chronological Order

EMIL KETTERING

Martin Heidegger, *Die Selbstbehauptung der deutschen Universität* (Breslau: Korn, 1933). 2nd ed. 1934; withdrawn from trade by the National Socialists, following Heidegger's resignation as rector. Translated as *The Self-Assertion of the German University* by Lisa Harries, this volume, p. 5.

Maurice de Gandillac and Alfred de Towarnicki, "Deux documents sur Heidegger, *Les Temps Modernes*, vol. I, 1946, pp. 713–724.

Karl Löwith, "Les implications politiques de la philosophie de l'existence chez Heidegger," *Les Temps Modernes*, vol. II, 1946, pp. 346–360. Written in 1939, when Löwith was in exile in Japan. See also "Der europäische Nihilismus" (1940), in *Sämtliche Schriften*, vol. 2, *Weltgeschichte und Heilsgeschehen* (Stuttgart: Metzler, 1983, pp. 473–540, esp. pp. 514–528. Also "Der okkasionelle Dezisionismus von Carl Schmitt" (enlarged ed. 1960), in *Sämtliche Schriften*, vol. 8: *Heidegger: Denker in dürftiger Zeit* (Stuttgart: Metzler, 1984, pp. 32–71, esp. pp. 61–69.

Alfonse de Waelhens, "La philosophie de Heidegger et le nazisme," in *Les Temps Modernes*, vol. IV, 1947/48, pp. 115–127.

Eric Weil, "Le cas Heidegger," *Les Temps Modernes*, vol. IV, 1947/48, pp. 128–138.

Karl Löwith, "Réponse à A. de Waelhens," *Les Temps Modernes*, vol. IV, 1947/48, pp. 370–373.

Alfonse de Waelhens, "Réponse à cette réponse," *Les Temps Modernes*, vol. IV, 1947/48, pp. 374–377.

Jürgen Habermas, "Mit Heidegger gegen Heidegger denken. Zur Veröffentlichung von Vorlesungen aus dem Jahre 1935," *Frankfurter Allgemeine Zeitung*, 25.7.1953. Reprinted in Habermas, *Philosophisch-politische Profile*, enlarged ed. (Frankfurt: Suhrkamp, 1981), pp. 65–72.

Christian E. Lewalter, "Wie liest man 1953 Sätze von 1935? Zu einem politischen Streit um Heideggers Metaphysik," *Die Zeit*, 13.8.1953.

Karl Korn, "Warum schweigt Heidegger? Antwort auf den Versuch einer Polemik," *Frankfurter Allgemeine Zeitung*, 14.8.1953.

Egon Vietta, "Heideggers Sätze von 1935." Letter to the Editor, *Die Zeit*, 20.8.1953.

Martin Heidegger, Letter to the Editor, *Die Zeit*, 24.9.1953.

Georg Lukàcs, *Die Zerstörung der Vernunft* (Berlin: Aufbau, 1954). Also in *Werke*, vol. 9 (Neuwied: Luchterhand, 1962), esp. pp. 165–195.

Christian Graf von Krockow, *Die Entscheidung. Eine Untersuchung über Carl Schmitt, Ernst Jünger, und Martin Heidegger* (Stuttgart: Enke, 1958).

Jürgen Habermas, "Die grosse Wirkung. Eine chronistische Anmerkung zu Martin Heideggers 70. Geburtstag," *Frankfurter Allgemeine Zeitung*, 26.9.1959. Reprinted in Habermas, *Philosophisch-politische Profile*, pp. 72–81.

Paul Hühnerfeld, *In Sachen Heidegger. Versuch über ein deutsches Genie* (Hamburg: Hoffmann und Campe, 1959).

Guido Schneeberger, *Ergänzungen zu einer Heidegger-Bibliographie* (Bern: Guido Schneeberger, 1960).

Jean Pierre Faye, "Heidegger et la 'révolution,'" in *Méditations*, vol. 3, 1961, pp. 151–159.

Jean Pierre Faye, "Attaques nazies contre Heidegger," in *Méditations*, vol. 5, 1962, pp. 137–154.

Guido Schneeberger, *Nachlese zu Martin Heidegger* (Bern: Guido Schneeberger, 1962). A collection of 217 documents from the years 1929–1961 of which 15 are by Heidegger. A selection of these documents was translated and published by Dagobert D. Runes as Martin Heidegger, *German Existentialism* (New York: Philosophical Library, 1965).

Theodor W. Adorno, *Jargon der Eigentlichkeit. Zur deutschen Ideologie* (Frankfurt: Suhrkamp, 1964).

Alexander Schwan, *Politische Philosophie im Denken Martin Heideggers* (Kön/Opladen: Westdeutscher Verlag, 1965). The 2nd ed., 1989, adds the important Postscript of 1988: "Um einen Heidegger von innen bittend," pp. 208–275.

"Mitternacht einer Weltnacht," in *Der Spiegel*, vol. 20, no. 7, 7.2.1966, pp. 110–113.

Martin Heidegger, Letter to the Editor, *Der Spiegel*, vol. 20, no. 11, 7.3.1966, p. 12.

Robert Minder, "Heidegger und Hegel oder die Sprache von Messkirch," in Minder, *Hölderlin unter den Deutschen und andere Aufsätze zur Literatur*, (Frankfurt: Insel, 1966). 2nd ed. (Frankfurt: Suhrkamp, 1968), pp. 86–153.

François Fédier. "Trois attaques contre Heidegger," *Critique*, no. 234, November 1966. Discusses Schneeberger, Hühnerfeld, and Adorno.

"À propos de Heidegger," *Critique*, no. 237, February 1967, pp. 284–297. Replies to the preceding article by Robert Minder, Jean Pierre Faye, and Aime Patri.

François Fédier, "À propos de Heidegger: une lecture dénoncée," *Critique*, no. 242, July 1967, pp. 672–686. Reply to the objections by Minder, Faye, and Patri.

Beda Allemann, "Martin Heidegger und die Politik," *Merkur*, vol. 21, no. 10, 1967, pp. 962–976. Reprinted in Heidegger, *Perspektiven zur Deutung seines Werkes*, ed. Otto Pöggeler (Cologne: Kiepenheuer and Witsch, 1969, pp. 246–260. 2nd. ed. (Königstein: Athenäum, 1984), pp. 246–260.

François Bondy, "Zum Thema 'Martin Heidegger und die Politik,' " *Merkur*, vol. 22, 1968, pp. 189–192.

François Fédier and François Bondy, "À propos de Heidegger," *Critique*, no. 251, 1968, pp. 433–437.

Hans-Peter Hempel. "Politische Philosophie im Denken Heideggers," *Zeitschrift für philosophische Forschung*, vol. 22, 1968, pp. 432–440. Review of the book by Schwan.

Jean-Michel Palmier, *Les Écrits politiques de Heidegger* (Paris: Éditions de l'Herne, 1968).

Hannah Arendt, "Martin Heidegger ist achtzig Jahre alt," *Merkur*, vol. 10, 1969, pp. 893–902. Translated by Albert Hofstadter, "Martin Heidegger at Eighty, *The New York Review of Books*, October 1971, reprinted in *Heidegger and Modern Philosophy*, ed. Michael Murray (New Haven and London: Yale University Press, 1978), pp. 293–303. See this volume, p. 207.

302   A Selective Bibliography

Jean Pierre Faye, *Languages totalitaires. Critique de la raison, l'économie narrative* (Paris: Hermann, 1972).

Karl August Möhling, *Martin Heidegger and the Nazi Party: An Examination.* Unpublished Dissertation, Northern Illinois University 1972.

Otto Pöggeler, *Philosophie und Politik bei Heidegger* (Freiburg and Munich: Alber, 1972). 2nd. enlarged ed. 1974.

Theodor W. Adorno, *Philosophische Terminologie,* 2 vols. (Frankfurt: Suhrkamp, 1973), vol. 1, pp. 148–160. (Frankfurt lectures of 1962/63.)

Alexander Schwan, "Martin Heidegger, Politik und Praktische Philosophie. Zur Problematik neuerer Heidegger-Literatur," *Philosophisches Jahrbuch,* vol. 81, 1974, pp. 148–171.

Michael Zimmermann, "Heidegger, Ethics, and National Socialism," *Southwestern Journal of Philosophy,* vol. 5, Spring 1974, pp. 97–106.

Pierre Bourdieu, *L'ontologie politique de Martin Heidegger.* First published in 1975 in *Actes de la recherche en sciences sociales,* the study was revised and republished by Les Éditions de Minuit, Paris, in 1988.

Interview with Martin Heidegger, "Nur noch ein Gott kann uns retten," *Spiegel,* vol. 30. no. 23, 31 May 1976. The interview dates from 1966. A translation by William J. Richardson in *Heidegger: The Man and the Thinker,* ed. Thomas Sheehan (Chicago: Precedent, 1981). For a translation of the version authorized by Heidegger for publication and an account of the circumstances surrounding the interview see pp. 41–66 in this volume.

Winifried Franzen, "Heidegger und der Nationalsozialismus," in *Martin Heidegger* (Stuttgart: Metzler, 1976, pp. 78–85.

Karsten Harries, "Heidegger as a Political Thinker," *The Review of Metaphysics,* vol. 29, no. 4, June 1976, pp. 642–669. Reprinted in *Heidegger and Modern Philosophy,* ed. Michael Murray (New Haven and London: Yale University Press, 1978), pp. 304–328.

Willy Hochkeppel, "Martin Heideggers langer Marsch durch die 'verkehrte Welt,'" *Merkur,* vol. 30, 1976, pp. 911–921.

Henry Pachter, "Heidegger and Hitler," *Boston University Journal,* vol. 24, no. 3, 1976, pp. 47–55.

Carl Ulmer, Letter to the Editor (Addendum to the Schelling lecture), *Der Spiegel,* 2.5.1977.

Henrich Bodensiek and Richard Breyer, Letters to the Editor (On Hitler's Hands), *Der Spiegel,* 2. 5. 1977 and 16. 5. 1977.

Bernard Willms, "Politik als Geniestreich? Bemerkungen zu Heideggers Politikverständnis," in *Frankfurter Allgemeine Zeitung,* 14. 5. 1977. Reprinted in *Martin Heidegger. Fragen an sein Werk. Ein Symposion* (Stuttgart: Reclam, 1977), pp. 16–20.

Karl Jaspers, *Philosophische Autobiographie*, enlarged ed. (Munich: Piper, 1977), pp. 92–111.

Frederick Olafson, "Heidegger's Politics: An Interview with Herbert Marcuse, *Graduate Faculty Philosophy Journal*, vol. 4, Winter 1977, pp. 28–39.

Georg Picht, "Die Macht des Denkens," in *Erinnerungen an Martin Heidegger*, ed. Günther Neske (Pfullingen: Neske, 1977), pp. 197–205.

Karl Jaspers, *Notizen zu Martin Heidegger*, ed. Hans Saner (Munich: Piper, 1978).

George Steiner, *Martin Heidegger* (Harmondsworth, England: Penguin, 1978).

Hans Köchler, *Skepsis und Gesellschaftskritik im Denken Martin Heideggers* (Meisenheim: Hain, 1978).

Reiner Schürmann, "Political Thinking in Heidegger," *Social Research*, vol. 45, 1978, pp. 190 ff.

Hermann Mörchen, *Macht und Herrschaft im Denken von Heidegger und Adorno* (Stuttgart: Klett-Cotta, 1980).

Mark Blitz, Being and Time *and the Possibility of Political Philosophy* (Ithaca: Cornell University Press, 1981).

Karl A. Moehling, "Heidegger and the Nazis," in *Heidegger: The Man and the Thinker*, ed. Thomas Sheehan (Chicago: Precedent, 1981), pp. 31–43.

Gregory Shufreider, "Heidegger on Community," *Man and World*, vol. 14, 1981, pp. 25–41. A critique of Harries, 1976.

Gerd Tellenbach, *Aus erinnerter Zeitgeschichte* (Freiburg: Verlag der Wagnerschen Universitätsbuchhandlung, 1981), pp. 40 ff. and 110 ff.

Wilhelm Schoeppe, Letter to the Editor (on Heidegger's Report on Baumgartner) *Frankfurter Allgemeine Zeitung*, 28. 5. 1983.

Willy Hochkeppel, "Heidegger, die Nazis und kein Ende," *Die Zeit*, 6. 5. 1983.

Alexander Schwan, "Die Verführbarkeit des deutschen Geistes. Zur verhängnisvollen Rektoratsrede Martin Heideggers am 27. Mai 1933," *Rheinischer Merkur/Christ in Welt*, 27. 5. 1983.

Hugo Ott, "Die Übernahme des Rektorats der Universität Freiburg durch Martin Heidegger im April 1933," *Zeitschrift des Breisgau-Geschichtsvereins* (*"Schau-ins-Land"*), vol. 102, 1983, pp. 121–136.

Otto Pöggeler, *Der Denkweg Martin Heideggers*, 2nd ed. with a new Postscript (Pfullingen: Neske, 1983), esp. 340 ff.

Heinrich W. Petzet, *Auf einen Stern zugehen. Begegnungen und Gespräche mit Martin Heidegger 1929–1976* (Frankfurt: Societäts-Verlag, 1983).

Martin Heidegger, *Die Selbstbehauptung der deutschen Universität. Das Rektorat 1933/34* (Frankfurt: Klostermann, 1983). Reprint of the Rectorial Address of 1933, supplemented with Heidegger's reflections on the time of the rectorate, written down in 1945. Translated by Karsten Harries. *The Review of Metaphysics*, vol. 38, March 1985, pp. 467–502. For new translations of these texts see pp. 5–32 of this volume.

Maurice Blanchot, "Die Intellektuellen im Kreuzfeuer," *Akzente*, vol. 31, 1984, pp. 403 ff.

Fred Dallmayr, "Ontology of Freedom: Heidegger and Political Philosophy, *Political Theory*, vol. 12, May 1984, pp. 204–207.

Hugo Ott, "Die Zeit des Rektorats von Martin Heidegger (23. April 1933 bis 23. April 1934)," *Zeitschrift des Breisgau-Geschichtsvereins ("Schau-ins-Land")*, vol. 103, 1984, pp. 107–130.

Hugo Ott, "Der Philosoph als Führer," *Frankfurter Allgemeine Zeitung*, 20. 7. 1984.

Hugo Ott, "Martin Heidegger als Rektor der Universität Freiburg i. Br. 1933/34," *Zeitschrift für die Geschichte des Oberrheins*, vol. 132, 1984, pp. 343–358.

Hugo Ott, " 'Es dürfte eher Entlassung in Frage kommen. . . .' Der Freiburger Rektor Martin Heidegger 1933/34 und das Verfahren gegen Hermann Staudinger. Ein Bericht über neue Aktenfunde," *Badische Zeitung*, no. 283, 8. 12. 1984.

Hugo Ott, "Martin Heidegger und die Universität Freiburg nach 1945. Ein Beispiel für die Auseinandersetzung mit der politischen Vergangenheit," *Historisches Jahrbuch*, vol. 105, 1985, pp. 95–128.

Hannah Arendt/Karl Jaspers: *Briefwechsel. 1926–1969*. Ed. Lotte Köhler and Hans Saner (Munich and Zurich: Piper, 1985).

Jürgen Habermas, *Der philosophische Diskurs der Moderne. Zwölf Vorlesungen* (Frankfurt: Suhrkamp, 1985). pp. 158–190.

Otto Pöggeler, "Den Führer führen? Heidegger und kein Ende," *Philosophische Rundschau*, vol. 32, 1985, pp. 26–67.

Edith Wyschogrod, *Spirit in Ashes: Hegel, Heidegger, and Man-Made Mass Death* (New Haven and London: Yale University Press, 1985).

Fred Dallmayr, "Heidegger, Hölderlin, and Politics," *Heidegger Studien*, vol. 2, 1986, pp. 81–96.

Philippe Lacoue-Labarthe, *L'imitation des modernes. Typographies II* (Paris: Éditions Galilée, 1986).

Karl Löwith, *Mein Leben in Deutschland vor und nach 1933. Ein Bericht*. With a preface by Reinhart Koselleck and a postscript by Ada Löwith (Stuttgart: Metzler, 1986), esp. pp. 27–46, 56–59, 147–150.

Alexander Schwan, "Heidegger," entry in *Staatslexikon*, vol. 2. 7., completely revised ed. (Freiburg: Herder, 1986), pp. 1225–1229.

Martin Heidegger. Ein Philosoph und die Politik. Freiburger Universitätsblätter, vol. 92 (Freiburg: Rombach, June 1986), pp. 8–90. The issue contains 1. "Ein Gespräch mit Max Müller," pp. 13–31. (For a translation see this volume, p. 175) 2. Alexander Hollerbach, "Im Schatten des Jahres 1933: Erik Wolf und Martin Heidegger," pp. 33–47. 3. Bernd Martin, "Heidegger und die Reform der deutschen Universität 1933," pp. 49–69. 4. Walter Biemel, "Erinnerrung an zwei Jahre in Freiburg 1942–44," pp. 71–73. 5. Ute Guzzoni, "Bemerkungen zu Heidegger 1933," pp. 75–80. 6. Gerhart Schmidt, "Heidegger's philosophische Politik," pp. 83–90.

Graeme Nicholson, "The Politics of Heidegger's Rectoral Address," *Man and World*, vol. 20, 1987, pp. 171–181.

Victor Farías, *Heidegger et le nazisme*, tr. from the Spanish and German by Myriam Benarroch and Jean-Baptiste Grasset with a preface by Christian Jambet (Lagrasse: Verdier, 1987). Reviews in *Le Monde*, 14. 10. 1987; *Liberation*, 16. 10. 1987; *Frankfurter Allgemeine Zeitung*, 28. 10. 1987; *Die Zeit*, 6. 11. 1987. The revised and longer German edition appeared as *Heidegger und der Nationalsozialismus* (Frankfurt: Fischer, 1989). It was translated from the Spanish and French by Klaus Laermann and includes an important preface by Jürgen Habermas, "Heidegger—Werk und Weltanschaung." The English edition, *Heidegger and Nazism* (Philadelphia: Temple University Press, 1989), edited, with a Foreword, by Joseph Margolis and Tom Rockmore, was translated from the French and the German editions, without, unfortunately, incorporating all of the corrections made in the latter. Of the three, the German must be considered the most authoritative.

Jacques Derrida, Interview, *Le Nouvel Observateur*, 6. 11. 1987.

Victor Farías, Reply to Jacques Derrida, *El Pais*, 19. 11. 1987.

Rudolf Augstein, "Aber bitte nicht philosophieren!" *Der Spiegel*, vol. 41. no. 48, 23. 11. 1987, pp. 212–221.

John Bailiff, "Truth and Power: Martin Heidegger, "The Essence of Truth," and "The Self-Assertion of the University," *Man and World*, vol. 20, 1987, 327–336.

Hugo Ott, "Wege und Abwege. Zu Victor Farías' kritischer Heidegger-Studie," *Neue Zürcher Zeitung*, 27. 11. 1987. For a translation see this volume, pp. 133–139.

Hartmut Tietjen, "Stellungnahme zu: Victor Farías, *Heidegger et le nazisme*," Press Declaration of the Martin Heidegger-Gesellschaft, 1987.

Rainer Marten, "Ein rassistisches Konzept von Humanität. Überlegungen zu Viktor Farías' Heidegger-Buch und zum richtigen Umgang mit Heidegger," *Badische Zeitungen*, 19/20. 12. 1987.

Jacques Derrida, *De l'esprit* (Paris: Éditions Galilée, 1987). Translated as *Of Spirit. Heidegger and the Question* by Geoffrey Bennington and

Rachel Bowlby (Chicago and London: University of Chicago Press, 1989).

Luc Ferry and Alain Renaut, *Heidegger et les Modernes* (Paris: Grasset, 1988).

Philippe Lacoue-Labarthe, *La Fiction du politique: Heidegger, l'art et la politique* (Paris: Christian Bourgeois, 1987).

"Heidegger et la pensée nazie," *Le Nouvel Observateur*, 22–28. 1. 1988. pp. 74–84. Contributions by Catherine David, Maurice Blanchot, Hans-Georg Gadamer, Philipe Lacoue-Labarthe, Emmanuel Lévinas, and François Fédier.

Michel Tibon-Cornillot, "Heidegger et le chainon manquant," *Libération*, 17 February 1988, pp. 41–42.

"Heidegger, la philosophie et le nazisme," *Le Débat*, no. 48, 1988, pp. 112–192. Contributions by Pierre Aubenque, Henri Cretella, Michel Deguy, François Fédier, Gérard Granel, Stéphane Moses, and Alain Renaut.

Jürgen Busche, "Also gut. Heidegger war ein Nazi," *Pflasterstrand*, No. 279/280, Frankfurt, 1988, pp. 46–48.

Manfred S. Frings, "Is there Room for Evil in Heidegger's Thought or Not?" *Philosophy Today*, Spring 1988, pp. 79–82.

Jean-François Lyotard, *Heidegger et "les juifs"* (Paris: Éditions Galilée, 1988).

Herbert Marcuse, "Briefe vom 28. 8. 1947 und 13. 5. 1948 an Martin Heidegger," *Pflasterstrand*, No. 279/280, Frankfurt, 1988, pp. 46–48. The letters were first published in *Pflasterstrand*, 1985.

Die Heidegger Kontroverse, ed. Jürg Altwegg (Frankfurt: Athenäum, 1988). A useful collection of relevant essays, including several of the items mentioned above.

Pierre Boncenne/Jean Blain/Alain Jaubert, "L'affaire Heidegger. Peut-on encore croire les philosophes? *Lire*, No. 153, June 1988, pp. 41–54.

François Fédier, *Heidegger—Anatomie d'un Scandale* (Paris: Laffont, 1988).

Dieter Hoffmann-Axthelm, "Farías und der Nazi—eine jakobinische Form der Konfliktvermeidung, *Die Neue Gesellschaft. Frankfurter Hefte*, vol. 35, no. 6, 1988, pp. 506–512.

Philippe Lacoue-Labarthe, *La fiction du politique* (Breteuil: Collection du Trois, 1988).

Hugo Ott, *Martin Heidegger. Unterwegs zu seiner Biographie* (Frankfurt: Athenäum, 1988).

Richard Rorty, "Taking Philosophy Seriously," *The New Republic*, April 11, 1988, pp. 31–34. A reaction to the book by Farías.

Thomas A. Sheehan, "Heidegger and the Nazis," *The New York Review of Books*, June 16, 1988, pp. 38–47. A reaction to the book by Farías.

Heidegger und die praktische Philosophie, ed. Annemarie Gethmann-Siefert and Otto Pöggeler (Frankfurt: Suhrkamp, 1988). The collection includes inter alia 1. Otto Pöggeler, "Heideggers politisches Selbstverständnis," pp. 17–63. 2. Hugo Ott, "Martin Heidegger und der Nationalsozialismus," pp. 64–77. 3. Winfried Franzen, "Die Sehnsucht nach Härte und Schwere. Über ein zum NS-Engagement disponierendes Motiv in Heideggers Vorlesung *Die Grundbegriffe der Metaphysik* von 1929/30," pp. 78–92. 4. Alexander Schwan, "Zeitkritik und Politik in Heideggers Spätphilosophie," pp. 93–107. 5. Ernst Nolte, "Philosophie und Nationalsozialismus," pp. 338–356. 6. Ernst Vollrath, "Hannah Arendt und Martin Heidegger," pp. 357–372. 7. Adriaan Peperzak, "Einige Thesen zur Heidegger-Kritik von Emmanuel Lévinas," pp. 373–389.

"Martin Heidegger and Politics: A Dossier," *New German Critique*, no. 45, Fall 1988, pp. 91–161. Includes an Introduction by Richard Wolin, translations by William S. Lewis of ten texts by Heidegger from Schneeberger, 1962, translations of two excerpts from Löwith, 1986, by Wolin, and Wolin, "The French Heidegger Debate."

Martin Heidegger und das 'Dritte Reich': Ein Kompendium, ed. Bernd Martin (Darmstadt: Wissenschaftliche Buchgesellschaft, 1989). A convenient collection of mostly already available material.

"Symposium on Heidegger and Nazism," ed. and int. Arnold I. Davidson, *Critical Inquiry*, vol. 15, no. 2, Winter 1989, pp. 407–488. Includes translations of the essays by Gadamer, Blanchot, Lacoue-Labarthe, and Lévinas that originally appeared in *Le Nouvel Observateur*, 22–28. 1. 1988, of Habermas' introduction to the German edition of the book by Farías, and of an excerpt from Derrida's *De l'esprit*.

George Steiner, "Heidegger, abermals," *Merkur*, vol. 43, 2. February 1989, pp. 93–102.

J. P. Stern, "Heil Heidegger," *London Review of Books*, April 20, 1989, pp. 7–9. Review of Ott, *Martin Heidegger*.

Catherine H. Zuckert, "Martin Heidegger: His Philosophy and his Politics," *Political Theory*, vol. 18, no. 1, February 1990, pp. 51–79.

Dieter Thomä, *Die Zeit des Selbst und die Zeit danach. Zur Kritik der Textgeschichte Martin Heideggers 1910–1976* (Frankfurt: Suhrkamp, 1990).

Index